AGENCY AND GENDER IN GAZA

with my best wishes

مع تمنياتي لك بالنجاح

Agency and Gender in Gaza
Masculinity, Femininity and Family during the Second Intifada

AITEMAD MUHANNA

ASHGATE

Published by
Ashgate Publishing Limited
Wey Court East
Union Road
Farnham
Surrey, GU9 7PT
England

Ashgate Publishing Company
110 Cherry Street
Suite 3-1
Burlington, VT 05401-3818
USA

www.ashgate.com

British Library Cataloguing in Publication Data
A catalogue record for this book is available from the British Library

The Library of Congress has cataloged the printed edition as follows:
Muhanna, Aitemad.
Agency and gender in Gaza : masculinity, femininity and family during the second intifada / by Aitemad Muhanna.
pages cm
Includes bibliographical references and index.
ISBN 978-1-4094-5453-3 (hardback) -- ISBN 978-1-4094-5454-0 (ebook) -- ISBN 978-1-4724-0720-7 (epub) 1. Man-woman relationships--Gaza. 2. Family--Gaza. 3. Al-Aqsa Intifada, 2000- I. Title.
HQ801.M83 2013
306.850953'1--dc23

2013007771

ISBN 9781409454533 (hbk)
ISBN 9781409454540 (ebk – PDF)
ISBN 9781472407207 (ebk – ePUB)

MIX
Paper from responsible sources
FSC www.fsc.org FSC® C013985

Printed in the United Kingdom by Henry Ling Limited, at the Dorset Press, Dorchester, DT1 1HD

Contents

Foreword

The 'plight' of women in conflict zones was first officially recognized by the international community with the passage of United Nations Security Council Resolution 1325 on Women, Peace and Security in 2000. Paradoxically, the increased international attention to the impacts of conflict on women has been accompanied by an increased silencing of voices of ordinary women living in conflict zones, except when they conform with liberal notions of agency or are victims of violence and patriarchy. Aitemad Muhanna's outstanding book presents, for the first time, a detailed and nuanced account of the impact on women in Gaza of decades of conflict, violence and, since 2006, blockade resulting from Israel's illegal occupation. She pays attention to women from the poorest sections of society, those whose voices are either not heard or co-opted, challenging dominant conceptions of women's agency.

Engaging with Gazan women over many years, Aitemad Muhanna, herself a Palestinian refugee who grew up in Beach Camp, reveals how gender and generational dynamics amongst poor Gazan households have shifted over time, particularly since the onset of the Second Intifada in 2000. The author weaves together the individual stories of women of different generations, speaking about their memories and their lives. She illustrates how gender roles within families have altered to cope with harsh economic conditions. The 'traditional' gendered division of household roles, consisting of male breadwinner and housewife, has been undermined since 2000. Palestinian men from Gaza, previously heavily integrated into the Israeli labour market, now find themselves unemployed or underemployed. In the face of rising household costs and increasingly precarious incomes, women are forced to engage in income-generation projects or to chase food coupons from humanitarian agencies. Rather than finding this 'empowering', the author finds that women either become indebted or obliged to act helpless in order to be deemed worthy of humanitarian aid.

The author also documents changes to household composition and generational dynamics, and how these have had an impact on women. After Israel's occupation of the Gaza Strip, and the incorporation of Palestinian men into the Israeli labour market, rising incomes enabled young couples to move out of the extended family home and to create a nuclear family household. This enabled daughters-in-law to escape the domination of mothers-in-law and gave more autonomy to young wives. The increase in male unemployment since the outbreak of the Second Intifada has encouraged many families to move back to live in extended households for the sake of family survival. Unlike in earlier times, mothers-in-law do not wield the same levels of power over their daughters-in-law. Now, daughters-in-law are valued for their ability to bring in extra income to the household and marriages are even arranged based on the potential earning ability of future wives. For female university graduates, this has given them a new level of autonomy in decision-making about their employment and marriage choices. However, this does not mean that young women are dismantling the gender order; rather, they are negotiating better terms and conditions for themselves and their future children.

Aitemad Muhanna looks beyond the statistics of humanitarian crisis and sees that Gazan families are also suffering a moral crisis, which is no less damaging to their lives. Men and women are unable to perform their 'traditional', socially-legitimate roles, yet do not find new gender roles that enable them to live in dignity. Unemployment, indebtedness and dependency on humanitarian aid are deeply humiliating for men and women. The author explains how this gives rise to a disjuncture between gender roles and gender norms. Men and women reproduce 'traditional' notions of femininity and masculinity, with their concomitant gender hierarchies, as a means to sustain a moral self-hood in the midst of destruction and despair.

Aitemad Muhanna's book illustrates how important it is to listen to the voices of women without assuming that women's agency and subjectivities are shaped by desires of autonomy and resisting male domination. Her findings and arguments challenge internationally hegemonic models of development and peace building, particularly with regard to 'gender mainstreaming'. International humanitarian and developmental organizations, as well as many international women's activists, continue to base their programmes and policies on an assumption of women's liberal agency. This book questions whether such policies 'empower women' or whether they create another layer of violence that operates in tandem with the violence of Israel's occupation and blockade.

Nicola Pratt
University of Warwick, Coventry, UK

Acknowledgements

So many people contributed to the accomplishment of this book. I would especially like to thank Professor Ann Whitehead of Sussex University, who voluntarily supervised my research. She provided me with a truly extraordinary experience, and without her I simply would not have been able to get to where I am now. Special thanks are also due to Professor Andrea Cornwell of IDS/Sussex University, for the financial, technical and spiritual support she offered me while I was conducting my research through the 'Pathways of Women's Empowerment' programme. I am also grateful to DFID and to the UNDP office in Palestine for providing me with a full scholarship, which enabled me to conduct this research. I would also like to thank my supervisors, Dr Jeremy Holland, Dr Gerard Clarke and Dr Tim Bower of Swansea University, for their support, insights and encouragement.

I am fundamentally grateful to my two friends, Laura Mitchell and Louisa Waugh, for all of their great editing. Finally, my great thanks to the young Gazan men and women who helped me to arrange my field research in the different regions in Gaza, and who facilitated my research in spite of the insecure situation of Gaza, especially Rami Murad from the Development Research Centre at Birzeit University, and Said Abu Ghaza from the Gaza UNDP office. I am truly thankful to all of you for your various contributions to making this empirical work about Gazan women and men into a book.

I am tremendously thankful to the women of Gaza who opened their homes and lives to generously participate in this study. These women spent hours sharing their insights, emotions and life experiences with me for the purpose of my research. Their cooperation allowed me to progress in my research, despite the mobility and communication difficulties we all encountered during the field work.

In my own personal life, I would like to thank my two children, Neda and Magd, and my sisters and brothers in Gaza, who contributed more to my book than they are probably aware.

Glossary and List of Abbreviations

a'ila ghalbana	Docile household
afiato	Physical and mental well-being
awanes	Spinsters, women beyond the socially accepted age of marriage
basta	A small stall consisting of a wooden table, usually placed directly in front of a house, where sweets and small grocery and school items are sold to neighbours
beit el a'ila	The house of an extended family, where the eldest parents live with their married sons
Beit Hanoon	Town in the north eastern Gaza Strip, situated close to the border with Israel
Beit Lahia	Small city in the northern Gaza Strip, also located close to the Israeli border
bent a'isha	A daughter of marrying age, socially nurtured to adapt to poverty and conflict in her future family-in-law household
bent nas	The daughter of a socially recognised, respected and honourable family
CBOs	Community-based organisations
Deir El Balah	The main city in the central Gaza Strip
Donum	A size of land of 1,000 metres square
el jami'at	Charity or community-based association
el mara el shatra	The adept wife
el Shabka	The gold given to brides at their wedding party
El-dywan	A place for male gatherings, where men of different clans discuss family disputes and other local issues
el-jehad	Holy struggle
el-Kenna, Kanayni (pl)	Daughter/s-in-law
el-yahood	The Jews, often with reference to Israeli soldiers
FAFO	The Institute for Applied International Studies, based in Oslo, Norway
Fatah	The Palestinian National Liberation Movement, which governed the Palestinian National Authority from 1994–2006
ghalbaneen	Docile women who are the head of their households because the male head of their families is either chronically sick or dead

hakma Jouzha	A wife who is perceived by her community as controlling her husband
Hamas	The Islamic Resistance Movement and current de-facto Government of the Gaza Strip
hamati, hamawat (pl)	Mother/s-in-law
hamula	Clan
Isteqlaliat el a'ila	Autonomy of a nuclear family household
IWS	The Institute of Women's Studies at Birzeit University in Palestine
JD	Jordanian dinar (the Jordanian currency)
Lajnet el Islah	Traditional re-conciliation committee, made up of local traditional and religious leaders
Madyooneen	Households in debt
Mahkoom	A man considered to be under the control of either his mother or wife
Makshofeen	Vulnerable households without sufficient resources to sustain their living
marato el musatata	His respected wife
Mastoreen	Households with limited sources of income that manage to survive without being in debt to strangers outside family and kin relations and networks
MOSA	The Ministry of Social Affairs
mudardahat	A subtle women
mukhtar / makhateer	Traditional leader / leaders
musatata / musatatat	A housewife who takes care of her children and depends on her husband to financially provide for the family
NAKBA	The catastrophe of the Israeli–Palestinian war in 1948
neswan / neswana	Women / our women
niqab	A scarf, usually black, used by women to cover their faces, except the eyes, and a radical Islamic form of veiling used by some women in Gaza
NIS	The New Israeli Shekel (the Israeli currency)
OPT	Occupied Palestinian Territories: the West Bank, East Jerusalem and the Gaza Strip
PCBS	Palestinian Central Bureau of Statistics
PCHR	Palestinian Centre for Human Rights
PFI	Palestinian Federation of Industries
PLO	Palestinian Liberation Organization
PNA	Palestinian National Authority
Rafah	A city located in the southern Gaza Strip, bordered by Egypt
rejal haqeeqi	A real man
se'ba	Tough

Set el beit	The mistress of the household
set muhtarama	A respected woman
Shabab el Watan	The young men of the nation
Shabab	Youth, a term used by Palestinians to describe young men aged 16–30 years old
SHAREK	A leading youth organisation in Gaza
Shari'a	Religious codes or laws that control marriage and other family affairs
Shu'un marriage	The marriage of sons before they reached the age of 20 years old, in order for their families not to be deprived of humanitarian assistance from the Ministry of Social Affairs
tartoor	A man with no power and authority inside and outside home
Tawjihi	The final year of secondary education in Palestine
tehrad	A woman who leaves her husband's home for a short period of time, and usually stays in her parents' or brothers' house
Toub and *ghata ra*s	Traditional Palestinian dress and head scarf
UNRWA	The United Nations Relief and Works Agency for Palestine Refugees in the Near East
Wasta	Influential network based on either family and kin relations, or political factions in Palestinian society
WFP	United Nation World Food Program
Zakat committee	Zakat is one of the five pillars of Islam. Muslims are obliged to pay 2.5 per cent of their wealth, or zakat, to charity (it can be paid in cash or in-kind forms of assistance to families in need)

Chapter 1
The Contemporary History of Gazan Society and the Complexity of Gender

Introduction

Since the beginning of the Second Intifada in September 2000, women, men and children in the Occupied Palestinian Territories of Gaza, the West Bank and East Jerusalem have experienced unprecedented insecurity at individual, familial and community levels. The Gaza Strip, with its specific geopolitical context, has been exposed to relentless armed conflict. The last 10 days Israeli armed assault against Gaza occurred few weeks before finalising this book in mid-November 2012. The Israeli assault resulted in killing 140 people, most of them civilians; wounding 1,202 people; completely destroying 120 homes and damaging 9,000 homes; in addition to damaging and destroying large number of businesses and public buildings.[1] The last assault occurred whilst Gaza was hardly relieving the destructive material and humanitarian effects of the longer and harsher Israeli assault against Gaza in December 2008. Although this book focuses on the humanitarian and livelihood situation of Gazan families and its gender impact in the period of 2000–2009, its analysis and findings remain extremely relevant to the current situation of insecurity and its gender and non-gender socio-economic impact.

Such persistent insecure and uncertain situations in Gaza have destabilised all aspects of social relations, especially gender relations. Gender outcomes have different dimensions, depending on individual life experiences, locations, employment patterns and opportunities, assets and coping mechanisms. This book is concerned not only with understanding how men and women cope with chronic insecurity and economic collapse, but more importantly, how changes in what men and women do have affected socially and morally constructed images of gender subjectivity inside Gaza.

The main aim of this book is to examine the effects on both women and men of the prolonged experience of living in a situation of chronic insecurity and uncertainty, and how they have adapted to these circumstances. To what extent have their experiences and strategies involved renegotiating aspects of their 'normative' historical gender roles, responsibilities and relations? How does the history of gender within the Palestinian family affect the trajectories of these relations

1 See UNRWA report on the November 2012's Israeli assault against Gaza: http://www.unrwa.org/etemplate.php?id=1523.

outside of the family? In what ways do the changing functions of gender, for the purpose of family survival and livelihood security, affect gender subjectivity? How did internalised images of masculinity and femininity differ during the crisis of the Second Intifada, as opposed to beforehand? What transformations occur as a result of shifts in gender according to situational changes? If none, what is the combination of objective and subjective factors that has constrained Gazan women from resisting historical and socially constructed gender images and practices? The analysis in this book focuses on both institutional and interpersonal relations. It seeks to understand how gender mediates the process of coping for survival where formal institutions have lost their 'normal' capacity to function within contexts of lawlessness and political division (Roy 2006).

My research explores the example of Gazan society during the Second Intifada, particularly in the period 2000–2009, when the combination of the Israeli military occupation of Gaza and the ensuing collapse of sustainable livelihoods, resulted in a crisis of masculinity and femininity: the former caused by men's loss of jobs and sources of income, and the latter by women's loss of their self-respect through their dependence on humanitarian aid provided by local, national and international institutions. These two crises have been resisted by the production, or reproduction, of alternative modes of gender agency and subjectivity. Although I have attempted to understand how and if gender has been renegotiated in order to develop resources for coping and resisting this chronic livelihood crisis, I have also sought to go beyond this limited understanding of women's agency, to explore the subjective aspect of resistance through women's agency, by paying attention to the moral meanings associated with gender identity.

The first section of this chapter provides a brief introduction to the main theme of the book which is to explore the impact of the Israeli military occupation on family, kin and survival in the Gaza strip. The second section offers an overview of the contemporary history of the Gaza Strip. The third section is about the socio-economic conditions of Gaza under Israeli military occupation, and especially during the Second Intifada. The fourth section is about family and gender in the Second Intifada. The fifth section is an elaboration of the research objectives and the sixth describes the research methodology and methods. The final section outlines the remaining book chapters and content.

Family, Kin and Survival under Israeli Military Occupation

Israeli restrictions and policies of massive closure of Gazan borders have destroyed all aspects of Gaza's economy and its social infrastructure.[2] This destruction has

2 See the recent report about the destruction of Gazan economy entitled 'The Peril of Forgetting Gaza', published by Sara Roy, the senior research scholar at the centre of Middle Eastern Studies at Harvard University, on Tuesday 2 June 2009, available at: www.thecrimson.com/article.aspx?ref=528434 [accessed 20 October 2009].

expanded to affect the social fabric of the society, thereby increasing internal violence among tribes and political factions. This has negatively influenced the historical features of social cohesion and collectiveness among and between families and local communities, as well as in the wider society (World Bank 2004; Malki, Shalabi and Ladadwa 2004). Furthermore, where the informal system of social security based on subsistence economy and kinship has been undermined by the collective impoverishment of Gazan society, social and economic sanctions within this informal system have lost their efficacy (Hasselknippe and Tviet 2007, Oxfam 2007). In 2007, 82 per cent of Palestinian families became fully reliant on the humanitarian aid provided by international and national institutions (UNRWA 2007). The role of family and kin relations and networks as the historical basis of social organisation and individual security and as a signifier of national and cultural identity (Rosenfeld 1968, Swedenburg 1990) has also been diminished and narrowed to the level of an individual household unit. Due to the closures imposed by the Israeli occupation, the mobility of goods and people has been severely restricted. As a consequence, the vast majority of men have lost their jobs and their households have become resourceless and vulnerable.

The prolonged history of the creation of a Palestinian economy that is dependent on the Israeli market since the Israeli occupation in 1967, has produced a crisis in the role of the male breadwinner even prior to the conditions of the Second Intifada. This is exemplified in the irregularity and insecurity of men's and women's participation in the labour force (Roy 1999). The current crisis caused by men's loss of their sources of income is a gendered crisis and consequently, a family crisis. The effects of unemployment – whether psychological problems, loss of self-confidence, disruption and tensions in family life, a rise in illness and morbidity, or the reconfiguration of gender roles and responsibilities – reverberate throughout all family members. The most common effect is the rise of the burden of care for women. Poor women have coped with economic shocks and loss of income by striving to replace home-based or informal work for loss of male income. In addition, they have substituted their time and intensity in their work for lost money and have diminished their sense of personal integrity by acting as 'beggars' reliant on humanitarian aid from public institutions. The massive burden on poor women at home has also been increased by the constant presence of jobless and helpless men at home, whose failure to provide for the family has been expressed in conflicts with family members, especially women and children.

The harshness of the crisis of adult men losing their sources of income in the Second Intifada is also linked with the structure and ideology of the formal social welfare system in Palestinian society. It assumes that the role of adult men is stable and unproblematic, as they are always able to find jobs, and that the role of adult women is only as care givers, concentrated in domestic non-productive activities (Johnson 2002). This system is not responsive to the specific situation of the Second Intifada, where the majority of adult men have lost their sources of income with no provision of benefits for their unemployment (Malki, Shalabi and Ladadwa 2004). The main two providers of social and humanitarian assistance for poor families (Ministry of Social Affairs and UNRWA[3]) forbid aid to families with able-bodied men over 18, whether they have jobs or not. Other humanitarian non-governmental institutions such as *Zakat*[4] committees largely target widows and orphans (Johnson and Hilal 2001). This social welfare system has multiple effects on poor families and on the gender order, since families headed by men have, arguably, become the most vulnerable. The historical conflation between household poverty and female headship in Palestinian society thus becomes inapplicable (FAFO 2003).

A further impact of the Second Intifada is exemplified in the changing priorities of Palestinian families, particularly in Gaza. Formerly, families living under Israeli military occupation prioritised investment in their children's education and employment as a sustainable source of family progression and development. This contributed towards challenging patriarchy and gender subordination (Rosenfeld 2002). However, during the crisis of the Second Intifada, loss of family income has forced many Gazan families to return to coping mechanisms which in effect exacerbate the reproduction of poverty based on gender and age. These dynamics include early marriage as a family preference for both men and women, male children dropping out of school, and women's persistent interest in having larger numbers of children, especially boys, as a long-term source of economic support (MOPIC, UNDP and DFID, 2002).

A Brief History of Political Conflict in the Gaza Strip

When the State of Israel was established, in May 1948, the Gaza Strip was under the control of Egypt. The borders between Gaza and Israel were established by the Israeli and Egyptian governments after the 1948 Arab–Israeli war. Prior to this war, the population of Gaza was approximately 80,000. During 1948, the majority of Palestinians were forced to leave their land to live in Diaspora. Whilst hundreds of thousands fled to neighbouring Arab countries, a minority of Palestinians fled to the West Bank and the Gaza Strip, where they sought shelter in camps

3 Following the 1948 Arab–Israeli conflict, UNRWA, the United Nations Relief and Works Agency for Palestine Refugees in the Near East, was established by United Nations General Assembly resolution 302 (IV) of 8 December 1949 to carry out direct relief for Palestine refugees. The Agency began operations on 1 May 1950. In the absence of a solution to the Palestine refugee problem, the General Assembly has repeatedly renewed UNRWA's mandate, most recently extending it until 30 June 2011. Since UNRWA's establishment, it has delivered its services in times of relative calm in the Middle East, and in times of hostilities. This includes food, housing and clothing in addition to education and health care provided to hundreds of thousands of young refugees (see www.un.org/unrwa/overview, accessed 20 October 2009).

4 *Zakat* is one of the five pillars of Islam. Muslims are obliged to pay 2.5 per cent of their wealth, *zakat*, to charitable causes in society. *Zakat* can be paid in cash or in the form of 'in-kind assistance' to families in need.

that have been administered by the United Nations Relief and Works Agency (UNRWA) since the early 1950s. Over the last six decades the population of Gaza has increased a staggering 20-fold (Hammami 1994). This has been caused by two factors: the mass influx of Palestinian refugees in 1948, who today represent around 70 per cent of the total population, and high birth rates coupled with low mortality rates, due to the provision of basic health services to the refugees by UNRWA (Elisha 2006).

The Gaza Strip is 360 km^2. It borders Egypt to the south, the Israeli Negev desert to the east and the Mediterranean Sea to the west. The strip is divided into five districts of almost equal size: Rafah, Khan Yunis, Deir El Balah, Gaza City and the northern district of Beit Lahia and Beit Hanoun. There are eight refugee camps administered by UNRWA across the Strip. According to the Palestinian national population census of 2007, the population of Gaza stood at 1,499,369[5], making it one of the most densely populated places on earth, with an average density of more than 26,000 people per km^2, the overwhelming majority of whom live in refugee camps and urban neighbourhoods.

Gaza remained under the administration of Egypt until the 1967 Israeli *Six-Day War*. Gaza was not however economically integrated into Egypt; most of the population were confined to the Strip, they had few viable political options and the majority of Gazan refugees survived on UNRWA rations. Whilst the period of Egyptian administrative rule was politically oppressive, the Egyptian regime did allow nationalist political expression, so long as it was couched in the language of Arab, rather than Palestinian, nationalism.[6] The Egyptian government built schools and hospitals and housing projects for the refugees, and also provided universal access to education and, therefore, a future for the first generation of refugee children.

In 1956, the Israeli military occupied the Gaza Strip for a period of five months during the Suez Campaign. This first Israeli military occupation of Gaza came to an abrupt end when the US Eisenhower administration pressurised Israel to withdraw. However, 11 years later, in 1967, Israel invaded East Jerusalem, the Gaza Strip and the West Bank, a historic event that placed the Palestinian population of these unified territories under Israeli military occupation. The civil affairs of Palestinians in the OPT (Occupied Palestinian Territories) were then administered by the government of Israel, whilst UNRWA was responsible for providing for the refugees' basic needs.

During the first few years of its occupation of Gaza, Israel did not encourage Palestinian employment, as it conflicted with Israel's policy of Jewish self-sufficiency. However, when the Israeli economy boomed in the 1970s, more Palestinians crossed the borders to work on Israeli farms and in construction

5 PCBS, Population Projections. Projected Summary Statistics; and PCBS, Press Release on World Environment Day, June 2007, available at: http://www.passia.org/palestine_facts/pdf/pdf2008/Population.pdf.

6 Until the 1967 war with Israel, the question of Palestinian nationality was not considered as separate from that of Arab identity or nationalism.

businesses. The Israeli government later adopted a policy of economically integrating the Gazan economy with its own (Roy 1999: 65). By the mid-1980s almost 70 per cent of the Gazan workforce was employed in Israel (Roy 1987: 61). Israel's control over the natural and economic resources of Palestine forced Palestinians to shift their economic activities towards wage labour inside Israel. In 1975 unemployment in Gaza fell to 1 per cent because of the huge demand for Palestinian labourers in Israel (Roy 2007). In addition, the flow of Israeli agricultural products to Gazan markets also undermined local Gazan agricultural production. Thousands of farmers were forced to abandon their agricultural livelihoods to work as cheap unskilled wage labourers in Israel (Haj 1992).

Despite the socio-economic differences between refugees and non-refugees in Gaza, the Israeli military occupation disadvantaged both groups, who were forced to develop mutual economic relations and networks after the 1967 war, although social relations between the two groups remained less integrated. Refugees maintained a distance from total integration into the social networks of non-refugees. They maintained kin marriages as a sign of resistance, so as not to lose their national identity as refugees (Hammami 1994). However this marriage pattern has gradually shifted. The social and cultural differences between refugees and non-refugees have recently dissipated due to the major involvement of Palestinian refugees in the local Gazan economy.[7]

After two decades of Israeli military occupation, its policies of land confiscation, and with no apparent progression in resolving the Palestinian-Israeli conflict, the situation in the OPT, particularly in Gaza, reached breaking point. The First Palestinian Intifada erupted in December 1987. It was characterised by mass Palestinian demonstrations, curfews imposed by the Israeli military, and armed clashes between Palestinian and Israeli military, often led by Gazan refugees. Poverty increased dramatically as a result of massive numbers of young men being arrested, martyred and/or injured.[8] The Palestinian economic infrastructure was also destroyed. Between June 1990 and June 1991, the number of families receiving food assistance from UNRWA increased from 9,383 to 120,000 (Roy 2007).

---

7 The official national statistics of 2002 show insignificant difference between refugees and non-refugees regarding their economic involvement in the Palestinian local economy. For example, 29 per cent of non-refugees were self-employed against 23 per cent among refugees. For more figures on the differences between refugees and non-refugees, see the IDRC book '*Palestinian Refugees: Challenges of Repatriation and Development*', published by I.Tauris, IDRC (2007), available at: http://web.idrc.ca/openebooks/231-0/.

8 A martyr is a specific term used to describe men killed by the Israeli Occupation whether during their participation in national resistance or in a situation of military attacks by the Israelis. This term is extended to include men who are killed during internal conflicts between political factions in Palestinian society. The term mother, wife or sister of a martyr is regarded as positive and valuable terms for women.

In 1993, following secret negotiations in Oslo between Palestinian and Israeli leaders, the Palestinian leadership returned to Gaza from exile in July 1994, and established the Palestinian Authority (PNA). The Oslo Agreement gave the PNA – led by the Palestinian Liberation Organization (PLO) and the Fatah political party – the right to administer over 60 per cent of the Gaza Strip.[9] However, Palestinian Islamist factions (Hamas and *el Jihad*) rejected the Oslo agreement, and began to revive their militant struggle against the Israeli military occupation, using suicide bombing tactics inside Israel. As a result, Israel imposed harsh restrictions on Palestinians' movements, including Palestinian labourers entering Israel. Thousands of Hamas and *el Jihad* members were arrested in the period 1994–2000.[10] Frustration at the failure of progress towards an independent Palestinian state, coupled with Israel's policy of closing its borders against Gaza from 1994–2000, led to the uprising of the Second Intifada in September 2000. The south of Gaza was the main focus of Israeli military attacks during this period. The Israeli military destroyed 1,500 Gazan homes to create a buffer corridor between the southern Gazan town of Rafah and the Israeli border, making 16,000 Gazans homeless in the process.[11] Continued military conflict between Israel, and particularly the Islamist resistance militant groups in Gaza, led to Israel disengaging from the Gaza Strip in August 2005. This effectively froze Palestinian/ Israeli peace process negotiations, including any discussion of an independent Palestinian state, and Palestinians' right of return.[12]

Israel's disengagement from the Gaza Strip is one of the most significant factors in Gaza's recent history. It was followed by the January 2006 Palestinian legislative election, when Hamas won a landslide victory.[13] When Hamas formed its government in March 2006, Israel began withholding custom tax revenues from the PNA – in direct defiance of the Oslo Economic Declaration and the Paris Protocol.[14] Foreign governments ceased all transactions with the new Hamas government, whilst international donors immediately ceased payments to PNA.

---

9 For more details see Declaration of Principles on Interim Self-Government Arrangements (Oslo Agreement), 13 September 1993, available at: http://www.unhcr.org/refworld/publisher,ARAB,,3de5e96e4,0.html.

10 For further details, see Palestine Centre for Human Rights, PCHR's Annual Report 2001, available at: http://www.pchrgaza.org/portal/.

11 Human Rights Watch, *Razing Rafah: Mass Home Demolitions in the Gaza Strip*, October 2004, available at: http://www.hrw.org/reports/2004/rafah1004/ (accessed 2 July 2007).

12 The 'final solution' of the Palestinian-Israeli conflict, as stated in the peace process negotiations, entails the creation of an independent Palestinian State alongside an independent Jewish state or next to the State of Israel. See http://www.mideastweb.org/campdavid2.htm (accessed 7 November).

13 See Steven Erlanger's article in the *New York Times*, 27 January 2006 entitled 'Palestinian Landslide: The elections; Hamas ruling faction, Casting Pall on Peace Process'.

14 The Paris Protocol is the agreement signed between Israel and the PLO in Paris on 29 April 1994. It defines the economic relationship between Israel and the Palestinian

The government of Israel prevented Gazan workers from entering Israel in March 2006, and its closure of the Gaza Strip remains in place, with only exceptional cases of Gazans being permitted to enter or leave the Gaza Strip via Israel.

After the January 2006 legislative election, violence continued inside Gaza. Sporadic fighting between Hamas and the previous ruling political party, Fatah, began with a protest by unpaid security forces, as a result of international donors withholding their salary payments. Other forms of internal security chaos and lawlessness emerged, and expanded, including military conflicts between clans inside Gaza.[15] Clashes and assassinations of members of the two main political parties occurred in early 2007, while all internal and external attempts at conciliation failed. Factional conflict and fighting in Gaza reached unprecedented levels. This conflict between the two main political factions culminated in a full-scale military assault by Hamas against the security forces of Fatah on 11 June 2007. Hamas secured full control of the entire Gaza Strip, and Gaza became completely isolated from the world outside.

The political crisis in the PNA, and the conflict between the two de facto Palestinian governments – the Hamas government in Gaza and the Ramallah government led by Fatah – have negatively affected the economic and social conditions of public service employees in the Gaza Strip, both military and civil. Certain measures taken by the two governments have had severe impacts on the living conditions of employees and their ability to provide for themselves and their families. These measures have included cutting off salaries for thousands of public services employees, employing new individuals in a manner which violates the national Civil Service Law, and the dismissal, marginalisation and substitution of hundreds of public service employees in the Gaza Strip.

In parallel with the internal conflict and political divisions within Palestinian society, the Israeli military continued to impose a tightened siege on the Gaza Strip. This denied Palestinian civilians access to basic items of food, medicines, fuel – including electricity – and other necessary commodities. The Israeli state also continued to impose severe restrictions on the movement of Palestinian civilians and goods, violating the economic and social rights of the civilian population. This chronic history of violent conflict, military occupation and insecurity culminated in Israel's largest military offensive against the Gaza Strip. Launched on 27 December 2008, the offensive continued for 23 days. According to documentation by the Palestinian Centre for Human Rights (PCHR), 1,417 Palestinians were killed, including 1,181 civilians, considered as protected persons under international humanitarian law. According to PCHR, civilian victims included 313

Authority. For more details, see the PLO website, available at: http://www.nad-plo.org/etemplate.php?id=48.

15 See the International Crisis Group; New Report 'Inside Gaza: The Challenge of Clans and Families, Gaza/Jerusalem/Brussels, 20 December 2007, and see the annual reports of the Palestinian Centre of Human Rights (2007 and 2008), available at: http://www.pchrgaza.org/.

children (26.5 per cent) and 116 women (9.8 per cent). The total number of injured was 4,336, including 1,133 children (26.1 per cent) and 735 women (17 per cent) (PCHR 2008). The population of the Gaza Strip continue to live under an Israeli military siege, with the majority suffering deteriorating standards of living, whilst political negotiations have stagnated. The following section explores in more depth the impact of the Israeli military occupation on the socio-economic conditions of Gaza.

The Socio-Economic Conditions of Gaza under the Israeli Military Occupation

The 1967 Israeli occupation of Gaza and West Bank was the critical historical event that exposed the Palestinian socio-economic structure to fundamental structural change. Israel occupied the whole West Bank and Gaza, putting the entire Palestinian population under the military control of the Israeli state. The occupation of Gaza changed the configuration of livelihood and employment options. Before the Israeli occupation, the Gazan economy had been reliant on agriculture as the main source of livelihood. According to an early study of Palestinian employment under the Israeli occupation, employment in agriculture in the Gaza Strip declined from 33.1 per cent in 1969 to 9.7 per cent in 1985 (Abed 1988).

After the Israeli occupation in 1967, refugees became largely involved in Israeli wage labour in the same way as non-refugees. The main difference between refugees and non-refugees in the 1967 post-war period was access to education. Refugees had had better access to basic education from UNRWA since the establishment of the camps in the late 1950s. Moreover, by then, basic education from UNRWA had become the main respected source of livelihood for refugees, for the present and into the future. The Israeli occupation forces were responsible for basic social service provision for non-refugees. In the 1970s and 1980s, these services were very limited and of low quality. Consequently, the non-refugees became less concerned about their education. The landlessness of refugees was an important factor that made their men and women very ambitious to finish high school or college in order to find a regular stable job with UNRWA. The landless refugees remained, nevertheless, largely dependent on UNRWA ration cards; but a few who had completed their education managed to get jobs in the education and health departments of UNRWA, as teachers, nurses, clerical staff or in catering and cleaning. Other men and women gained employment in the Arab oil countries (Rosenfeld 2002: 520). From the early 1970s, Gazan non-refugees started to leave their agricultural lands which had become unproductive (Roy 1987: 61). The flow of Israeli agricultural products to the Gazan market also undermined local Gazan agricultural production. Owing to the Israeli control of the export and import and all other aspects of the movement of goods in the territory, thousands of farmers were induced to leave their agricultural livelihoods to work as cheap unskilled wage labourers in Israel (Haj 1992).

Despite the socio-economic differences between refugees and non-refugees before the war in 1967, the Israeli occupation disadvantaged both refugees and non-refugees. Both were forced, after the war, to develop mutual economic relations and networks, while social relations remained less integrated between refugees and non-refugees. Refugees until the late 1980s had to keep themselves from being totally integrated in the social networks of the non-refugees. Refugees maintained kin marriage as a sign of resistance, and so as not to lose their national identity as refugees (Hammami 1994). The refugees have gradually shifted from kin marriage to marriage with other refugee tribes, but they continued to reject marriages with non-refugees. It was not really socially supported for a refugee woman to get married to a non-refugee until very recently. Marriage between kin and between refugees was maintained for decades as a symbolic sign of refugees' connectedness with their original land and their right of return (Swedenburg 1990).

As mentioned before, Palestinian men in Gaza had rapidly and massively shifted their livelihood sources and had become more reliant on their wage labour in Israel (Lesch and Tessler 1987: 249). Many men, especially non-refugees, dropped out of schools to work as wage labourers and were able to earn relatively good incomes. In the beginning, men worked as unskilled cheap labourers, but over time, many became skilled labourers and earned much better wages by increased participation in the modernisation of the Israeli market and its technology, especially in the agricultural and construction sectors. Simultaneously, the business of subcontracting between the Israeli firms and small to medium-sized Palestinian workshops – particularly in the three sectors of construction, garment-manufacture and agriculture – flourished, thereby absorbing most of the local cheap labour in Gaza, particularly that of women (Roy 1991: 66). Home-based female labour was the main source for this competitive market, in which women were paid only pennies, or became unpaid workers in family businesses, especially in the garment manufacturing sector (Haj 1992, Rosenfeld 2002).

Israeli policies continued to make Palestinians fully reliant on Israeli capitalist market relations. This meant that the Israeli state could successfully stabilise its control not only over the natural resources of Palestinians, but also over Palestinian manpower. Wage labour in Israel became not only the main source of livelihood in Gaza, but also the determinant of wealth distribution and social arrangements (Roy 1991). Many skilled labourers became sub-contractors to Israelis, employing many unskilled and semi-skilled labourers from Gaza. Wage labour in Israel also attracted more highly educated men. Wage labour in Israel absorbed the largest proportion of the Palestinian labour force until the mid-1990s when the Israeli occupation started to re-regulate the entry of Gazan labourers into Israel (Farsakh 2002).

Sara Roy considers Israel's policy of integrating the economy of Gaza into its own economy as a deliberate process of undermining Gaza's economic base. Roy describes this Israeli policy as the *de-development* of the Occupied Territories, which 'undermines the ability of an economy to grow and expand by preventing it from accessing and utilizing inputs needed to promote internal growth beyond a specific structural level' (Roy 2007: 2). This helps to explain why the June 2007 closure of Gaza struck its economy much harder than it might have hit other economies. She argues that 'the closure policy proved so destructive only because the 30-year process of integrating Gaza's economy into Israel had made the local economy deeply dependent' (Roy 2007: 313–314).

The Second Intifada (2000–2008)

Since the beginning of the Second Intifada and the enforcement of the closure regime, Gazan people have been living in economic, social and cultural isolation. It started with the elimination of work permits so that Gazan labourers could not work in Israel anymore; it was followed by the international boycott of the PA after Hamas won the democratic elections in January 2006. This resulted in the halt of payments to PA employees, who constituted 26 per cent of the total labour force in Palestine, and around 40 per cent of the labour force in Gaza, according to the official records of the Palestinian Central Bureau of Statistics (PCBS) (PCBS 2007). The situation has since deteriorated through indiscriminate attacks on civilians in Israel via rockets launched from Gaza and the frequent Israeli targeted killings, air strikes and incursions (Hasselknippe and Tveit 2007). The tight restrictions on the movement of people and goods into and out of Gaza, has resulted in the collapse of the private sector, disruption of the local market through high prices for basic products and a lack of basic services, as well as the degradation of the physical and social infrastructure (PalTrade 2007, World Bank 2007b).[16]

A field assessment conducted by Oxfam in several Gaza Strip communities in 2007, revealed that the average income of Gazan families had reduced by 75 per cent since the year 2000 (Oxfam 2007). A United Nations agencies report published in 2008 stated that almost 70 per cent of families in Gaza are living below the poverty line of 1.2 USD per person per day; 61 per cent of the non-refugee population is food insecure, with a sharp increase in the prevalence of anaemia and malnourishment amongst children (WFP, FAO and UNRWA 2008);[17] 48.4 per cent of the Gaza labour force is concentrated in the public sector, especially in the security forces of Hamas government. The highest unemployment rate is among

16 See PalTrade Gaza Report, 20 February 2007; 'Investing in Palestinian Economic reform and development', World Bank, 17 December 2007; and 'The closure of the Gaza Strip: The Economic and Humanitarian consequences', OCHA Special FOCUS, December 2007.

17 WFP/FAO/UNRWA rapid food security survey conducted March/April 2008 as reported in World Food Program, 'Food Security and Market Monitoring Report', July 2008: Report 19.

the 15–29 age group and among those who are more highly educated (PCBS 2009). Young men and women with higher education have no job opportunities due to the destruction of the private sector and an overloaded public sector.

The exposure of an increasing number of families to the threat of Israeli incursions and bombings as well as the internal militant chaos has added to the increase of vulnerability amongst the Gazan population. Israeli military incursions resulted in the destruction of many houses as well as the death of civilians. The internal conflict between political factions and family clans also resulted in a high number of deaths amongst the local population.[18] Recent reports show that since the beginning of the Second Intifada in December 2000 until March 2008, over half of those who were killed, at 55.3 per cent (2,966 deaths), are from the 18–29 age group. According to the Palestinian Centre for Human Rights' Annual Report (2008), the Israelis destroyed 216 houses in the OPT (107 in the West Bank and 109 in the Gaza Strip). They also heavily damaged 680 houses and razed 3,424 donums of agricultural land in the Gaza Strip (PCHR 2008). Additionally, they destroyed civilian facilities, including public buildings, charities and sports clubs.

Growing poverty and livelihood vulnerability has also increased crime, especially amongst Gazan children and youth. The reported cases of crimes by Gazan police for the year 2006 showed more than a 100 per cent increase in certain categories. Children were exposed to increasing violence from their jobless fathers inside their homes, in schools and in the streets. The PCBS report on violence for the year 2005 showed that 32.2 per cent of children between the ages of 5 to 18 were exposed to increasing violence (PCBS 2005).

Family and Gender in the Second Intifada

The Second Intifada has had a fundamental effect on gender relations in Gazan society. Men and women use both the structure and ideology of gender to cope with the consequences of chronic personal and familial insecurity. Some coping mechanisms have enhanced the hierarchical structure of the Palestinian family, and some have transcended it, depending on which mechanism has the capacity to achieve the immediate goal of family survival and security from within the existing structure of household and local community gender relations. The Second Intifada has facilitated the fluidity of gender relations in which each gender is reconfigured to resist the threat to family stability. Women in Gaza have developed strategies to cope with poverty and vulnerability by simultaneously referring to the systems of tradition and modernity. The former relies on the *embodied history* of the Palestinian family, as exemplified in the domestic economy and family and kin relations and networks (Johnson 2006). The latter depends on contemporary sources of personal and family livelihood security, such as education and formal

18 See the Palestinian Centre for Human rights' annual report 2007, available at: http://www.pchrgaza.org/files/Reports/English/pdf_annual/Ann-Rep-07-Eng.pdf.

employment (IWS 2008). These two paths have been effectively utilised by women in order to challenge the threats against their families' survival and security. Women began coping by intensifying the exercise of their agency as managers of their households. This included: the reduction of household expenditure and consumption; activating the domestic economy; selling household assets; selling their personal jewellery; borrowing from relatives and neighbours; and increasing the support they receive from informal charities (IWS 2001, Obrien and Pickup 2002, Kuttab 2006). For example, the quantity and quality of the food women consumed decreased, whilst their domestic workload increased (Oxfam 2007).

Continuous violence and economic insecurity has also affected men's and women's education, employment, and marriage patterns. Research conducted by the Institute of Women's Studies (IWS) in 2008 on the impact of the Second Intifada on gender shows that interest in basic and higher education for both men and women has continued to climb since 2000, despite the economic collapse of the family and restrictions on movement. The rise of male and female educational attendance is attributed by Palestinian men and women to the destruction of both the unskilled local labour market and the informal sector. As a result, men and women want to work in the public sector, the only secure source of income. Educational attainment has also become a coping mechanism against the loss of families' sources of income and the destruction of their local economy. Families have invested in their children's education, especially female education, either as a potential source of economic support for the family, or as a marriage resource. Women's participation in the Palestinian labour force is, however, still amongst the lowest in the world, at 11 per cent of the total labour force (PCBS 2007). It has, however, slightly increased during the years of the Second Intifada (IWS 2008).

During the Second Intifada women have also had better opportunities to participate in public life and to control their sexuality. This has in turn affected patterns of marriage and reproductive health. PCBS figures from 1997, 1999, 2004 and 2006 show a remarkable decline in the number of women marrying by the age of 20 – with a drop of 20 per cent between 1997 and 2006 in Gaza.[19] This shift away from early marriages for women is largely situational, arising from the increasing number of women pursuing higher education, and those who have become employed in order to contribute to, or provide for, their families. It is also a reflection of the inability of families to cover the financial costs of marriage (dowry, wedding and housing expenses). Early marriage has remained the dominant preference for uneducated women, with no opportunities to work in the public sector. PCBS data of 2004 and 2007 suggests 10 per cent of women in Gaza are still marrying at a very young age. Women's fertility rate has also been affected by the increasing poverty. From 8.37 in 1992 it reduced to 5.4 in 2006 (PCBS, 2004b and 2006). An IWS survey on domestic violence also exposed how profound insecurity in Palestinian society diminished women's sense of personal

19 See all the PCBS official statistical reports available at: http://www.pcbs.gov.ps/.

security. In the Gaza Strip women's education appeared to reduce the levels of violence they were subjected to (IWS 2008: 96).

The personal security of family members appears to be a central concern, particularly amongst women with young children. Family relations continue to mediate the effects of public insecurity and long-term unemployment in ways that either facilitate or prevent violence and conflict in the family (IWS 2008: 98). In such contexts, the decisions taken by women are mainly family-centred. The prioritisation of the security of family members may be reflected in contradictory behaviours: the increasing willingness of women to participate publicly in education and employment, to enable their families to survive materially; and the tolerance or accommodation of domestic violence and contestation based on gender and age in order to maintain the connectedness between the family members, as a source of social and spiritual support.

These empirical studies of the Second Intifada all affirm the reconfiguration of gender through the challenging of stereotypical gender roles, gender access and control over resources and decision-making, and sexual divisions of labour. Lamis Abu Nahleh points out:

> Loss of work and decline in household income has strong resonance in the gendered reallocation of household material and labour resources and reflects the gendered reaction of dealing with the dilemma … men suffer the crisis of job and income loss and women absorb the shock, carrying the burden of providing for the family. (Abu-Nahleh 2006: 180)

Women cope with the consequences of war and crisis by using a combination of strategies: accommodating, resisting and negotiating family patriarchy and hierarchy (Giacaman and Johnson, 2002a, Taraki 2006, Abu-Nahleh 2006). Abu Nahleh considers both men and women to be victimised within the family patriarchal system. Both sexes act to reinforce it, accommodate its norms and codes, or negotiate and resist its restrictions and boundaries (Abu Nahleh 2006: 182). Resistance to male domination, exemplified in women's enactment as a primary family provider, increasing interest in education and employment, and increasing mobility, are most likely decisions taken in relation to the immediate purpose of family survival and security. These decisions are, however, associated with the inability of men to practice their male gender norms.

Research Problem, Objectives and Analytical Framework

My research is an intervention in the ongoing theoretical debate on the relationship between structures, gender relations, and the constitution of gendered subjectivities. This research is grounded in a multi-disciplinary and multidimensional notion of the feminist theory of intersectionality, through which I can understand and analyse the complexity of gender relations and women's agency and subjectivity in the specific political and historical context of the Gaza Strip. Although gender relations and women's agency in Gaza have been influenced by multiple micro and macro-political and historical factors, this research focuses on the empirical analyses of the gendered micro-politics of poor and vulnerable women who have become dependent on international, national and local sources of humanitarian aid: their 'negotiation, cooperation, and contestation in different but intersecting institutional arenas' (Hart 1995: 61, quoted in Kandiyoti 1999: 137). The research examines how changing gendered responsibilities for the material and social survival of the households/families affect the meaning of women's agency and subjectivity, and how the reconfiguration of gender stereotypes is reflected in the representation of the gendered self and others from relational and inter-subjective perspectives.

There are multiple dimensions to the impact of the specific economic and political context of Gaza. Gazans have not only lost their material sources of power for economic survival, but also their self-respect and dignity based on the historically and socially constructed meanings of masculinity and femininity (Adibi 2006: 4). This work explores the significance of these meanings, and specifically considers two potential processes within which agency may be exercised: resistance against household poverty and vulnerability and resistance against the crisis of gendered self-representation. In this context, if the newly emerged gender performativity forcefully created by external colonial forces (Israeli military occupation and the international community) is not experienced as desirable and pleasurable, but rather as humiliating, women as well as men may seek to find an alternative, in order to resist this humiliation without abandoning the daily necessities of economic survival. This may be reflected in the enhancement of the presentation of internalised images of masculinity and femininity, as an attempt to maintain a meaning for social and moral existence, whilst other meanings based on nationality, class, kinship and patriarchy are diluted by the destruction of the political economy. However, these possibilities cannot be validated in my research on the basis of existing feminist theoretical frameworks, unless sufficiently empirical evidence from women's day-to-day life experiences are provided (Kandiyoti 1998, Al-Ali 2007).

The dominant framework of analysis used in gender literatures of the Second Intifada, particularly its impact on gender roles and dynamics within households and local community institutions, provides sufficient evidence on the agentive nature of women and their capability of achieving valued outcomes for family survival and security (Taraki 2006, Hasselknippe and Tveit 2007, Mitchell 2009).[20]

20 See FAFO report no. 41 (2007): 'Against the Odds: How Palestinians cope through Fiscal Crisis, Closures and Boycott', a study conducted in three phases: one a year into the Second Intifada, the second after three years, and the third in March 2007. It includes details about effects on health, education, poverty and food security, and also explores coping mechanisms used by Palestinian families, including dependence on humanitarian aid, reliance on family networks and reduction in household expenditure.

However, this literature mainly concentrates on material aspects of agency. It has not given sufficient emphasis to the complexity of the relationship between the enactment of material, practical aspects of agency and the subjective aspects of experiencing gender within inter and intra-personal relationships that result in specific self-presentations for each gender (Moore 1994). This research tries to fill this gap by exploring the multiple dimensions of women's agency – the subjective meanings beyond changing gender structures and the forms of women's agency produced by the livelihood crisis during the Second Intifada. The research considers the different political, institutional, historical and inter-subjective elements that influence the form of women's agency being enacted in the specific context of absolute poverty, reliance on international humanitarian aid, personal and familial insecurity and high levels of uncertainty inside Gaza.

The research examines a number of questions: why do vulnerable women in Gaza naturalise and undermine the form of oppression based on gender to concentrate on resisting other forms of oppression, like the ones practiced by the Israeli occupation, the national government, and the international humanitarian agencies, despite the evidence that women in Gaza have historically experienced gender-based oppression from their husbands and their mothers-in-law? (Holt 2003). How can we analyse the contradictions between the actuality of gender performance, where women act as the primary provider and the core decision-maker of the family and where men are helpless, and the presentation of gendered subjectivity, where women willingly and consciously enhance their feminine subjectivity as subordinated and masculine subjectivity as dominant? These questions are grounded on the relational constructionist theory of Connell (2000). Connell rejects the essentialist concepts of gender, where masculinity and femininity are its basic terms, by arguing that masculinity, like femininity, is not fixed in character. Both are socially constructed and reconstructed in relation to the changes in institutions, economies, and everyday life experiences (Connell 2000: 24). In the Middle East, masculinity is not only constructed by the patriarchal culture and religion of Islam, but also influenced by local realities, religious and political agendas, the consequences of colonialism, and the market effects of globalisation (Kandiyoti 1994, Ouzgane 2006: 6, Adibi 2006: 3). Thus femininity and masculinity take different characters in different places and at different times, whether in the form of domination or subordination. Men as well as women represent the characters of the two genders through the relationship between their day-to-day activities and their language of presentation, in order to 'validate self-worth and encourage resistance against other forms of oppression' (Cornwall and Lindisfarne 1994: 5).

The research on which this book is based has sought to excavate the complexity of women's exercise of their agency through accommodation of, and resistance to, patriarchy. This complexity may be attributed to the contradiction between the structural interpretation of gender and gender relations and the actual exercise of women's agency on the ground. To better understand the complexity of gender and gender relational dynamics and their effect on the process of self-formation, it is important to differentiate between the actual power that women gain and practice, and the ideological and subjective presentation of their selves. Although the fluidity of gender structures is confirmed by many Middle Eastern empirical studies, including Palestinian studies (Kandyoti 1998, Joseph 1999, Shalkomy 2003, Taraki 2006), it is not yet clear whether the fluidity of gender structures in these different Middle Eastern contexts creates fluidity within ideological and subjective images of women's subordination and male domination. If not, why do women retain the image of male domination despite the actual material and social power they gain and the social legitimacy of their practice of agency?

I refer in both my analytical framework, and in shaping my research questions and objectives, to anti-essentialist feminist approaches within the anthropological and sociological disciplines, which emphasise that the study of women's agency and gender relations has to be both contextualised and historicised. The actuality of women's lives must be explored in order to expose, analyse, and critique multiple forms of oppression based on gender and non-gendered factors. This framework also helps to analyse the effects of the various local, national and transnational actors/institutions in shaping particular models of agency, which act instrumentally as well as morally to meet specific individual and collective goals in a specific context (Kandiyoti 1998, Moore 1999, Al-Ali and Pratt 2009). I also agree that there is a need to reject the conventional dualistic approaches of some feminists which dichotomise gendered concepts: domination and subordination, femininity and masculinity, autonomy and dependence, superior and inferior, emotional and rational. The diverse experiences of women, especially in the recent war and conflict situations in Middle Eastern countries, particularly Palestine, are not only shaped by gender, but are also significantly influenced by other considerable factors, such as colonialism, racism, class inequality, religion, and sexual orientation (Al-Ali and Pratt 2009: 10).

Deniz Kandiyoti points out that the messiness of modern social realities exceeds the explanatory power of the conceptual frameworks. She suggests that it is hard to have a starting point for analysis, while self-determining, autonomous individuals may or may not be the starting point for analysing women's agency and gender relations. For Kandiyoti, although contestation and resistance based on individual capacity are possible, they are always circumscribed by intersecting institutional and cultural constraints at local, national and international levels (Kandiyoti 1999: 174). Women's decisions and choices to resist or to accommodate the gender order, according to Kandiyoti, 'may derive neither from false consciousness, nor from conscious collusion but from an actual stake in certain positions of power available to them' (ibid. 143), in both the domestic and public domains.

All this is made more complex by the character of gender relations as both structural and interpersonal, as well as being characterised historically with fluidity and resilience. Love, care, respect and intimacy between men and women may be enacted in parallel with the practice of male domination, and perhaps in parallel with male violence within a specific context, and these enactments may be rationalised as well as moralised in relation to the different positionalities of both men and women throughout their life cycles, according to the specific structural changes that occur in certain times and in certain places (Kandiyoti 1994, Moore 1994, Joseph 1999, Kholy 2002, Mahmood 2005).

Research Methodology and Fieldwork

Research Sites

The research fieldwork took place in two Gaza Strip communities: El-Shujae'ya neighbourhood and the Beach camp. The Beach camp was selected as a representation of Palestinian refugee life, and El-Shujae'ya neighbourhood as a representation of a non-refugee urban neighbourhood. According to the PCBS 2007 census, the Beach camp has a population of 34,648 and El-Shujae'ya has a population of 19,800. Both communities are located in Gaza city, the largest city in the Gaza Strip. Gaza city covers 45 km^2, and has a total population (excluding the Beach camp), of 449,221 (228,630 male and 220,591 female) (PCBS 2009).[21] El-Shujae'ya is an impoverished neighbourhood on the east side of Gaza city, with few resident refugee families. It is situated on the eastern border with Israel, and has been exposed to numerous Israeli military assaults and incursions. The Beach camp is located to the west of Gaza city, on the seafront, historically a safer location compared to that of El-Shujae'ya.

The criterion of population classification in the Gaza Strip is between refugees' localities (the camps) and predominantly non-refugee localities (where some refugees also live). The Gaza Strip has become increasingly urbanised due to the destruction of its agricultural sector, and its prolonged dependency on the Israeli economy (Roy 1999). Just 5 per cent of the population is considered rural (PCBS 2007). Most rural communities are located near the borders between Gaza and Israel, and their land is frequently razed during incursions by the Israeli military. El-Shujae'ya is the only urban neighbourhood within Gaza city situated adjacent to the border with Israel.

According to the local municipal classification, Gaza City has 11 neighbourhoods, including the Beach camp. There is very little documented

21 The Gaza Strip is divided into four districts: North district, Gaza district, Middle district, and South district. Gaza district consists of the Beach camp, Gaza city, Zahra city, Mughraqa, and Juhr el Deik. The total population of the Gaza district is 496,411, classified in three categories: 449,221 urban population, 12,542 rural population, and 34,648 camp population (see PCBS, January 2009). According to the 2008 records of the Ministry of Local Governance Categorization, Gaza city does not include rural areas, and all its segments are named as neighbourhoods, except the city centre, see the World Bank project documents of 'Village and Neighbourhood development', available at: http://web.worldbank.org/external/projects/main?pagePK=64283627&piPK=73230&theSitePK=294365&menuPK=294396&Projectid=P104257.

information specific to the background of the research sites. Thus, I depended on information regarding the history of both sites from older residents and from traditional community leaders.[22] A brief history of the two sites selected for this research follows:

The Beach camp As one of the eight officially recognised refugee camps in the Gaza Strip, the camp is administered by UNRWA, and the local municipality. These two bodies provide basic health and education services, as well as distributing food and cash aid. The major source of employment for refugees used to be men from the camp labouring in Israel and contracting or sub-contracting for Israeli garment factories, whilst women worked from home on both a paid and unpaid basis. A substantial number of the residents' male refugee population has historically been employed in the local fishing industry, utilising traditional Palestinian skills from before the 1948 establishment of Israel (Hammami 1994). After the establishment of the PNA, in 1993, many public employees came from the camps. Most, however, consisted of employees on the lowest salaries. The Beach camp location is advantageous, because it lies very close to the centre of Gaza city, thus facilitating residents' movement and access to central health and education services, and institutions.

El-Shujae'ya neighbourhood Prior to the Israeli closure of Gaza, the majority of El-Shujae'ya residents worked as wage labourers in Israel. Like other rural border neighbourhoods in the Strip, they cannot now use much of their land for farming or agriculture, as it has been appropriated by the Israeli military as part of their buffer zone, and cannot be used by its Palestinian owners. Due to its location, local residents have been killed and injured by the Israeli military and a large number of local homes have been demolished. Many families have been displaced and forced to live with other family members. Like other urban neighbourhoods in Gaza, El-Shujae'ya has been extensively urbanised by the historical change from local agricultural labour to wage labour in Israel.

Despite the changing mode of production, from farming to wage labour and trading as a result of the Palestinian economy being integrated into Israel's economy, El-Shujae'ya maintained its traditions, dominated by local clan culture. The few El-Shujae'ya families who own substantial amounts of land did not sell it in order to invest in their children's education, as other Gaza city landowners have done, considering this to be a shameful practice. Local families are characterised by large numbers of children, and traditional leaders and elders still act as judges in order to resolve family and neighbourhood disputes. Local women in El-Shujae'ya are actively involved in the informal trading sector.

---

22 I conducted a number of field visits and informal conversations with the traditional leaders of the main clans in the two sites: El-Shujae'ya and the Beach camp in order to gather information about the two sites' contemporary history.

Sampling and Research Methods

The research sample consists of 60 women from the two sites: 30 refugees from the Beach camp and 30 non-refugees from El-Shujae'ya. The women are from very poor and vulnerable households. However, the research participants are not quantitatively representative of the overall population. The conclusions from this research do not depend on quantitative methodology. The 60 cases were selected based on specific features of poverty and vulnerability that characterise the vast majority of Gazan families who are dependent on humanitarian aid. For the qualitative purposes of this research, reliability and validity of the research findings are more dependent on the wide level of socio-economic and cultural diversity between the 60 cases selected. Compiling precise data on the research subject, and on the life stories of the women, is a primary methodological element to serve the objective of this research. The comparison between the different cases – based on factors of locality, age, marital status, poverty trends, and dynamics of actions – is another important element in the provision of reliable research analysis and findings.

This book does not attempt to reach any generalisation regarding women's individual actions. These actions cannot be standardised as they are highly context-specific, as responses to the type and forms of structural constraints and facilities; to the scope of women's capacities to exercise their agency in coping with or to challenging poverty and vulnerability, and to the diverse history of different individuals. My research is more qualitative, aiming to understand the actual life experiences of poor women and how these experiences shape and reshape their actions regarding the meanings they ascribe to their own actions, and their sense of agency. The sample cases provide precise, in-depth and detailed information about the relational, attitudinal and behavioural processes of change that women have been encountering. The research participants were also chosen with a view to considering the multi-generational dimension that serves the historical elements of the research questions.

This book specifically focuses on women whose families are classified and selected as extremely poor and vulnerable following the national Palestinian definition of poverty and vulnerability. The PCBS defines extreme poverty is when a household of two adults and four children live on New Israeli Shekels (NIS) 1,000 (US$250.6) per month or less, approximately NIS 5.5 (US$1.38) a day per person. Vulnerability, on the other hand, is defined by the PCBS as being when a household does not have enough to live on. According to the 2007 UNDP survey of poverty in Gaza and West Bank, 41 per cent of extremely poor households are barely surviving on their income, whilst 18 per cent do not have enough to live on. These definitions of *poor* and *vulnerable* are couched in terms of the absence of sources of income, such that families are basically reliant on humanitarian assistance from formal and informal institutions (PCBS 2007).

The following are the criteria used for the selection of the purposive research sample considering the different material and social features of poverty and vulnerability:

a. All the women were aged 18 to 65 during the research; they were married, divorced or widowed and live with their children, who are either dependent or married. This age range is important in order to highlight differences in the experiences of three generations of women. It also serves to compare women's past and present actions and self-perceptions within the historical contextual analysis of changes in the Palestinian family and women's life cycles.
b. All the women in the sample are classified as housewives. They have no formal employment status, and they have not been registered or involved in the national labour force. However, they are most likely involved in the informal economy.
c. Women who are the heads of household, widows, divorced, or living with chronically sick husbands. The wives of 'martyrs' are also considered as heads of household. Their number increased during the Second Intifada, and they are usually registered as hardship cases by the Ministry of Social Affairs and UNRWA safety net programs.
d. Women who live with able-bodied husbands and/or sons and have no regular sources of income. They are dependent on humanitarian aid. Some of these women were better off before the Second Intifada, when their husbands and/or sons had wage labour in Israel.
e. Women who live in large extended families, reliant on one or more sons working as low-income public employees, but their total income classifies the family as extremely poor in relation to the size of the family. This criterion helps to differentiate between extremely poor families with regular low-income earners and vulnerable families fully reliant on humanitarian aid.

Specifying the classification as *housewives* serves to narrow the scope of the research to focus on women who have historically been perceived as *domesticated*, regardless of their level of education. According to a 2008 study by the Women's Affairs Centre, housewives constitute more than 90 per cent of women over 18 years of age in Gaza (WAC 2008). This broad category includes women who are involved in domestic and non-domestic economic activities, but only in the informal sector. Focusing on housewives helps to provide a better understanding of the profound gender changes in the practice, and the imaginary of gender in Gazan society during the Second Intifada, as housewives with jobless husbands have represented the poorest and most vulnerable families in Gaza during this period.

Most development planners and scholars continue to use the Gazan household as the central unit of analysis. This is a methodological problem that ignores individual differences based on gender and age in understanding household dynamics. As result, policies and strategies of humanitarian aid are often gender-biased, and gender changes are analysed and interpreted as in connection with family interests, disregarding their link with the different subjective aspirations and desires of both individual men and women.

Although the household unit provides the essential context within the community at large, women as individuals are the central unit of analysis in this research. Women's self-perceptions and their objective and subjective interpretations of the different actions and interactions they undertake throughout their lived experiences are the critical elements for understanding the dynamic interplay between women's individual agency and the structure of power relations. In addition, their presentations and interpretations clarify or redefine notions related to female autonomy and their resistance of the gender order.

Three qualitative methods were used during the research: semi-structured in-depth interviews, life stories, and focus groups. These approaches better served the research, as they are contextual and historical methods, with the potential to capture the social, personal and interpersonal aspects of women's daily lives and their relationship with the past. Six women were selected in order to conduct individual interviews as a narration of life stories from which detailed information and analysis was extracted.

The analysis of women's life stories is central to realizing the contextual and historical approach to this research. Through them, I aim to understand better the dialectical relationship between current life and memory of the past in the making and remaking of gendered selfhood. The empirical data used in this research is also supported by other relevant sources of qualitative data compiled in the same period of fieldwork. Beside my PhD research, in which this book has its origins, I was asked to conduct two other qualitative researches for UNRWA and the World Bank in Gaza and the West Bank. These two studies aimed to examine the socio-economic and cultural impacts of the Second Intifada on gender in Gazan society. I received permission from these two agencies to use the qualitative data from both research projects for my own PhD research analysis. The two studies used several quantitative and qualitative methods (survey, individual interviews, workshops and focus groups). However, only the data from the focus groups (FGs) was used for the purpose of this research.

Phases of Conducting Fieldwork

Phase 1: An overview of vulnerable women's daily lives (July 2007 – April 2008) This first phase of the field work aimed to collect, analyse, and compare data regarding the actuality of poor and vulnerable women's lives during the Second Intifada. The research sample of 60 women was asked one open question as a starting point for semi-structured interviews between the researcher and the research subject: 'How has your household been affected since the beginning of the Second Intifada, and how do you and the members of your household survive?'

Semi-structured in-depth individual interviews (SSIIs) were conducted with 30 women in each site, to profile women's poverty and vulnerability, along with the actions and interactions they use in order to cope with, and confront, their family situations. The SSIIs also served to make a comparison between women, based on differences in household structures, age and marital status, which clarified the analytical and historical context of the research, thus enriching the data analysis.

Around 60 per cent of the SSIIs were accomplished in one meeting, with the remainder taking two or three meetings. Some of the women were not comfortable speaking about their household problems in the presence of other family members, which meant that SSIIs had to be postponed on a number of occasions. In El-Shujae'ya the SSIIs were conducted in women's homes, and also in two local women's community organisations, visited regularly by local women, who registered there in order to receive humanitarian assistance (in the form of food coupons, temporary jobs, and home-based production projects or grants and agricultural assets). However, the majority of SSIIs in the Beach camp were conducted at women's homes, and a minority in local community-based women's organisations. This also served to clarify the formal and informal institutional constraints and opportunities Gazan women encounter whilst communicating and negotiating with regard to their problems and their needs.

Phase 2: Women's life stories and gender historical contexts (January – August 2008) During the period of conducting individual interviews, I selected six of the original research participants (three from each research site) and asked them to provide detailed life histories, in order to collate in-depth information of intra and inter-generational diversities, to understand better the intra-family dynamics and its effects on gender and gender relations. These six cases were selected after I had completed 20 SSIIs in each site, requiring further meetings between myself and the six research participants. These informal visits, and the subsequent interactions, led to the selected women better understanding and analysing the complexity of their gender, and in some cases changing their attitudes and perceptions about themselves and their society.

The three women selected from each research site where chosen in order to represent Gazan women at different stages of their lives, and in different household circumstances. They comprised:

- Two married women in their early 30s with a large number of dependent children. One lives in a nuclear household and the other in a separate co-located household.[23]
- Two female heads of household, both widows in their mid-50s with a large number of children. They live in extended families with their married children.

23 The definition of different household structures is explained in Chapter 3.

- One married woman in her late 40s whose husband is chronically ill and who lives in a separate co-located household.
- One married woman in her late 40s living in a nuclear household.

Phase 3: Cross-checking and further analysis (March 2008 – August 2008) In addition to the preliminary data collected by the SSIIs, and the six life histories, I conducted four focus groups with groups of vulnerable poor women from both El-Shujae'ya and the Beach camp: two focus groups in each community, with 10 to 12 women participating in each focus group. A total of 50 women participated in the four focus groups. They were selected using the same criteria as the research sample selection. These focus groups were later followed by focus groups that I conducted during research projects that I carried out for UNRWA and World Bank.

The UNRWA focus groups were conducted in March 2008. A total of 99 women participated in nine FGs, divided equally between three Gaza Strip locations: North and South Gaza, and Gaza city. In each location women were categorised into three groups:

- Married or previously married (divorced or widowed) housewives aged 22 and above;
- Single women aged 17–22, with the focus on less educated women in this age group;
- Employed and unemployed women aged 22 and above, searching for a paid job.

Although I did not originally plan to interview men during this research, the UNRWA research involved focus groups with men, which helped me to cover this methodological gap, and the qualitative data compiled from these FGs enriched my gender analysis. Thirty six men participated in three FGs, one in each of the three regions. The participants to a large extent represented the diversity in men's education, economic and social status and age. The World Bank focus groups were conducted from mid-April till the end of May 2008. A total of 14 FGs were conducted in the five districts of the Gaza Strip: four with housewives, four with female youth, four with male youth, one with teachers, and one with micro-credit borrowers. This data helped me to cross-check my compiled information and deepen the analysis.

This process of conducting fieldwork enabled me to have access to large amounts of qualitative data from a large number of participants in addition to the 60 SSIIs. It also presented me with a serious challenge regarding the analysis of the high degree of diversity in the information gathered from a wide range of social groups. The quantity of raw data was coded and classified throughout the writing of this book, following the sequential development of the research outline. Some data was coded in the beginning, in order to understand the developmental cycles of Gazan households before and after the Israeli military occupation; to typologise Gazan households during the Second Intifada; to categorise different coping strategies for survival during the livelihood crisis, and the gender and generational effects of coping. My treatment of the qualitative data was a process in which I tested emerging thematic interpretations against the content of the collated material.

Research Timing, Constraints and Ethics

The qualitative research data was collected during the three phases, from July 2007 – August 2008. During the period of fieldwork no clear differences were noticed between the refugee and non-refugee women in terms of their openness to communicate their life experience in detail. Slight differences were presented based on age and economic status. Older women with years of experience working in public, who were at ease communicating in the public sphere, were generally more open and fluent in their dialogue than younger women, whose experience was mainly domestically-based. Formal education did not appear to be a significant factor during my interactions with the female research participants.

Men did not constrain, or object to, the interviews in either of the research sites. This may be explained by the work practices of humanitarian programmes that routinely send fieldworkers to make regular home visits to families in need of humanitarian assistance. The field-workers often meet women at home, particularly older women, as opposed to the men, because it has become socially accepted that women are more knowledgeable about the actual needs of their families. When men did intervene during the interviews, it helped me better to understand and analyse the gendered relationship between them and their wives.

I deliberately tried to break down any image of unequal power relations between myself and the research participants. However, some of the women I interviewed asked me to assist them in gaining access to coupons or temporary jobs, assuming that I had influence with local humanitarian organisations. I agreed to help them explore possibilities of assistance, and discussed individual cases with heads of local community associations, and made recommendations supporting women and families whom I believed to be in dire straits. But I did not attempt to interfere in any associations' decision-making processes. Through these interventions I assisted several especially vulnerable families in gaining access to humanitarian aid.

Many of the common ethical difficulties that researchers encounter whilst carrying out qualitative research were not present during my fieldwork experience. The research participants were ready to talk openly about their lives. I was also emotionally in tune with local Gazan women, thereby excluding many formalities and increasing the reliability of the information collated. As a result, the women brought up sensitive personal issues for discussion. My social background, which is similar to many of the research participants' backgrounds, enhanced the mutual process of interpretation during the field work, during which women contributed, in many cases, to challenging my own way of thinking about my gendered selfhood.

I am a Gazan woman and lived in El-Shujae'ya until I was 22 years old. My family was well known among most El-Shujae'ya inhabitants, which helped to create trust with the research participants. I have lived, worked and experienced life in both of the research sites. This however created both methodological and ethical implications. My personal and historical experience in both El-Shujae'ya and the Beach camp was always present in the research analysis and findings, because I was myself part of the process of interpretation and reinterpretation, reflecting on, and comparing, my own personal experience (Warren 1988, England 1994). Regarding the ethical implications, I deliberately attempted to be sufficiently detached from my research as to neither completely obscure my position as a researcher, nor to undermine the dialogical intersubjective relationship between myself and my research subjects. I was careful when and how to use and communicate my personal knowledge of the research themes in order not to undermine the centrality of the women's knowledge and interpretation.

Although I was experiencing multiple and contradictory positions of power in my own subject positions – that of being a Gazan wife of a political prisoner (regarded as a 'martyr' after his death), and a mother of two children – I said little in detail about my personal life during the field work. I did not want my research subjects to think that I was familiar with details that could affect their willingness to discuss their social and personal lives. Nevertheless, I was, of course, subjective in my research. My personal experiences and memories were always present during the research process, and in the drafting of the final text.

Overview of Chapters

Chapter 2 presents a conceptual framework outlining the theoretical underpinning of this book. It offers a more detailed analysis of the dimensions of women's agency in relation to the ideology of gender transformation, and with respect to the differences in context between the Middle East and other parts of the world, by reviewing the main social scientific theories regarding agency, followed by my setting out the context of the Middle East scholarship regarding different trajectories of feminist activism and theory. This chapter also includes analysis and critique of accounts of women's agency in the Middle East and how these overlap with international intellectual feminist debate on women's agency. I explain how my research contributes to the intellectual debate on women's agency, particularly in re-examining women's agency and subjectivity in contrast to mainstream liberal perspectives.

Chapter 3 delineates the historical structure of the Palestinian family and of gender relations. It includes two main sections; the first describes housing and the gender relational structure of the households of refugees and non-refugees in the post-1948 period. The second examines structural changes in the Palestinian household and family relations under the Israeli military occupation (1967–2000).

It also examines the effects of both the first and the second intifadas on the Palestinian gender order.

Chapter 4 discusses and analyses the effect of the Second Intifada on the economy of women's everyday lives. It covers a number of themes: the gender-differentiated basis of household livelihood during the Second Intifada; coping mechanisms that women adopt for household survival, how these mechanisms create both enabling and disabling environments for men and women from different generations, and the gender and generational effects of the coping strategies used.

Chapter 5 examines changes in the dynamics of gender relations in a situation of masculinity in crisis: first, it describes the different bargaining tactics used by women within the family and how these tactics shape the positions of women throughout their life cycles; second, it discusses the crisis of masculinity during the Second Intifada and its effects on changing forms of presentation and representation of gendered selfhood by both men and women.

Chapter 6 presents the research conclusions. It attempts to theorise the concept of women's agency and subjectivity, reflecting on the model of women's agency in Gaza. It opens an important debate about the relationship between structure, individual practice, and the constitution of gendered subject and subjectivity.

Chapter 2
Agency and Meaning in Women's Lives: A Comparative Analytical Perspective

Introduction

For decades, many social scientists have attempted to conceptualise the relationship between structure and human agency, to debate the nature of the relationship between the two, and to refute one-dimensional theories of individualism and structuralism. Individualist theories consider structures the aggregates of individual actions and decisions (Homans 1958), while structuralists posit that social systems determine individual actions (Parsons 1951). Theoretical debates of the structure/agency relationship have developed in various forms within different theories: functionalism, Marxism, methodological individualism, modernism, socialism, post-modernism and post-structuralism, and intersectionality. This chapter contributes to these debates by challenging the essentialist and dichotomist theories of agency that confine agency to resisting structured power relations. Instead, agency is historicised, contextualised and personalised by understanding the objective and subjective intersectional elements (gendered and non-gendered) that contribute to shaping and reshaping human agency and subjectivity. Human agency in this chapter is analytically and politically specified and located *in situ* rather than by drawing upon normative, feminist politics.

The conceptual framework which emerges in this chapter aims at addressing the historical, contextual, political and moral elements underpinning the gendered tensions experienced by Palestinian women during the Second Intifada. In the extreme livelihood crisis in Gaza, particularly during the years 2007–2010, these tensions arise and are located between: women's actual capability to take powerful independent actions and decisions publicly and domestically; and their subjective representation of themselves as ideal wives and mothers reproducing and transmitting the imaginary of masculinity and femininity based on the ideology of male domination.

This chapter is organised into three main sections. The initial section reviews contemporary theorisations of the structure/agency relationship with a focus on feminist theory and post-structuralism and specifically their critiques of rational liberal approaches to subjectivity and agency. The explanatory and analytical potential of each theory is examined in terms of its ability to address the complexity of women's day-to-day experiences in the Middle East, and specifically in the Gaza Strip.

The chapter's middle section presents how Middle Eastern women and their agency have been historically constructed in hegemonic discourses of nationalism, liberal feminism and Islamism. The predominant liberal feminist theorisations focus selectively and exclusively on the repressive aspects of two Middle Eastern institutions, namely, patriarchy exemplified in family-kin and community relations, and Islam. While recognising their contributions, I critique these theorisations as being largely empirical and descriptive and having significant shortcomings, namely: the need to historicise and contextualise women's agency; the need to address the multi-faceted and productive nature of women's agency and subjectivity (i.e. class, gender, race/ethnicity, generational, rural/urban); the need to analyse and integrate the substantial effects of other key institutions like the state, the economy, the legal system and different state policies on women's agency. I draw on critical theorists to highlight these theoretical problems and present an intersectional feminist approach adopted by Middle Eastern feminist scholars. This intersectional approach – which is the key focus of this chapter – emphasises a combination of historical-political analysis of women's agency and intersubjective analysis and allows for more reflective forms of agency which are shifting, multiple and contradictory.

In the chapter's third and final section, I critique accounts of the specificity of women's agency in the Middle East and discuss how these accounts actually overlap with international intellectual feminist debates on women's agency. The critique draws upon the intersectional feminist framework of analysis which focuses on understanding and analysing multiple objective and subjective dimensions affecting the form of agency, and the different dynamics women use to interact with the multiple discourses they experience.

In the concluding section, I consider the need to re-examine current discussions and conceptualisations of women's agency in the literature in light of the critiques and discussions within the chapter. The specific case of the Gaza Strip provides important insights in answering the following research questions, namely: On what basis should women's agency in Palestinian society be defined or redefined in relation to resistance and/or accommodation of male domination? Why are women in Gaza interested in maintaining the image of male domination despite the actual power that they wield?

Agency between Structure and Intersubjectivity: Theoretical and Feminist Implications

The complexity of understanding the relationship between structure and human agency is apparent when answering questions such as: 'what do humans do?' However, this complexity becomes even more evident when one considers how and why humans act in a certain way. The answers to such questions are situational, functional, political and/or moral. The form of agency determines how social change will happen. For the purposes of this research, I frame agency in terms of either reproduction or transformation of the social order. I briefly review some theories of human agency and their implications for feminist theorisations of difference and potentialities of resistance to male domination as a form of social injustice.

Agency is analysed in Weber's individualist theory of rational choice (1978), Giddens's theory of structuration (1979, 1991), Bourdieu's theory of '*habitus*' (1990, 1998) and Foucault's theory of the subject as an effect of disciplinary power (1980, 1983, 1997). Influenced by these various theorisations, feminist theorists worldwide have further historicised, contextualised, politicised and moralised the meaning of women's agency and its effect on the actuality of women's lives (de Certeau 1984, Young 1990, Kandyoti 1998, Kabeer 1999, Yuracko 2003, Meyers 2002, 2004).

Feminist scholarship has critiqued rational liberal conceptualisations of women's agency where actions are presumably taken for the greatest individual benefit. Feminist theorists argue that this notion of free and autonomous actors has failed to provide the potential for achieving justice for women (Hampton 1993, Radzink 2005). The feminist debate on women's agency has shifted beyond materialistic and distributive perspectives to emphasise the constitution of women's selves. These important theoretical developments have influenced Middle Eastern feminist scholars – a point to which I will return later.

In contextualising women's agency, feminist scholars shifted their focus from the individual to the inter-subjective and relational dimensions of women's lives. Essentialist dichotomist theories of structure/agency have been thoroughly critiqued by feminist scholars since these theories are unsupported by empirical evidence (de Certeau 1984, Kandiyoti 1998, Cornwall 2007). According to de Certeau (1984), in situations of necessity or uncertainty, women's tactics for managing their day-to-day activities take pragmatic precedence over the pursuit of strategic choices; so, in these circumstances, the exercise of agency may not lead to actual improvement in women's lives or to transformations of the gender order. Middle Eastern feminist scholar, Nadje Al-Ali, also cautions against approaching women's agency in a linear chronological manner as a function of changing socio-economic and political structures, as different historical periods are experienced differently by women (Al-Ali 2007).

Despite diverging theorisations of women's agency, feminist scholars do agree that regardless of the repressive nature of the social system, women act and make choices and decisions that influence their lives (Allen 1998, Kabeer 1999, 2000). Two critical lines of inquiry emerge in these feminists debates. Firstly, are women making these choices 'freely' or as a result of other dynamics and processes? And secondly, do women's choices always imply resistance to patriarchy? If not, how do we explain women's choices? These questions open up complex intellectual and empirical debates about the agency of gendered subjects within the process of self-construction. Henrietta Moore argues, for example, that the agency of both men and women has to be analytically and politically specified in context rather than assumed in advance (Moore 1994: 50).

Over the past two decades, most literature on women's agency in the Middle East has portrayed women as active agents capable of negotiating their position in a gendered order to achieve their interests for a better quality of life. Some empirical studies (Boddy 1989, Macleod 1991, Singerman 1995) analyse women's exercise of agency contextually through their relations with family-kin networks and the use of religious rituals. These studies assert that women's agency entails resistance to male domination or patriarchy, while others (Kandiyoti 1988, Early 1993, Haj 1992, Shalkomy 2003, Johnson 2006) claim that women only bargain and compromise with the patriarchal system. The implications of the latter group's claims are rather bold since, for them, no Middle Eastern woman actually challenges or resists the patriarchal system. A dichotomy underpins much of this research and literature which simplifies and reduces women's agency to either resisting or accommodating patriarchy. Feminist anthropologists however have emphasised that women's agency and the dynamics of its practice never take a singular form or remain constant. Agency is always in motion with ambiguous and unpredictable outcomes. Women are social beings dynamically interacting with their social environments, responding to multiple discourses, and reflecting on diverse individual histories (Hollywood 2004, Moore 2007, Bucar 2010). This interaction and reflection process generates possibilities for more creative theorisations of women's agency and multi-faceted identities, as well as moving beyond simple, reductionist dichotomies of resistance and accommodation of patriarchy.

Divergent models of agency in the Middle East identify a range of contextual factors, such as: structural constraints exemplified in state structures, policies and regulations; the patriarchal structure of family and society; and the internalisation of the prejudicial culture of religion and patriarchy (Kandiyoti 1993, Afshar 1993, Moghadam 1996, Joseph 1999). By the early 1990s, the presumed relationship between agency and resistance to male domination was common to both liberal feminist and socialist feminist perspectives. While the former considered patriarchy and Islam as the main constraints on women's autonomy and freedom (Duval 1998), socialist feminists asserted that while patriarchy and Islam provide discursive foundations for women's subordination, they also create institutional sites for women's practice of agency and power (Kandiyoti 1991a, Afshar 1993).

Since the 1990s, this literature has increasingly addressed women's diverse life experiences, roles and status in light of differences in class, religious interpretation, race and ethnicity, and over time (Keddie and Baron 1991, Kandiyoti 1993, Afshar 1993, Meriwether 1999). More recently, Middle Eastern feminist scholarship has shifted its emphasis from structural-individual frames, to focus on the subjective, interpersonal and intrapersonal elements (e.g. connectedness, intimacy, love and care) that contribute to the shaping of women's agency whether as resistors or accommodators of male domination (Macleod 1991, Cooke 2000, Mahmood 2005). However, the feminist debate remains engulfed in a dichotomy which reduces women's agency to either resisting or accommodating patriarchy. My research suggests that women's agency and subject formation constitute a much more complex process in which women move between the various discourses in a conscious, agentive way to best respond to their objective and subjective interests and desires.

Trends in Feminist Theory towards Intersectionality and Intersubjectivity

As stated earlier, the essentialist dichotomist model of agency has been critiqued by feminist scholars – be they postmodernists, poststructuralists or intersectional analysts. They all reject singular and dichotomist understandings of agency, for example: subordinated or dominated; masculine or feminine; passive or active; rational or emotional. These scholars all focus on the need to understand the diversity of women's individual and collective experiences. While post-structural feminists have largely decentred the liberal notions of the free, autonomous agent, the normative model of agency for post-structuralists remains fixed on assumptions of strategic choice and/or on resisting gender norms and male domination. Subversive or emancipatory acts which resist relations of domination are but one modality of human action – a tendency which Saba Mahmood calls the theory of the liberatory (2001: 208).

Empirical analyses of women's agency in Africa, Asia and the Middle East provide sufficient evidence of women in diverse situations acting to shape different forms of agency to meet their personal and familial goals over the short and long term (Agarwal 1997, Kabeer 1999). Nevertheless, the outcome of women's exercise of agency remains unpredictable precisely because that agency is always simultaneously both constrained and enabled by multiple intersecting factors: class, gender, age, race, ethnicity, religion, cultural system, national and transnational forces, geopolitical divisions, the personal history of individuals and groups, and many other factors specific to each context. The intersection of these factors makes it impossible to constitute a unified form of agency, and as a consequence, a unified form of outcome.

The trajectory of contradictory modalities in women's everyday lives reinforces the need for an analytical and political perspective for the contextualisation of women's agency. Since the beginning of the twenty-first century, feminist scholarship has largely sought to challenge the singular dimensions of thought by shifting its concern towards intersectionality. As a multidisciplinary framework of analysis, intersectionality is concerned with understanding and analysing the different dimensions affecting the form of agency and the constitution of gendered subjectivity in a specific time and place, without necessarily being generalisable to other contexts or moments. Patricia Hill Collins's conceptualisation of intersectionality asserts that the forms of oppression that men and women experience are not independent of one another, but are bound together and influenced by intersecting systems in society, such as race, gender, class, nationality, religion and ethnicity (Collins 2000: 42).

Intersectional feminist analysis and frameworks recognise and attempt to identify the ways in which different systems (i.e. race, class, gender) and conditions intersect and work together at specific times and places to create various forms of gendered inequality and experience. These frameworks allow for combining various approaches, including an individual (embodied or experiential) level of analysis; a relational or interactional analysis; and/or a social structural analysis. Intersectional feminist frameworks all emphasise the ways in which diverse social locations shape lived experience and the construction of power and oppression through social interaction (Glenn 1992, Smith 1999, Collins 2000, McCall 2001). To avoid essentialising dichotomies in analysing women's life experiences, intersectional feminist analysts deal with structural, institutional, behavioural and subjective elements as an inseparable package. According to Patricia Hill Collins, in any society, the dominant ideology and culture are demonstrated by the interlinkages 'between their social institutions (structural domain), their organizational practices (disciplinary domain), and the level of everyday social interaction (interpersonal domain)' (Collins 2000: 284). No domain operates in isolation, and quite the contrary, all constantly interact and influence each other.

Intersectional feminist approaches overlap with intersubjective feminist approaches in so far as the subject's meanings, morals, emotions, desires and fears are not constituted in a vacuum, but within the subject's historical interaction with the diverse collective situations (structures and discourses). As Moore argues, the gendered self only emerges as a consequence of the way it identifies and invests in social and ideological values (Moore 1994: 507, Moore 2007: 20). This may explain why women in specific political and historical contexts through their everyday life experiences show their preference often to act to maintain their subordination by enhancing the agentive and subjective aspects of their femininity, that is, their sensitive emotions and feelings towards others, and their sense of collectiveness and dedication inside their homes and in the local community (Held 1993, Hampton 1993). This practice of women's agency is interpreted differently by feminists. Sandra Lee Bartky, the liberal feminist, points to structural constraints that force women to behave in a feminine fashion, to diminish their aspirations, and to embrace gender-compliant goals (Bartky 1990). Others refer to the internalisation of gender oppression which renders women less capable of overcoming or resisting it (Kabeer 1999, Meyers 2002).

In contrast, other feminists do not see women's enactments of femininity as inferior or as devaluing the gendered self. These enactments are rather viewed as a conscious strategy women use to enhance their autonomy and self-respect (Hartsock 1983, Hoagland 1988, Friedman 1993). These authors consider the moral and emotional aspect of women's agency – for example, the provision of care and love, mothering, friendship, and forming separate women-only gatherings – as a form of resistance to the liberal form of a masculinised self that puts women in conflict with their femininity. For them, the intimate interpersonal relations, through which women value themselves and act accordingly, are also seen as linked to social transformation. The power of women's selfhood to change social arrangements is achieved through women's connectedness to others, but this is not always a reflection of common gender interests (Hartsock 1983). The valuing of intersubjectivity in women's selfhood stands in considerable contrast to the rational liberal model in which women's individuated self is based on free choice, accompanied by a reality of social isolation and self-alienation.

Some feminist theorists view intersubjectivity as an important element for achieving justice (Friedman 1993, Card 1996, Kitty 1999). These authors are concerned with diluting the masculinised self that is reinforced by the liberal discourse of rationality. For them, the masculinisation of women's selves leads women to sacrifice the distinctive values of their femininity and to restrict social transformation processes aiming at greater justice (LIoyd 1992). However, the increased emphasis on the value of women's enactment as self-sacrificing care-givers prompts important questions. Do women's feminine enactments serve a devaluing function and, as a result, reflect a devaluing of self? And does their empowerment imply that women have to pursue the universal model of masculinised agency (i.e. to be rational, recognised in public, and act as dominant)? Do such framings and questions themselves reflect a dichotomous approach to understanding both women's agency as either rational or emotional and women's actions as either resistance or accommodation of male domination? To answer these questions, a rethinking and a re-examination of how women conceptualise their exercise of agency and power are required.

Empirical evidence suggests however that there is no singular form of masculinity or femininity: rather, both are contextual (Moore 1994, Connell 2000). In the current hegemonic global system of militarisation led by men (Zarkov 2007), women may prefer to keep their exercise of power through the enhancement of the subjective features of their femininity, through caring and giving love, through dedication and self-sacrifice, and through collective and emotional attachments. While structures of male domination may remain uncontested, this exercise of power seemingly gives women a sense of moral distinctiveness to challenge the immoral aspects of masculinisation of the self. In this respect, Virginia Held argues that unlike men, women do not seek hierarchal control and contractual constraints, but 'the power of a mothering to empower others, to foster transformative growth, [which] is a different sort of power from that of a stronger sword or a dominant will' (Held 1993: 209). Nevertheless, women's enhancement of their feminine selfhood does not necessarily obstruct their capacity to practise the socially-constructed masculine aspects of power, particularly in situations of necessity and scarcity. The masculine character of women's exercise of agency is situational and may be instrumental, as illustrated in the performance of gender roles. This performance is deliberately used to meet the necessities of living. In the process, women's capacity to choose and decide is reinforced, while the feminine character of agency and women's sociability is maintained and enhanced by them to meet their personal desires and fantasies.[1] It is these multiple and sometimes contradictory aspects of agency that I examine in the example of women's agency in Gaza.

In the context of this analysis, I would like to emphasise that the concepts of masculinity and femininity used above are not fixed. They are, rather, situational, relational and as mentioned earlier, shaped by gender and non-gender systems (e.g. class, race, ethnicity), as well as factors like location. These fluid concepts of masculinity and femininity are invested at the intersection of these systems and factors. Masculinity and femininity are negotiated, reproduced and communicated in everyday life (Kandiyoti 1998). Regardless of the differences of their sexed bodies, men and women can act as both genders, albeit under specific circumstances, since each gender's experiences must be contextualised and located in a specific time and space. Masculinity, like femininity, is not fixed in men and boys, and cannot therefore be essentialised. Rather, gendered subjects are socially constructed and reconstructed in relation to changing institutions, economies, and everyday life experiences (Connell 2000: 24). Femininity and masculinity assume different characters in different places and at different times. Men and women represent the characters of the two genders through the relationship between their everyday social interaction and their language of self-representation. For Nancy Lindisfarne, a space always exists for a 'subordinate version of masculinity – as an alternative gendered identity – which validates self-worth and encourages resistance against other forms of oppression' (Cornwall and Lindisfarne 1994: 5). Through social interaction, both men and women learn how to modify their femininity and masculinity within different domains of discourses and contexts in order to stabilise or destabilise the existing gendered and non-gendered system of domination (Cornwall and Lindisfarne).

In situations of gender instability,[2] as with the masculinity crisis in Gaza, women may feel more empowered by enhancing the socially-constructed characters of their femininity: as dedicated mother and care giver dependent on intimate interpersonal relations. Yet, these women show a high capacity to maintain their autonomy and freedom. On this reading, I argue that gendered selfhood operates from a consciously motivated position. Under circumstances of war, deinstitutionalisation and stark familial deprivation, Palestinian women have learned to compare and assess the anticipated outcomes of performing the socially-constructed masculine and feminine aspects of agency to attain their personal

1 See Henrietta Moore's 2007 book, *The Subject of Anthropology: Gender, Symbolism and Psychoanalysis*. Moore's psychoanalysis of subjects' desires and fantasies does not refer to the private ones, but to those created by the hegemonic cultural ideologies. For her, cultural ideologies are built upon the impossibility of realising one's desires. The gendered fantasies of being a different sex are the representational means by which society – where men and women interact with the continuously changing social and gender structure – culturally and ideologically represents itself to itself (2007: 19–20).

2 Gender instability as described by Moore occurs when the appearance of the gendered subject does not match with the origin of the social (2007: 22).

and familial goals. Women also examine the intersectional factors affecting their lives and accordingly decide when and how to resist or accommodate forms of oppression based on gender and non-gender interests.

Women's decisions to accept or reject male domination are not *only* a question of their capacity and interest in resisting domination. In today's modern and postmodern societies, women have proven highly capable of achieving autonomy – that is, making strategic choices and shaping their goals in life (Kabeer 1999). Nevertheless, in certain socio-economic and political contexts, women may intentionally decide not to resist the image and the structure of male domination. This raises the question of how women strategise their resistance and why they select certain strategies that support male domination. To answer this question, I refer to my assumption that women often perform as strategic actors, even though their performance is based on a system which subordinates them.

In situations of continuous deprivation and poverty imposed by an oppressive system, women learn from their life experience about when and how both to invest in the historical image of their subordination and to facilitate the achievement of their personal and familial immediate and strategic goals. Lewin et al. emphasise that:

> Women, like other people, have goals and desires which go beyond their immediate situations – they might seek political power, control over other persons, financial security, love, whatever. Feminine behavior, then, must be interpreted in relation to the goals women are moving toward – to an extent, their actions are bound to be strategically chosen. (Lewin et al. 1971: 13, as quoted in Rogers 1975: 337)

Nevertheless, with poor and vulnerable women, the achievement of their strategic choices is most likely restricted by the high level of uncertainty and contingencies in their life experience, as in the Gaza Strip.

De Certeau (1984) and Andrea Cornwall (2007) both explore women's agency in situations of necessity, describing their enactment as situational, relational and provisional. According to Cornwall, poor women's fulfilment of their strategic choices is not only constrained and enabled by 'asset endowments and opportunity structures' and by their capacity to act as autonomous agents, but also by the contingencies of their circumstances in the household, the work place, and within the web of relationships (2007: 29). The capacity of poor women to pursue their strategic choices is extremely limited (Cornwall 2007: 42) not because they are incapable of shaping these choices, but because the situation of uncertainty and contingent circumstances are restrictive at the structural and intersubjective levels. Uncertainty and contingent circumstances make women consciously or unconsciously take 'a pragmatic precedence over the pursuit of strategic choices by the use of tactics to manage uncertainty' (Cornwall 2007: 43). This nuanced analysis is important for my own research since it suggests that apparent inconsistencies between women's tactical actions and strategic actions may not be caused by a lack of consciousness of their strategic choices, whether gendered or non-gendered.

Having presented this intersectional feminist framework as relevant and appropriate for analysing Middle Eastern women's agency, in the next section I will examine this framework's relevance in relation to the specific historical and contextual factors affecting the process of constituting women's agency.

Discourses of Women's Agency in the Middle East

Much of the literature theorising Middle Eastern women's subjectivity attributes just two institutions with shaping and limiting it, namely: patriarchy exemplified in family and kin relations; and the role of the various forms, practices and interpretations of Islam. Middle Eastern women are represented as active agents struggling in multiple spaces with the persistence of patriarchy and Islam (Kandiyoti 1993, Afshar 1993, Meriwether 1999, Shalkomy 2003). Arab Muslim culture is represented as being produced by and embedded within cultural institutions in the Middle East conditioned by a patriarchal society that legitimises the domination of men over women. In these representations, this association of patriarchy and Arab Muslim culture is attributed a central role in shaping and reshaping the particularities of women's and men's agency in the Middle East. While agency is of course shaped and reshaped by Arab Muslim culture, multiple other contextual and historical systems and factors also play key roles (Adibi 2006: 5). Adibi's constructivist analysis challenges the single-faceted, homogenising and culturalist approach to agency.

The experiences of women's agency in contemporary Arab Muslim societies reveal, however, a variety of modalities that make gender relations historically and contextually fluid and ambiguous (Keddie and Baron 1991, Joseph 1993, Abu-Lughod 1989). Contrary to the claims of liberal feminists and much contemporary literature, gender, gender relations and constructions of masculinity and femininity in the Middle East are not determined by the religion of Islam, the Qur'an or other sacred texts. Gender relations and subjectivities are influenced by multiple systems and factors (e.g. social class, labour market and economic relations, the state and state policy, ethnicity and culture, sexuality, history), as well as individual experiences and relations with family peers. These multiple systems and factors are integrally implicated in the formation of male and female identities in the Muslim and Arab world (Keddie and Baron 1991, Kandiyoti 1991, Afshar 1993, Adibi 2006). Historically, Nikki Keddie emphasises that in the Middle East 'there was never one set of Muslim women operating under one set of rules' (Keddie and Baron 1991: 207), because of the differences both within and across Arab Muslim societies related to different histories, state policies, class differences, ethnicity, sexuality and so on and over time.

Within the diverse historical trajectories of nation state and specific policies, the practice of patriarchy and various interpretations within Islam have rationalised, relationalised, and moralised women's agency while also being exposed to multiple, complementary and contradictory discourses: modernity, nationalism, traditionalism and Islamism (Ahmed 1992, Moghadam 1993, 1996, Afshar 1993, Badran 2007).

Although the feminist project in the Middle East succeeded in refuting colonial perceptions of Middle Eastern women as voiceless and submissive, this refutation is insufficient to understand the link between women's enactments as active agents and the specific constitution of the gendered self. Much of the literature presents women's agency as either: politicised motherhood in national liberation struggles – particularly, in the Palestinian, Egyptian and Algerian literatures (Sayigh 1998, Lazreg 1994, Baron 2005); or as bargaining with patriarchal structures and culture to wield their autonomy and to achieve their familial and personal interests (Kandiyoti 1988, Haj 1992, Early 1993). One reading of the contemporary literature suggests that the debate on women's agency and subjectivity is centred on the conciliation and tension between feminism and the prevailing discourses of nationalism, modernity and Islamism (Kandiyoti 1991, Ahmed 1992, Moghadam 1992). While Islam and patriarchal family kinship systems appear to serve as the central socio-economic, political, institutional, and ideological grounds of the intellectual debate, both have been used to defend national and cultural identity from the consequences of modernisation and more recently, globalisation.

In what follows I will present and explore the characteristics of Middle Eastern feminist discourses vis-à-vis nationalism, liberalism and Islamism. I am aware that the colonial and post-colonial multiple feminist discourses experienced by Arab and Muslim women throughout contemporary Middle Eastern history have overlapped and been contested; each has had diverse interpretations and reinterpretations at different historical moments. I present this categorisation only to enable differentiation and comparison. Different feminist discourses developed in the contemporary Middle East are also examined to illustrate how gender is negotiated and how agency is shaped and reshaped by the various political and ideological discourses, as well as by different life experiences and histories of women in connection with their collective situations.

Feminism and Nationalism

The first group of self-consciously feminist writers in the Middle East emerged during the colonial period when these societies became concerned with national liberation. Within nationalist discourses, there were persistent tensions between modernist and anti-modernist trends. The former trend suggests that the advancement of Middle Eastern women is achieved by combining the cultures and structures of patriarchy with modernity, while the latter is concerned with diluting and contaminating cultural values and identity through modernisation. As a result, women's opportunities and participation in nationalist independence struggles were complex and contradictory (Kandiyoti 1995). The modernist, nationalist trend, however, remained dominant before, during and after formal independence until the 1960s. The focus was on enhancing women's participation in national liberation struggles and constructing and developing the modern nation state by involving women in education and employment (Antonius 1979, Talhami 1984, Haddad 1980, Warnock 1990, Baron 2005).

Despite its predominance, by the 1960s, this national liberation discourse had largely subsided in much of the Arab World. In Palestinian society, however, this discourse persisted and was further fuelled for various reasons, including: the situation of statelessness and dispossession of Palestinians in 1948, the loss of land, and the 1967 Israeli Occupation of the West Bank and Gaza Strip. The continuation of the 1967 Israeli Occupation served to ensure the Palestinians' necessary prioritisation of national struggle (Hammami 1995). Within this nationalist frame, women's demands for participation were largely legitimised by the needs of society, rather than on the basis of individual rights and equality (Gluck 1995). Significant and successful female activism is well documented historically in Egypt, Algeria, Palestine and Iran, where women participated energetically in national struggles only to struggle later with national authorities for access to social welfare and to education and employment (Haddad 1980, Talhami 1984, Baron 2005). Nevertheless, women's nationalist activism remained delinked from any analysis of their social subordination (Ahmed 1984, Hale 1986).

According to Lazreg (1994), within nationalist discourse, women have been identified and become symbols for culture both by secular nationalists and their Islamist opponents – restricting the possibility of social transformation. Some scholars criticise the joining of modern nationalist with traditional Arab Muslim patriarchal discourses – which maintained the dominance of the markers of religion and patriarchy in defining cultural identity (Kandiyoti 1993, Lazreg 1994). For many Middle Eastern feminist scholars, this combination diminishes the substantial engagement of women in the process of social transformation; women are selective in their engagements in order to maintain the distinctive features of their national cultural identity (Hale 1986, Naryan 1997, Hasso 1998). More specifically, the possibilities of independent feminist scholarship (Kandiyoti 1995) are seriously constrained by the complex entanglement of discourses of anti-imperialism, Islamism and national development, combined with state repression and the fear of Islamist movements.

Women's identity in nationalist discourses is basically understood as motherhood (Abu-Lughod 1998, Peteet 1997, Jean-Klein 2000), although feminist scholars critique and analyse this differently. For Peteet, the identity of women as mothers has been used in Palestinian society to serve national liberation goals. Women act as a subject for wider change, including national liberation. The meaning of motherhood for Palestinian women resisting the Israeli occupation has been reconstituted by their active engagement in that resistance. According to Julie Peteet, mothers acted as 'national icons' during the First Palestinian Intifada. As symbols and icons, mothers and especially older mothers of adults were mobilised both to empower and to constrain women. These older mothers were labelled as 'mothers of the nation' – a label and a role which not only failed to challenge but further enhanced gendered and age-based power structures. Through their engagement during the First Intifada, these older mothers of the nation claimed public roles for themselves, while effectively enhancing the domestication of younger women (i.e. daughters, daughters-in-law) and reiterating that women's positions and responsibilities were located in the domestic sphere. Mothers' sacrifice for the nation was represented by the male national leadership as an aspect of the 'nature' of women. This representation of mothers' sacrifice served a wider national goal, namely that of reinforcing and supporting their sons' struggles against the occupation. Nonetheless, Peteet views mothering in Palestinian society during the political conflict and livelihood crisis as gender transformative. She argues that 'mothering and sacrifices and the hardships this entailed, were the ground on which to make claims for political and social rights and for the critiques of resistance' (Peteet 1997: 110). These mothers exercised their power over the younger generation of women (namely, daughters and daughters-in-law) by maintaining family honour which signified the honour of the nation.

In addition, nationalist discourse has constructed women as active agents locating and using their reproductive abilities to resist colonialism in the Middle East. In the Palestinian case, women's position as the mothers, wives and sisters of martyrs is romanticised. Some argue that women's involvement in national resistance has not transcended the boundaries of patriarchy, but has reproduced it (Sayigh 1983, Joseph 1986, Hale 1986, Lazreg 1994, Abu-Nahla 2006). Others interpret women's anti-colonial engagement and resistance as creating opportunities for challenging patriarchal gender-based structures (Peteet 1997, Jean-Klein 2000, Taraki 2006). This group of scholars built their arguments on the fluidity of gender relations in situations of war and conflict, especially vis-à-vis the mother-son relationship.

The literature on women and nationalism in the Muslim and Arab world provides sufficient evidence that gender and gender relations in these societies during the process of state-building were fluid and failed to take a singular form. The fluidity and ambiguity of gender relations during state-building processes differed both between and within different countries, influenced by the intersectional, national and transnational factors, namely: colonialism, government policies and politics, class, ethnicity, geographic locations, religious interpretations, and historical experiences (Keddie 1991, Ahmed 1992, Abu-Lughod 1989, Meriwether 1999, Baron 2005, Al-Ali 2007). Nevertheless, in many cases, women's agency and the fluidity of gender relations during periods of national struggle and state-building do not appear to significantly dilute the ideological and moral features of femininity and masculinity embedded in patriarchy and Islam. In this respect, Lila Abu-Lughod criticises nationalist discourses in their constructions of women but also argues that 'women publicly enact their own moral, and ultimately social, inferiority' (Abu-Lughod 1992: 203).

The relationship between nationalism and gender is however more complex than implied by liberal feminists focused on patriarchy, Islam and culture. This is a reductionist, ahistoric and often decontextualised understanding not only of Islam and patriarchy, but also of culture. The understanding of patriarchy and Islam, at a certain time and place, must be linked to the global system of imperialism and militarisation and its consequences for women's position and status. Many recent studies confirm that women's position and agency in Middle Eastern societies, and particularly those experiencing war and conflict with external imperial forces (as in Afghanistan, Palestine and Iraq), have rapidly deteriorated for reasons other than patriarchy or Islam (Abu-Lughod 2002, Mahmood 2006, Al-Ali and Pratt 2009). These studies point to the destruction of social and economic infrastructure in these societies by the militarised global system and various other national, regional, transnational, and international actors. Such analysis is highly relevant to the current Palestinian context and prompts similar questions as this book. In the specific situation of war and livelihood crisis caused by the Israeli occupation and blockade, why do Gazan women continually present themselves as inferior and label this presentation 'feminine'? Why this persistent enactment by Gazan women while important changing gendered relations of power and participation in public institutions are culturally legitimised by nationalist and Islamist discourses during the period of the Second Intifada?

Liberal Feminism in the Middle East

Forms of liberal feminist thought have been encouraged by the urbanisation of Middle Eastern societies and by the increasing interventions of western countries and their institutions in the socio-economic development of Middle Eastern countries. Liberal feminism has become the mainstream feminism largely institutionalised in Middle Eastern societies (Arebi 1994, Moghadam 1996). Liberal feminism was a dominant form during the second wave of western feminism and had as a central focus women's equal access to public opportunities and equal participation in public life. The achievement of individual autonomy, women's integration into the labour market, and ending all forms of gender discrimination are also important features. The underpinning framework is one of modernisation, while the overriding liberal modernist representation of women (adopted by western and non-western feminists in the region) is as a homogeneous social category, according to which all women have been subordinated by men through the institution of the patriarchal family and other social institutions. Liberal feminism represents Arab Muslim women in literature as passive, submissive and silenced by these dominant patriarchal structures. Liberal feminists argue that modernisation and women's liberation is incompatible with the persistence of tradition and religion (Duval 1984, Rubenberg 2001). These authors emphasise that the trajectory of gender transformation implies the dismantling of what is understood to be the main constraint to women's individual autonomy and freedom – the family and kinship relations and networks based on gender and age. To modernise society, liberal feminism also assumes that patriarchy and religion must be broken down, since women are understood as weak and inferior (Duval 1984).

Certain radical feminists also centre their analyses on heteronormativity, specifically located in the structures and culture of patriarchy and religion. For them, patriarchy and religion are timeless universals determining the subordination of women as a unified category. Nawal Sadawi is one of the few feminists who can be classified as radical in the Middle East. She has set out to liberate the mind, sexuality and legal position of Arab women (Sadawi 1993). Although Sadawi's work breached taboos on discussing sexuality and heterosexuality, her analysis tends to exaggerate the influence of culture in the form of religion and patriarchy, at the expense of institutional, historical and ideological factors responsible for women's subordination. Neither radical, nor liberal feminists see any facilitating or productive roles within patriarchy, whereby women gain and may use their agentive capacity to negotiate and manoeuvre their power and identity within the family and in society. Women are also represented as a homogeneous social group always positioned as subordinated to men in the family and society.

These singular dichotomist analyses of liberal feminism have been reviewed and critiqued by many, including Turkish feminist Deniz Kandiyoti (1993, 1996, 1998), Iranian feminists Hala Afshar (1991, 1993), Valentine Moghadam (1993, 1996), and by the Lebanese feminist Suad Joseph (1996). Kandiyoti and Joseph critique liberal modernist and radical feminist discourses for failing to analyse historically the gendered realities in the Middle East. Kandiyoti criticises liberal feminism for failing 'to appreciate the systemic deep-rooted nature of gender subordination, and for not providing a framework to explain it' (1995: 6). Moghadam also criticises liberal feminism in the Middle East for its one dimensional insight. For her, it denies the existence and effects of other wider structural, systemic and institutional factors that affect the status of women in Arab Muslim societies, by concentrating exclusively on patriarchy and religion as the determining factors positioning women (Moghadam and Sadiqi 2006). Supporting Kandiyoti's analysis (1991), Afshar (1995) emphasises that Middle Eastern women's subordination can neither be solely attributed to the ideology of Islam or its practices, nor explained by referring to the universalistic premises of liberal feminist theory. Islam, for Afshar, has been integrated into the lives of women differently, mediated by history, state, and individual practices.

Women in the Middle East have experienced and taken up diverse ideological and political discourses and positioned themselves differently within these discourses. These engagements have created multiple forms of consciousness and diverse responses, whether resisting, accommodating or engaging otherwise with the prevailing system (Kandiyoti 1991). I would argue that the diversity of forms taken up by Middle Eastern women partly explains why women's agency has not historically taken a singular form (Keddie and Baron 1991, Kandiyoti 1998). Women have constituted their agency through an active, conscious process of moving and taking up multiple subject positions created by the competing complex ideological and political discourses around them.

Islamism and Feminism

In the early 1990s, feminist scholars in the Middle East began to study the relationship between Islam and feminism, and this body of scholarship has grown significantly. However, most literature analyses this relation merely as a reflection of the combination of the socio-economic, political, historical and cultural factors (Kandiyoti 1991, Keddie and Baron 1991, Afshar 1993, Stowasser 1996).

Similar to faith-based movements in other parts of the world, the revival of Islam and the emergence of Islamist movements in the Middle East are contextual, situational and relational (Adibi 2006) and need to be approached and studied as such. The popularity of Islamist movements emerges within and responds to a particular context while developing instrumentally for social, economic and political purposes. Islamist discourses also develop to provide a moral, ethical and conceptual framework to guide social life (Mahmood 2005, Jad 2005). To understand the popularity and rapid emergence of these discourses and movements, one must understand that context.

Over the past few decades, much of the Middle East has experienced growing insecurity and vulnerability caused by global militarisation, military intervention and neoliberal economic policies. This insecurity was further exacerbated by the 'War on Terror' with its focus on Arab and Muslim suspects and networks. Besides socio-economic and cultural responses to poverty and vulnerability caused by war and repressive corrupt states, Muslim women in the region have also acted to shape a moral form of agency; in this process, women and men individually and collectively turn to religion as a form of faith both to defend themselves against the harshness of life and to achieve self-realisation (Mahmood 2001, 2006, Jad 2005).

The debate on feminism and Islam has been taken up by secular feminists on the one hand and Muslim scholars and activists on the other. These two groups or camps should not however be homogenised or dichotomised. Within each, there are divergent readings of feminism in Islam ranging from the more radical to more liberal interpretations and with varying emphases on historicisation and contextualisation. Amongst Muslim scholars and activists, Islamic paradigms constitute the central source of their diverse, even contradictory understandings of feminism in Islam. Muslim women scholars and activists are classified by Azza Karam (1998) into two main categories: Muslim feminists and Islamist feminists. Karam's clustering of the two groups is supported by several Muslim feminists albeit without these labels (Wadud 1999, Abu-Baker 2001, Barlas 2002). Both Muslim feminists and Islamist feminists are Muslim believers but with different politics and diverse views of feminism in Islam (Karam 1998).

Muslim feminists do not distinguish between the sexes on the basis of ability, but on their characteristics and roles in society. Most view the religion of Islam as having established a framework of gender equality. Social justice and gender equality are seen as intrinsic to Islam, and interpretations which suggest otherwise must be revisited and reinterpreted. Muslim feminists do not consider Islam or the

Qur'an as patriarchal; patriarchy for them stemmed from the pre-Islamic period and continued through patriarchal interpretations of Islam. These feminists view and promote their own role in interpreting Islam not only for pragmatic reasons, but because, as believing women, it is also most meaningful to them personally (Wadud 1999, Barlas 2002). Muslim feminists view Islam as compatible with modernity. As the English feminist scholar converted to Islam, Kate Zebiri (1993) argues, Islam has granted rights and duties or responsibilities to Muslim women in the family, in education and in society as a whole.

Islamist feminists, on the other hand, have different interpretations of feminism in Islam. The term, Islamist women or Islamist feminists, is mostly used to refer to women who are affiliated to Islamist political parties. However, this term is used more loosely here to include women activists who may share the broad aims of Islamist parties even if they are not members. These women, mostly activists in Islamist political movements in Middle Eastern countries, share an interest in clarifying the position of women through *ijtihad* – the already existing interpretations of Islam which are historically done by men. As a result, these women activists spend much time studying, analysing and referring to religious texts to support their arguments.

According to Karam's analysis, the difference between Muslim feminists and Islamist feminists lies mainly in their sources: that the latter only refer to traditional, authoritative interpretations of religious texts and find them still most suited to the modern day context (Karam 1998: 12). Inevitably, by holding to the interpretations already established by religious figures, Islamist women come up with a much more conservative interpretation of women's rights than Muslim feminists. Azza Karam points out that some Islamists argue that the Qur'an does not allow for gender equality and they, as women, should not strive for it (ibid.: 10). Gender equality is viewed as a western concept that has brought nothing good for western women, condemned as they are to struggle for equality with men, and to fail. They argue that it is not necessary or even desirable to equal men in their various endeavours, as they have different but complementary roles in life.

Yet the conservative discourse of Islamist feminism, as described by Azza Karam, is not generalisable to all Islamist feminists. Empirical evidence shows diversity among Islamist feminists due to differences in the political context. In Islah Jad's study of Islamist women in the Palestinian Islamist political party, Hamas, these women activists think and act differently due to their involvement in political Islam. Jad argues that the daily reality of life for women eager to work, be educated and participate politically has shaped a gradual and growing critique inside the movement. While committed to disseminating the movement's gender ideology, Islamist women were actively involved in changing the conservative gender vision of the movement. In both their writings and public activities like workshops and conferences, they admit that their movement has no vision or agenda for women's issues, and they encourage the reinterpretation of the religious texts to allow for a new reading relevant to processes of modernisation. Jad also refers to a paper written by an Islamist activist in Hamas which identifies

Islam as the religion which grants women all their rights, namely to: education; free choice of a husband; inheritance (albeit widely denied by customs); mobility to participate in matters related to religious calling; proselytising; and social or professional work. The same paper also stresses a more controversial issue – that of 'mixing with men' – and concludes that Muslim women were moved to prove themselves in all aspects and fields of life. Islam allows women to meet men and to exchange in dialogue if they are committed to the morals of Islam and Shari'a (Jad 2005: 36–40). Jad's analysis emphasises that as with secular feminists, Islamist feminists do not embrace or exhibit a singular model of agency and should not be homogenized. Differences in class, race, geographic location, religious and daily material practices are significant.

As various Muslim and secular scholarship from a range of theoretical perspectives has indicated and highlighted, feminist discourses in Islam and Islamic history are very fluid (Mernissi 1987, Ahmed 1992, Macleod 1992, Wadud 1999, Barlas 2002, Mahmood 2005). A central topic of discussion in the intellectual debate on feminism and Islam relates to veiling. While Muslim feminist approaches view veiling as a matter of personal choice, some conservative Islamist feminists see veiling as a compulsory act which distinguishes and defines Muslim women's identity (Barlas 2002). In her early 1992 outstanding book, *Women and Gender in Islam*, Leila Ahmed noted that for emerging middle class women in urban Egypt, veiling provided women with the freedom to operate in comfort and with the approval of family members in sexually-mixed environments such as universities, work places and on public transport. In this sense, depending on the context, veiling can sometimes be enormously liberating (Ahmed 1992: 224–225). Seen from this perspective, Islamic dress is not a return to traditional dress, but a modern phenomenon (Macleod 1991, Ahmed 1992).

Many other scholars focus their attention on the link between Islam and women's agency, arguing that women in Muslim societies are always in a position of power. Women, especially the poor, accommodate and resist male domination by referring to and practising religious rituals and codes to achieve autonomy and freedom in such areas as inheritance, veiling, dowry, men's financial responsibility or *Quwama*,[3] and entitlement for separate marriage houses (Macleod 1992, Moors 1995, Wassef 2001, Cooke 2000). Other scholars argue that Muslim women's practice of their faith helps them challenge the history of colonialism and destabilise the resulting gender order (Torab 2006). Saba Mahmood (2001, 2005), on the other hand, sees women's practice of piety as a sign of self-realisation, that is, of aspirations to be an ideal faithful Muslim woman. She argues that women's practice of pious agency is not motivated by resisting male domination, but is a means to achieve authenticity, purity and happiness.

3 *Quwama* is an Arabic term meaning guardianship or leadership. It refers to the Islamic tradition in which men have the financial responsibility for their female relatives. According to mainstream male Islamist interpretations, men's financial responsibility for women implies men's control over women's decisions and mobility.

I argue here that feminist discourses in Islam have historically taken multiple and contradictory forms as a result of the overlap between modernity and Islam in Middle Eastern countries. In contrast to the liberal feminist framework discussed earlier, Islam is indeed compatible with modernity (Ahmed 1992, Abu-Lughod 1998, Haddad and Esposito 1998, Hatem 2002). Many Middle Eastern feminist scholars agree that the main problem for women does not emerge from the holy texts and sources of Islam, but from the politicisation of Islam (Hammami 1990, Ahmed 1992, Litvak 1998, Mir-Hosseini 2010, Shalkomy 2010). Leila Ahmed posits the strong, empirically-grounded argument that it is not the practice of veiling as an Islamic symbol that is problematic, but the use of this symbol by hardline Islamist parties.

Ziba Mir-Hosseini and other secular Middle Eastern feminists warn of the perils of faith-based feminism, which she views as a vehicle for strengthening the agenda of political Islam. Mir-Hosseini is of the opinion, however, that secular feminist scholars have no option but to cooperate with Muslim women activists and to eliminate the dichotomy between 'Islam' and 'feminism' that characterises the politics of gender in the region. As part of a broader struggle for gender equality and justice, collaboration with Muslim feminists is an appropriate strategy. With Islam as the source of its legitimacy, Muslim feminism has great potential to challenge both the hegemony of patriarchal interpretations and the authority they imply to maintain gender inequality. Otherwise, Muslim women's quest for equality risks becoming a hostage to the fortunes of various political forces and tendencies.[4]

While neither Islam, nor the Islamicisation of Gazan women during the Second Intifada were the prime focus of my research, the unfolding of Islamist politics in Gaza since I began my research is undoubtedly a growing political and ideological factor affecting women's agency in Gaza. However, my analysis of Gazan women's agency and practice of Islam overlaps with the work of various feminist scholars, who have different interpretation of the relationship between Islam and women's agency (Mahmood 2005, Jad 2005, Shalkomy 2010, Mir-Hosseini 2010). I analyse the individual and institutional Islamicisation of women's agency from two interlinked dimensions: first, as an instrument used by poor women for the material survival of their families in situations of dire necessity; second, as an ethical and moral framework enhancing poor and vulnerable women's capacity to endure pain, suffering and hardship, while maintaining meaning for their social existence within the Islamist hegemonic ideology.

4 See the first issue of *Islam and Feminism: Dialogues on Women's Empowerment*, available at: http://www.contestations.net. The March 2010 issue includes Hania Shalkomy's article and a response from Ziba Mir-Hosseini.

The Intersectional Feminist Approach: Combining Historical-Political Analysis with Intersubjective Analysis

Feminist scholarship in the Middle East has also witnessed another philosophical offshoot since the early 1980s challenging essentialising, universalist discourses of liberal modernity and conservative Islamism. Anti-essentialist feminists are concerned with diversity in understanding and analysing gender relations and women's agency. Women's agency and subjectivity are no longer approached or understood from the singular perspective of gender oppression (limited to the domination of men over women and older generations over younger ones). Gender relations are instead understood as always in a process of negotiation and contestation to meet the interests of both men and women, as well as the interests of others at certain times and places (Keddie and Baron 1991, Kandiyoti 1998, Taraki 2006). Gender relations in this literature are analysed as situational and contextual, as well as political and historical. Tradition, religion and the past are embodied in the present strategies for survival, for earning a livelihood and for political participation (Singerman 1995, Johnson 2006). This understanding of women's agency requires an appreciation of the interconnectedness of the 'symbolic and instrumental: behavioural and ideological; and cultural, social and political process' (Abu-Lughod 1990: 41). Within the same framework, Nadje Al-Ali emphasises that women's agency in the Middle East cannot merely be understood as a static reflection of the changing socio-economic structures, but more importantly as the actual life experiences of women and the differences in their responses based on the intersecting factors of class, race, ethnicity, location, and interpersonal relations (Al-Ali 2007: 1).

As forms of patriarchal and hierarchal interpersonal relations, family and kin relations and networks have remained a central area of analysis, but based on different methodological, theoretical and political underpinnings. Family and kin relations as presented by Diane Singerman (1995, 2006) and Suad Joseph (1986, 1999, 2001) are the most effective source of personal and family security in situations of statelessness and/or weak or ineffective state governance. Suad Joseph recognises the constraining role of patriarchy, family and kin relations, as well as the power and connectedness which family relations can offer. She also comprehends its facilitating socio-political and economic effects. Joseph does not see patriarchy as merely centred or rooted in the family, but also in the wider society – in both market and state apparatuses. The patriarchal forms of kin and communal relationships are fluid, arising from differences in class, race, ethnicity and location. Suad Joseph sees patriarchy as both a constraining and facilitating structure for the fluidity of gender relations. In the region's political context, although patriarchy constrains women's equal access to healthcare, the education system, the labour market, human rights and democracy, patriarchy remains crucial for persons, men and women, to sustain the sense of self and identity (Joseph 1996, 1997). Family and kin interpersonal relations such as connectedness and voluntarism are crucial for social and economic security and for political membership (Joseph 1996: 15).

Joseph's studies attribute the persistence of patriarchy to the weak, often corrupted governance of states in the Arab Muslim world that fail to provide decent welfare systems to poor people; as a result, the informal social system of kin and family relations serve to fill the economic, social and political gap left by the formal system of social security.

In these accounts, patriarchy is no longer presented as singularly associated with women's disempowerment. Empirical studies have provided sufficient evidence to show that women use different power dynamics within the family and with kin and non-kin patriarchal relations to enable their families to survive within the local community (Singerman 1995, 2006, Taraki 2006). Arab Muslim women are situated within a wider perspective of patriarchy not only as active agents managing household and family needs and interests for survival, but also as political actors influencing politics in the public sphere. Hania Shalkomy (2003) and Penny Johnson (2006) assert that women in Egypt and in Palestine often prefer kin-marriage as a long term strategy of personal security where state sources of welfare and social protection are unavailable. The practice of kin marriage as a patriarchal social arrangement is maintained, even in the urbanised modern societies of the Middle East, as a source of family and personal security.

The central point in these discussions is that women's reliance on family and kin relations in the Middle East should not be perceived only as a function of cultural choice. Women's reliance on familial-kin networks must be understood within the system of power relations grounded in the modes of production, the type of nation state, and ideological frameworks and discourses. In poor communities, patriarchy is rationalised at the level of household economic survival and the survival of the family as a strategy for coping with and perhaps resisting the oppressive prevailing economic and political system (Singerman 1995). Historical and political analysis of multiple gender relations within patriarchy erodes dichotomous understandings of patriarchy as a form of domination of men over women and of older over younger generations (Kandiyoti 1988, Haj 1992, Shalkomy 2003, Johnson 2006).

An enduring issue in Middle Eastern feminist literature is the persistence of interpersonal relations grounded socially, emotionally and morally in patriarchal ideology and practice in mother-son, sister-brother, husband-wife and father-daughter relations (Joseph 1994, 1999, Peteet 1997, Jean-Klein 2000). Feminist approaches towards interpersonal relations have taken two forms. The first views the emancipatory potential of interpersonal relations for resisting patriarchy and the prevailing gender order (Boddy 1989, Singerman 1995, 2006, Kholy 2002). The second approach examines the moral subjective effect of interpersonal relations, specifically through the practice of piety, but without assumptions about resisting patriarchy, its structures or the prevailing gender system (Mahmood 2005, Deeb 2006, Za'atera 2006).

Singerman (1995, 1996) and El-Kholy (2002) exemplify the first approach and argue that poor Egyptian people, especially women, use interpersonal patriarchal relations to resist the broader prevailing system of oppression. Singerman attributes women's dependence on informal family and kin interpersonal relations to the failure both of the nation state to provide welfare for poor people and of the liberal discourse of women's empowerment supported by the global free-market economy. For Singerman (2006), reliance on formal social institutions and the prevailing free-market economy has neither liberated women, nor provided personal and familial security. In her previous writings, she has also emphasised that women, especially poor women, must always search for alternatives to secure their lives and livelihoods, and that they mostly find these sources of security in the reproduction of intimate, collective and reciprocal patriarchal relations and networks (Singerman 1995: 46). While an important empirical contribution, Singerman's 1995 study of poor Egyptian families overstates the role of the informal family and kin relations and networks in promoting change in the Middle East. Singerman argues that poor families use their family and kin networks to manage and secure their livelihoods – constituting a form of political resistance, even if through 'illicit' means. She adds that these individuals' actions necessarily lead to political influence related to the distribution of resources (Singerman 1995: 7–14). Within the same framework, El-Kholy emphasises that understanding women's agency as a form of resistance requires an understanding of the intersection between socio-economic and political structures, cultures, ideologies, and interpersonal relations (2002: 16–17).

The second approach to gendered interpersonal or intersubjective relations fluctuates between the conceptualisation of agency as resistance to and accommodation of social norms. This approach is centred on women's religious practices as an effective means for distinguishing a gendered self in the Middle East. Even though gender scholars' interpretations of religious practices are not homogeneous, scholars agree upon the importance of religion in either stabilising or destabilising gender relations, as well as in re-shaping the constitution of gendered self (Deeb 2006, Torab 2006, Za'atera 2006). Lara Deeb, in her study of *Shi'ite* Lebanese women, disagrees with the dichotomy of modernity against Islam. She considers women's practice of piety as a moral sign of 'authenticity' in which Islamic values and beliefs are rooted in women's minds and spirits and are pure and uninfluenced by fantasies of modernity. Women's practice of Islam is not a set of unconscious iterative performances as in Bourdieuian sense, but has a moral value that enables women to revive their sense of self-satisfaction, purity and selfhood without rejecting modernity. In this respect, Muslim women interpret and reinterpret their participation in higher education, employment and public politics as a requirement of being an ideal faithful Muslim woman, just as with veiling and sex segregation (Macleod 1991, Cooke 2000). While Deeb presents a mode of acting and being that may disturb the gender order and resist male domination, Saba Mahmood, in her study of Egyptian women, offers a very different trend of analysis. She focuses on the constitution of a distinctive gendered self that is not necessarily associated with resistance to the gender order.

Saba Mahmood (2001, 2005) problematises the universalised interpretation of women's desire as always emancipatory and tied to resistance. Through the practice of religiosity and piety, women are understood as active agents capable of realising their own interests against the weight of customs, tradition, and/or other obstacles. While women's religious practice may be analysed vis-à-vis its role in reinforcing or undermining the structure of male domination, this is not her main concern. Mahmood's analysis does not deny the possibility of transformation resulting from women's practice of piety. She draws on both Foucault's conceptualisation of power as productive rather than merely repressive and Butler's notion of agency. Regarding Butler's work, Mahmood claims that subject subordination can be a means by which a woman can become self-conscious and surpass stereotypical gender and male domination. Mahmood concentrates on how individuals operate, pointing out that agency operates neither 'to invoke a self-constituting autonomous subject nor subjectivity as a private space of cultivation', but to 'attain a certain kind of state of happiness, purity, wisdom, perfection, or immorality' in accordance with a particular discursive tradition (Foucault 1997: 24 as quoted in Mahmood 2001: 210).

Saba Mahmood's analytical framework explicitly contributes to understanding patriarchal domination as a subjective moral image which does not contradict women's exercise of agency based on their religiosity. However, willing subjects construct multiple, contradictory and shifting desires, capacities and virtues that are never static. Given the historic, cultural and political specificity of societal change, considering change based on singular measures (including moral measures) is illogical and necessarily reductionist. Perceiving women's agency as purely a function of moral or rational subjectivity is inconceivable precisely because morals themselves – whether religious or not – are also not fixed. They are influenced by changing socio-economic structures at national and global levels, by political and ideological discourses and by diversities in women's positions and individual experiences. Therefore, the two forms of women's subjectivity –moral and rational – consciously interact to shape the specificity of women's agency in time and space.

Critical Analysis of Dynamics and Constraints

The discussion in this chapter leads me to suggest that women in the Middle East have multiple forms of agency reflecting intersecting political, ideological and subjective dimensions. One way in which women's agency is presented within Middle Eastern literature is as the practice of subtle manoeuvres in adverse circumstances. Middle Eastern women's responses to their subordination support Ann Cudd's insights and analysis of oppression. Cudd found that some women may refuse to resist male domination, yet, utilise all incentives offered by the system of subordination to meet their interests and to achieve their goals (Cudd 2006). In her study of *baladi* women (women of the popular classes) of Cairo, Evelyn Early describes this specific social group of women as 'tricky, playing with egg and stone' to meet their personal and family needs and to wield power within the family (1993).

Another theorisation of agency suggests that women practise their agency as unconscious actors, having internalised their gender oppression and with little, if any recognition of their gender interests (Kandiyoti 1988, Haj 1992, Johnson 2006). While these authors do not deny the rational aspect of women's actions, actions are presented as tactical behaviours related to the necessities of social reproduction (de Certeau 1984). Despite their tremendous skill at negotiating strategic and tactical manoeuvres, women in the Middle East and their enactments continue to be viewed by these theorists through a lens of implicit assumptions about consciousness, personhood and subjectivities. In this respect, Kandiyoti reconsidered her earlier theorisation of women 'bargaining with patriarchy' and argued that gendered experiences of power, subordination and resistance cannot be captured under a singular analytical framework (Kandiyoti 1998: 136). Echoing Kandiyoti's reflections, I would argue that the enactments of bargaining and compromise by women – including those based on internalising their gender oppression – are a reflection of their *conscious* assessment of the situations in which they live and of a prioritisation of their own interests and desires. Women resist change in certain contexts because they are conscious of the social and moral rewards of acting within the existing gender order.

One widely-debated aspect of women's agency in the Middle East is the representation of women as practising self-denial and self-sacrifice for others, and especially for their children. Self-sacrifice is perceived differently by different scholars. For some, it is a moral sign of the ideal practice of motherhood (Peteet 1997, Jean-Klein 2000), as well as a sign of women's capacity to strategise about their power through the life cycle (Kandiyoti 1991c). Moreover, the valuation of self-denial for the sake of a better quality of life for their children cannot be solely attributed to the internalised gendered ideology of patriarchy and religion, as suggested by Kabeer (2000). Women's valuing of the denial of self as mothers also reflects women's evaluative capacity as autonomous agents. As part of their life and cross-generational experiences, women reflect on the effects of their actions and conclude that sacrificing for their children is more beneficial and effective over the long term for the quality of their personal and familial life. Through self-sacrifice, women minimise conflict and simultaneously ease the management and negotiation of their gender roles, responsibilities and relations.

If the subject is the site of multiple, even contradictory positionalities, then complex, multi-faceted and even ambiguous forms of women subjects always exist and are marked by different discourses (Moore 1994: 55). Discourses, as I understand them, are a set of interpretations and re-interpretations of the meanings and practices of power relations constructed within the prevailing structure. Although the socio-economic and political structures in Middle Eastern societies can be characterised as male dominated, these structures have historically been created and developed as mentioned earlier in this chapter – alongside multiple feminist and anti-feminist discourses and implying multiple forms of women's agency. These discourses have been used deliberately by women to preserve the normal operation of the prevailing gender order without restricting the exercise of their agency to achieve their own preset goals. In other words, multiple and contradictory discourses have given women throughout history the social and cultural legitimacy to shape and re-shape multiple and contradictory positions as subjects. Following Henrietta Moore's argument, the multiple and contradictory nature of these subject-positions creates an environment conducive to women gaining personal emotional satisfaction and material socio-economic benefits. These benefits are the reward of both men's and women's enactments of certain subject positions: authoritative husband, powerful mother-in-law, subordinated young daughter-in-law, faithful Muslim woman, or any other subject-position possibly constituted by the changing structures and changing discourses (Moore 1994: 65).

Concluding Remarks

In recent debates on agency in relation to gender structure and culture, the principal common element worldwide is the understanding that women's agency is always practised and situated at the dynamic location of action and interaction. Women's agency is influenced by several interlinked factors and interlocking systems that determine the forms of outcome achieved – whether regressive or progressive, emancipatory or oppressive. These factors and systems include the subjective aspects of gender ideologies, contextual social and economic realities (i.e. structural opportunities and constraints) and the individual strategies of negotiation towards action (Thompson 1991, Hochschild 1989). These systems work concurrently to produce both contradictory and complementary forms of women's enactment. Women in certain socio-economic contexts negotiate and/or compromise their gendered positions to achieve their immediate and strategic goals. The limits and boundaries of women's action extend or mitigate the moral and ideological aspects of their gendered constituted subject.

The critical conceptual and methodological point is that women's agency cannot be studied in a linear chronological manner (Al-Ali 2007). Women are not mere passive victims of circumstance but also perform as agentive actors throughout their struggle against these circumstances. Women's responses to their circumstances vary, not only because of their gender, but because of other political and historical factors that affect the forms of actions and interactions taken – producing different forms of gendered identity and selfhood. Women's agency is not necessarily motivated by resisting the dominant gender order. In situations of dire necessity and vulnerability, for example, women may act differently from women living under more secure conditions. While struggling for the survival of their families in crisis situations, the first group examines and questions its subjectivity and shapes its objectives accordingly, either to resist or to accommodate. New meanings and values may also be intentionally created, re-shaping the constitution of subjectivities to respond to newly-emerging circumstances and discourses. These may include the revival of their sense of femininity and their mothering roles as a sign of self-respect and dignity, despite having to enact socially-constructed masculine roles, as in the case of Gazan women. Given the impossibility of a standardised model of women's agency and of a single femininity or masculinity, women's agency can only be adequately conceptualised through an informed empirical analysis of the actual experiences of women in a specific time and place. As argued by Henrietta Moore,

> Understanding the agency of others and how they act in the contemporary world is thus a matter of comprehending the spaces and oscillations between integrating notions and diverse experiences. Selfhood is a situationally, not essentially, defined project. (Moore 1999: 15)

The discussion in this chapter also leads me to conclude that women always act on the conscious interests of their gender, including their consciousness of internalised gender oppression. Nevertheless, in certain contexts, they may act intentionally to reproduce prevailing systems that reinforce their subordination. They may also use the internalised image of gender subordination to restabilise the gender order. Why do women act this way? To answer this question is the focus of this book. I refer to Ernesto Laclau who analyses the relationship between ideology and structure. Laclau argues that the reproduction of social relations is impossible, but at the same time it is a necessity. Reproducing social relations is 'impossible because structural arrangements are essentially dislocated; [and a] necessity, because without that fabricated fixing of meaning there would not be meaning at all' (Laclau 1996: II).

In relation to gender, Laclau's argument can be interpreted to suggest that when the structural arrangements of gender are forcefully dislocated, men and women in a specific context may have no other option than to protect the prevailing ideology. This is reflected in men's and women's concern to enhance the ideologically-constructed image of masculinity and femininity in situations where gendered power relations are seriously disturbed. This dynamic is used by both men and women to ensure a meaning for one's social existence. These conclusions provide important empirical analysis and insight into the theoretical underpinnings of the meaning of women's agency and the representation of masculinity and femininity in Gaza, where the situation of prolonged livelihood crisis and insecurity is not one of a simple forceful dislocation, but a complex historical conjunction of circumstances.

Chapter 3
Family Structure and Gender Relations in Gaza under Israeli Military Occupation

Introduction

For more than half a century now, Palestinians have been living under conditions of tremendous stress, as a result of the Israeli military occupation of their land. The Palestinian family is one of the crucial social institutions that has preserved and reproduced Palestinian society under these highly adverse conditions. Fathers struggle to build and maintain a home for their family as breadwinners, and mothers sacrifice their own desires in order to invest in their children's education and marriage. But in the specific context of Palestinian society, the family cannot be considered at all times and all places as a site only of gender oppression.

Mudallala is a 58-year-old woman from the old neighbourhood of El-shuja'eya in the east of Gaza city. She narrates memories of the life of her non-refugee family in Gaza before the 1967 Israeli occupation of Palestine. In her narrative, 'the man was a man and the woman was a woman, each knew and respected his or her responsibility'.

Mudallala's narrative reflects the gendered features of the Palestinian peasant family among non-refugees in the pre-1967 period. Her traditional dress asserts that she is a peasant woman from El-shuja'eya. She is one of the very few local women who still wear the *toub* and *ghata el rass* (a long black dress and light white head scarf covering half her face). When I asked Mudallala to describe her memory of the Palestinian family before and after the Israeli occupation, she said:[1]

> Walla ya habibti, el yahood ma khallo el rejal rejal wala el mara mara, ma khallo la ard wala mal wala rejal. Kul she rah men hadeq el ayam. [Oh darling, believe me, since the Israelis came to Gaza, neither men stayed as real men nor women stayed as real women. The land, the money and the men, all were lost since these days.] We women have been just grieving the loss of our men from one side, and bearing the consequent misery of managing our living afterwards on the other. Oh my God, how hard the life of Palestinian women has been.

1 You will notice that in some narrations, I intentionally write down the Arabic words used by women and accompany them with the English translation. I found this technique very expressive, as it reflects the emotions, fears and pain women experienced, which can't be easily felt in the English translation.

Mudallala added:

> In the past, before the Israeli occupation, we [women] were working hand in hand with our men. I remember when I was ten years old [in the early 1960s], my mother used to wake me and my young brothers very early in the morning, to go and help my father harvesting the maize and wheat. My father and uncles were responsible for the wholesale of the produce, and my mother used to carry heavy loads of wheat and maize, and sometimes vegetables to the local market or to other family members or neighbours for sale. I never saw her sitting with idle hands. She was either sewing, cooking, or on the land with my father ... She used to sew my young brothers and sisters' clothes on a manual sewing machine.

Mudallala continued her narration, talking about her parents' relationship as an ideal model of gender relations before the Israeli military occupation:

> In the past, there were no schools and no universities, but women behaved better. Problems and disputes within families were much less, as we lived calmly [and] we used to earn our living in dignity. My father was so good with my mother, and my mother shared everything with him. I don't remember that he ever said 'no' to any of her requests. My mother wanted my father to show off his power with her, her children and the neighbourhood. This [in turn] gave her power at home. My father was a strong man who had a strong say at home, not like the men of today. Before the Jews, men were always with their families, providing them livelihood and security.

Although Mudallala's narrative does not necessarily reflect an accurate portrayal of the past, I do not want to undermine the authenticity of her words. Hers is a discourse that is often used in situations of conflict and contestation, like Gaza, to reflect the loss of any prospect for the future. Mudallala's memories of pre-occupation Palestinian peasant society are of a society where men visibly dominated the peasant family, and where both men and women negotiated different aspects of everyday life within the socially constructed boundaries of public and domestic domains. For Mudallala, the continuing presence of men with their families elevated the status of women.

Palestinian Family Structure Pre and Post the 1967 Israeli Military Occupation

This chapter identifies changes in the 1967 pre- and post-war periods that included the creation of a substantial refugee population inside Gaza; the dual responsibilities for service provision between the United Nations Relief and Works Agency (UNRWA) and the Israeli military occupier; the changes that occurred in the structure and livelihood of Gazan households; and changing configurations of gender relations within the family. This chapter will also discuss changing dynamics in household structure and family arrangements during two separate periods; the 1967 pre-war period, and the 1967 post-war period until the start of the Second Intifada in 2000. Regarding the latter, my focus is on household changes following the significant political events that took place during this period: the First Intifada (1987–1994) and the establishment of the Palestinian National Authority (PNA) from 1994 to 2000.

This first section of this chapter concerns itself with the different housing and household structures between refugees – who migrated from their home lands to Gaza in 1948 after what Palestinians refer to as el-Nakba (the Catastrophe) – and non-refugees, during the 1967 pre-war period. It also examines family relations of gender and power based on traditional peasant culture. The second section examines structural changes in Palestinian households and family relations between 1967 and 2000. This second section includes five sub-themes that trace these structural changes: first, the shifting of livelihoods from agriculture to wage labour and its effect on housing and household structure; second, the nuclearisation of households and the effects on women's autonomy; third, household structure and gendered power relations; fourth, the destabilising of the gender order as a result of the First Intifada; and fifth, the stabilisation of the gender order after the establishment of the PNA.

This chapter is based on secondary sources, as well as field data compiled from individual interviews conducted with women aged over 40 years. Secondary sources provide data on Palestinian peasant family composition and gender relations in the period following 'el-Nakba', until the Israeli military occupation of Gaza and the West Bank in 1967 (Rosenfeld 1960 and 1968, Swedenburg 1990). However, these sources rarely specify Gaza (Abu-Namil 1979, Al-Sourani 1991), with the exception of one outstanding anthropological study that focussed on family and gender relations in Gaza during this period, especially among refugees who fled from their original lands to Gaza after el-Nakba (Hammami 1994). Therefore, I have utilised life-story narratives from older women, in order to better understand the composition of Gazan families before 1967. These women experienced transitions in household structure and gender relations in the period 1948–1967.

Palestinian Household and Family Relations in the Period 1948–1967

The main focus of this chapter is the post-war period of 1967 onwards. But, in this first section, it is important to present a brief picture of the Palestinian family structure before 1967, for the purpose of comparison and analysis. In 1948, Gaza witnessed a massive influx of refugees who were displaced from their own lands by the establishment of the State of Israel. Prior to 1948, the population of Gaza was between 80,000 and 85,000 (Al-Sourani 1991). However, after the 1948 Arab–Israeli war, Gaza's population more than doubled and the shrunken new borders of the Gaza Strip were delineated in 1949. As a result, the non-refugee Gazan population lost their agriculturally based livelihood, whilst the refugees lived in squalid conditions inside the Gaza Strip (Abu-Namel 1979: 251). In 1952, UNRWA began building permanent housing for the refugees, and by 1954, the refugees were settled in eight refugee camps across the Strip (Al-Sourani 1991: 17). Refugees were dependent on UNRWA ration cards as their main source of livelihood. Although some refugee families were located in non-refugee rural areas for the duration of the Arab–Israeli war, the majority of refugees remained physically, economically and socially separated in the camps with no independent sources of livelihood.

Despite the separation between refugee and the non-refugee families in the early period of the post-1948 war period, it appears that the dynamics of housing and family arrangements amongst refugees were not significantly different from those of non-refugees. The shared values of both communities in shaping their housing and household structure can be attributed to the peasant origins of Palestinian society before 1948, especially amongst refugees who fled to live in Gaza. The harshness of their situation during the post-1948 period forced the population of Gaza, especially refugees, to shape and reshape their household structures based on family and kin relations and connectedness (Resenfeld 1968, Swedenburg 1990, Hammami 1994).

Post-1948 non-refugee housing and family arrangements In the post-1948 period, rural non-refugees lived in clans, and their agricultural land was mostly combined for collective farming. The housing structure in El-shuja'eya, one of the oldest cultivated areas in the Gaza Strip (Skeik 1982a), was, according to one of the older women in the research sample, structured around the co-habitation of three generations in *beit el a'ila*, the house of the extended family. *Beit el a'ila* consisted of the parents (in some cases with more than one wife) their married sons, and their children. The younger sisters-in-law usually rotated the housework between themselves, whilst the older ones joined their mothers-in-law working out in the fields. The composition of *beit el a'ila* did not remain static: for instance, after the marriage of her eldest son, the mother often moved with her married and unmarried sons to live in a separate house attached to *beit el a'ila*, where older parents and grand-parents lived together. This demonstrates that the composition of households in Gazan society is a developmental cycle, by which its individuals go through various life cycle events to reproduce themselves (Kinoshita 1995, Verdon 1998).

With the expansion of the extended family, *beit el a'ila* remained the central location where the eldest parent lived with at least one of their sons, most commonly the youngest married son. It was also the location where all of the sons and their adult married children gathered to resolve family problems. Marriage amongst cousins from the extended housing unit was common in order to keep land and property within the family. Kin marriage was a strategy used by mothers in particular, to secure family bonds across generations.

As the size of families increased, the older married sons began to move out of *beit el a'ila* into separate housing. The new housing units were only a few metres from their former home. In front of the extended family housing combine women created a large open-air space, where they shared the cooking of large meals, especially during religious and social occasions such as weddings or funerals. The women also used this space to wash clothes by hand, to socialise and as a place to arrange future family marriages.

Among non-refugees, the agricultural work was managed by men but all family members were involved in agricultural production. The gendered division of labour was based on the traditional peasant system, where women were concentrated in domestic agricultural production and men were responsible for marketing and goods exchange in public. Most family houses were close to agricultural land and women interwove domestic care and agricultural production responsibilities. The poor peasant family structure was based on connectedness. *Beit el a'ila* was commonly headed by the eldest men – the dominant form of the peasant extended family system. It took the form of 'a classic patriarchal family' in which the eldest male acted as the core decision-maker and the distributor of the family's resources.[2]

The refugee population Landless Palestinian refugees, displaced from their original villages by the 1948 war, were located in refugee camps in Gaza, where they struggled to maintain their former peasant household structure whilst waiting to return to their original homes and villages. The refugees' persistence in practising their traditional socio-cultural rituals was highly symbolic of their attachment to their original land. As the refugees gradually lost this attachment, they replaced it with physical and social intimacies with relatives who had been displaced from the same clans and villages. This helped the refugees to meet their desires for unification amongst themselves, and to struggle against the Israeli colonial occupation of their land. The refugees disregarded historical class divisions between themselves, and formed strong family connections based on their traditional peasant cultural identity (Swedenburg 1990).

According to narratives from older women, after being forcefully removed from their villages during *el-Nakba*, different extended refugee families from the same clans or villages chose to live near one another in one of the camps and even within the same section of a camp. Um-Mahmoud, a woman in her 60s from the Beach camp, said:[3]

2 See Deniz Kandiyoti who argues that the central feature of classic patriarchy is the patrilineal/patrilocal extended household which is associated with the reproduction of the peasantry (land inheritance to male members of the family). Deniz Kandiyoti, 'Bargaining with Patriarchy', *Gender and Society* 2, No. 3 (September 1988): 274–289.

3 '*Um*' is an Arabic prefix accompanied with the name of the eldest son, and means the mother of the eldest son 'Um-Mahmoud', while the father is named as 'Abu-Mahmoud', the father of Mahmoud.

> In the Beach camp, until today we named the blocks [of the camp] with the name of the *Hamula*, clan. After 1948, our parents and uncles spent months searching for each other. But we all followed our *Mukhtar*, the clan leader, and we lived closed to where he and his family lived.

In the early 1960s refugees were offered small houses, measuring just 50–70m^2, and many parents lived with their married sons in the same house, without running water or sanitation facilities, and sometimes without electricity. Schools and health centres were established in the late 1950s and early 1960s. Refugee parents were encouraged to educate their young children in local UNRWA schools, as this offered them a better future; one that would provide them with opportunities to work as teachers or nurses with UNRWA institutions (Hammami 1994, Rosenfeld 2002).

The co-dependence of the refugees reinforced the interest in maintaining their family connectivity, and also motivated them to have more children, especially sons. Having sons was a way of providing the family with labour. The refugees' persistence in practising their traditional peasant culture meant that their livelihood was manual drudgery: but their connections to each other provided them with a sense of dignity and social security that would otherwise have been lost. Um-Mahmoud described how, when she was newly married in the mid-1960s, her large extended family-in-law lived in a small refugee house of just two bedrooms in the Beach camp:

> I was living with my parents-in-law and their unmarried adult sons and daughters. I and my husband and our two young children lived in one small room. Another room was for my mother-in-law with her daughters. In winter, my father-in-law and his adult sons slept on mattresses in front of the two rooms. In summer, they used to sleep outside, in the small sandy yard in front of the house. The kitchen was too small to fit more than one person at a time. So I rotated the cooking with my sisters-in-law. Most of the time the men sat outside the home because there was no space for them to relax during the day.

The majority of refugees had no independent resources. Families were dependent on UNRWA ration cards that were not sufficient for the massive number of new refugee families. The men enjoyed no opportunities to earn income, except for a few who worked as unskilled agricultural labourers for Gazan landlords. Women, on the other hand, carried the bulk of responsibility for the survival of their families. They revived traditional peasant skills in order to earn small amounts of money, and also involved themselves in food and livestock production, and in local trading.

To conclude; during the pre-1967 war period, Palestinian refugees and non-refugees shaped their housing and household structures based on family and kin connectedness, in order to maintain inheritance across the male lineage and to use the symbolism of their peasant culture to challenge attempts by the Israeli occupation to dissolve their national and cultural identities. In both cases, women often endured the bulk of the burdens, including gendered responsibilities to attain goals of production and reproduction. Women used different strategies, including acting as the transmitter of family inheritance and togetherness by encouraging kin marriages. They bore large number of sons, as a source of long term family security, and enhanced the household economy and income-generating activities in order to maintain the livelihood of the extended family and to keep it socially connected.

The Israeli Military Occupation and Changing Dynamics of Household Structures and Family Gender Relations

A few years after the 1967 Israeli occupation of the Gaza Strip, Israel opened its borders for Gazan men to work within the Israeli labour market. By the mid-1970s, Gazan men represented a major contribution to Israel's wage labour market (Roy 1991). This was the main factor affecting the livelihood basis of Gazan households and their investment strategies. The priority amongst both refugees and non-refugee families was to invest their wages in two main areas: their children's education, and family housing. Refugees were more interested in investing in education, whilst non-refugees invested their energies and resources into housing. In the early 1970s, UNRWA developed a social service system for refugees in Gaza. At the same time, the Israeli occupation forces were responsible for the civil administration of non-refugees. At this point, Palestinian refugees enjoyed better access to primary health and education services, compared with non-refugees. However, refugees continued to live in squalid housing conditions due to the political dimension of refugee status, and lack of available land for refugees to build new homes.

Until UNRWA began to construct rehabilitation services for refugee housing, in the mid to late 1970s, most refugees lived in small, poor-quality houses with asbestos ceilings. The bigger houses in the camps had four rooms, and housed larger extended households composed of 15 members or more. Each household unit (parents and their young children) within the extended family lived in one room, and the rest of the unmarried adults, and the older people, usually slept in a small covered space in front of the bedrooms.

Refugees also became more involved than non-refugees in education and in formal employment in UNRWA service institutions, and in Arab countries. Education for refugees was considered a route to a sustainable livelihood, and a source of better social status. Refugees became increasingly concerned about educating their children when job opportunities opened up, particularly in Gulf countries. Some Arab countries, like Egypt, also offered free university education for Gazan refugees (Rosenfeld 2002). The increasing commitment to their children's higher education is encapsulated by a refugee woman in her mid-40s: 'Refugees felt humiliated by leaving their original lands and by becoming resourceless … [they] wanted to improve their status in Gaza through their education'.

I myself am a refugee woman, who grew up in El-shuja'eya in the 1960s, when most of the local residents were non-refugees. My father only finished his primary education and my mother was illiterate; nonetheless, my parents both insisted on educating all of their children. I remember my father telling us: 'If you really want me to hold my head up in the future, take care of your schooling. We refugees have nothing except your education. Education is the only thing that makes others respect us'.

The fundamental structural change of the Gazan political economy caused by the Israeli military occupation impacted on every aspect of Palestinian society, amongst both refugees and non-refugees. This section will mainly focus on the effects of the occupation on housing, household structure and gendered relations of power within the family.

The Proletarianisation of the Labour Market and Housing and Household Structure

Creating housing With the concentration of Gazan men working in the construction sector in Israel and the availability of modern construction materials from the Israeli market, the obvious trend was for Gazan families to extend their physical housing. In Shuja'eya, non-refugees, who had better access to land, invested the majority of their income in constructing large houses with several floors. Better off non-refugee families constructed an apartment for each adult son, with a view to all the brothers living connected to each other within one building.

Refugees in the camps also extended their houses, but on a smaller scale, for two reasons: lack of land within the camps, and the political dimensions of refugee status. Despite the increasing income of refugee families, very few families decided to leave their camp homes in order to buy a house outside of the camp: extending their homes vertically was cheaper than buying a new house either in or outside the camp. Refugees remained loyal to their camp for political reasons.

Prior to the beginning of Israeli-Palestinian peace negotiations in 1993, refugees remained inspired by their political right of return to their pre-1948 lands and homes, or their right to compensation – both of which enhanced their adherence to their refugee status. This political factor also encouraged refugee families to remain closely connected for decades, without being heavily influenced by the urbanisation of housing patterns in non-refugee Gazan society. Instead, refugees tried to improve their housing conditions without leaving their camp.

Although non-refugees were not restricted by the same land shortages as refugees, they did not want to use their agricultural lands for housing. This encouraged them to expand their housing vertically. Married sons continued to give their income to their parents, and the mother was often responsible for managing the whole family's expenses and consumption. Many of the women interviewed in this research asserted that the changing style of housing did not offer autonomy to the individual household units, as I will describe later in this chapter.

Impoverished refugees in the Beach camp endured far worse housing conditions than non-refugees. Limited housing space combined with large families made housing conditions extremely difficult. Increasing income among refugee families from their wage labour in Israel tended to be absorbed by the large number of family members, at the expense of any sustainable long-term investment strategies. Besides scarce financial resources, and the political dimension of the refugees' status, the persistence of patriarchal culture as a symbolic means to maintain their national identity made refugees' housing conditions harsher. This is illustrated by the interest and desire of older parents, in keeping with their peasant cultural heritage, to maintain the sense of collectiveness amongst family members, so that the married sons and their children remain socially connected and economically interdependent, living together in extended families.

Um-Jehad, aged 54 from the Beach camp, narrated the story of her struggle with housing in the camp:

> I married my cousin after I finished *Tawjihi* (high school), in 1973. He was 18 years old. He dropped out of school and worked in Israel in a bakery. I lived in a family of 15: my parents-in-law and their sons and daughters. The house had only four rooms and I had a very small bedroom. In 1978, my husband left his work in Israel and opened a sewing workshop at home; it was a small room in the tiny yard in front of the family home. I used to spend more than six hours a day sewing, and my children helped me cleaning up and packing, to make the goods ready for the Israeli firm. Our work was going very well, but all the money was spent on the big family.
>
> I was the first *kenna,* wife of the eldest son, the family's first daughter-in-law, and my mother-in-law wanted me to have a large number of children. By the mid-1990s, I had five boys and seven girls. As my children grew up, I needed to save money to reconstruct the house and to make it bigger, but we didn't have space to do so. At that time, it would not have been possible to leave the camp [anyway]. My mother-in-law threatened us, saying that if we left the camp we would lose our share in the family camp house. My husband is the eldest and he wouldn't live away from his parents and younger brothers and sisters.

The shifting of livelihood sources from agriculture to wage labour in El-shuja'eya contributed to the creation of individual household units that were physically separated from each other, but which did not have a household economy independent of the extended family. Married brothers with their wives and their children remained economically and socially interconnected with the extended family in *beit el a'ila*. The individual incomes of units with male heads of household were collectively distributed for the expenses and consumption of the whole extended family. Young wives' mobility, their control over their household unit and child-rearing and their social activities, were all defined by their being subordinate members of the family headed by the eldest father or mother.

Women's social obligations in the extended family restricted their interests and desires for autonomous housing spaces independent of their family-in-law. In the camps, house extensions, either horizontal or vertical, did not allow women to have any private space. They were seen by other members of the family in all their day-to-day activities. This also made non-kin marriage difficult. Brides who were close relatives, mostly cousins, would not feel like strangers amongst other family members, and could move and talk more freely within the family house. It was also assumed among refugees and non-refugees that having female relatives as brides for their sons reduced contestation between family members. However, the empirical data did not provide evidence to support this assumption, as we will see later in this chapter. Another inference from women's narrations is that although women presented the extended household pattern as the main constraint preventing their control over their own household unit, they in turn intentionally reproduced the pattern of extended family through the marriage of their sons. Women invested their own labour, and their husbands' incomes, in order either to expand the house with additional rooms, or in cases of better off families, to construct separate co-located houses for sons who were to marry. The next section will highlight the changing household structure among refugees and non-refugees over time, since the beginning of the 1967 Israeli military occupation.

Creating the household Some indication of the kind of changes that took place during the period of the Israeli military occupation can be found by examining the data on household structure in my interview material. This material has not been compared with official data on household structure, as the research sample has been purposively selected to give priority to the poorest Gazan households. The research sample is therefore not representative of the whole Gazan population, but it is probably representative of the overall features of the poorest and most vulnerable households in Gaza. There is a considerable difference in the numerical findings on household structure between my research and the national census findings of the Palestinian Central Bureau of Statistics (PCBS). I attribute this difference to a) different definitions and categorisations of household compositions used by PCBS; and b) the purposive selection of the most vulnerable households for my research. Around half of those interviewed considered themselves poor before the second Intifada.[4]

4 PCBS defines household composition in two categories; extended and nuclear households. The national census of 1997 showed that 75 per cent of households in Gaza were nuclear and 25 per cent were extended. The average family size of households in Gaza was larger than in other parts of the West Bank (7.3). Female-headed households were slightly more extended (28 per cent) compared with male-headed households (24 per cent) (See Rita Gaicaman and Penny Johnson (2002a) 'Inside Palestinian Household: Initial Analysis of a Community-Based Household Survey', Volume I, pp. 39–43. Also see the National Poverty Report of 1998. This report asserts that larger households are more vulnerable to poverty.

According to the fieldwork data, I have divided households into three categories to serve the analysis:

1. *Extended households*: These are composed of parents (elderly father or mother or both), their married sons and their dependent children. Some households include unmarried aunts, but it is rare in the research sample. The majority of extended households have one or two household units (i.e. married sons with their young dependent children). A few cases have more than two household units and these are considered very large extended families. The extended family has more than one bread-winner and the household income is managed collectively, mostly by the eldest mother, father or brother.
2. *Separated co-located households*: These household units are physically separate, but still attached to the family-in-law house, whether in a horizontal or vertical form. Some of these households share meals together. This form of household is common in both El-shuja'eya and the Beach camp. The separated co-located household is not an officially recognised category in Palestinian census records, where these units are considered to be nuclear families. However, I found this category to be different from the nuclear family. It is a form of household usually established for three reasons: lack of space within the extended household to accommodate newly married sons; tension emerging within the extended family, particularly between mothers-in-law and daughters-in-law; and the persistence of the patriarchal culture among older parents who desire to keep their married sons physically close to them, as this enhances their own social status. Men, in most cases, remain connected economically and socially with their family members, managing their income or working together. This form of household is very fluid in terms of its relations with the extended household. It operates in cooperation and contestation with the family-in-law, depending on the availability of income for the individual male head, and the intimacy of the relationship between the daughters-in-law and the in-law family members.
3. *Nuclear households*: These households consist of a married couple with their dependent children. It can be located either close to, or relatively far from, the natal family, but is not physically attached to it. The household is fully reliant on the parents' (mainly the male) sources of income for household expenditures and consumption. The nuclear household does not share meals with other family members. This form does not undermine the social connection with the in-law family and kin members, but it does operate as an independent economic unit. Wives are usually authorised to manage the household affairs by their husbands, but not by other members of the family-in-law. Women have more spaces for freedom of mobility compared with the first two, as they are solely responsible for the day-to-day domestic affairs of their household unit. However, in a few cases in

> El-shuja'eya and the Beach camp, women remain restricted by their in-law family, even after they moved to a nuclear family configuration.[5]

Of the 60 women interviewed in my research, 25 women live in extended households; 19 in separate co-located households; and 16 in nuclear households. The number of separate co-located households is higher in El-shuja'eya than in the Beach camp. This, as mentioned earlier, can be attributed to the ability of non-refugee families to accommodate their married sons in one building consisting of several floors, whilst refugee families did not have space for this.

Of the 16 women living in nuclear families, nine of the women lived in the Beach camp, and seven women lived in El-shuja'eya. This particular finding is not consistent with official records of household composition (Gaicaman and Johnson 2002a), but it appears reliable when linked to the specific characteristics of the research sample. The number of Gazan nuclear households has decreased among poor and vulnerable households since the beginning of the second intifada, because, as we will see later in Chapter 5, some nuclear families returned to *beit el a'ila* in order to cope with livelihood crises.

In the 1960s and 1970s, almost all the married women who were interviewed for this research were living in extended families. In the 1980s extended family households shrank to around 50 per cent in the Beach camp, however there was only a slight decrease in extended family households in El-shuja'eya. In the 1990s, due to flourishing construction, there was a rapid increase in co-located households, especially in El-shuja'eya. Meanwhile, in the Beach camp, there were more changes in the structure of the nuclear household. This data reflects the developmental cycle of the reproduction of extended households in both El-shuja'eya and the Beach camp. Women who married in the 1970s lived in extended households, before moving to either nuclear or separate co-located households, and in the last phase of their marriage they moved back to the extended family form, through the marriage and accommodation of their sons in *beit el a'ila*. All of the women in the research sample experienced these three forms of households through their life cycle. Although the data from the individual interviews is concerned only with the developmental cycle of household composition during women's married lives, the life stories of these women show that they also experienced this developmental cycle before they married. Most of the women compared their own experiences with the experiences of their mothers, who had also lived in different types of households.

---

5 Secondary literature shows inconsistent findings with regard to the nucleation of household in Palestinian society. Although Annelies Moors (1995) argues that the nucleation of the family weakened wives' kin-based social and economic relations, the national survey of Palestinian households carried out by the Institute of Women's Studies shows that nuclear households often live in kin environments, but these environments are more related to a male-head of household (see Rita Giacaman and Penny Johnson, 'Inside Palestinian Household' 2002: 44).

Refugee women lived in extended households for long periods of time, until they moved to separate co-located or nuclear households. The main indicator of refugees' poverty is the condition of their housing. Most of the refugee women interviewed for this research asserted that they had been living in poverty for decades. They saw the continuity of their poverty as being due to the large number of family members, and their inability to save money to invest in housing. Some women asserted that their housing poverty was due to the structure of the extended family, and the control of parents over their sons' income. Most of the household income was consumed by daily expenses. Refugee women asserted that it took a period of 7 to 10 years until they were able to have a separate co-located or nuclear household. The limited support for house rehabilitation from UNRWA also contributed to the persistence of extended households in the camps. This support used to be provided exclusively for female heads of household with no source of income. Households with one income earner or more were not eligible for house rehabilitation. The three female heads of household who live in extended families in the Beach camp confirmed that they had extended their houses to accommodate their married sons through UNRWA assistance. Among the poorest households, mothers tried to marry their sons at an earlier age, whilst they were without an income, and accommodate them with the extended family in order to be eligible for house rehabilitation from UNRWA.

The changing dynamics of household structures in both El-shuja'eya and the Beach camp imply that the household's reliance on wage labour in Israel contributed to improvements in their housing conditions. Household structure in the 1980s and 1990s tended to shift from extended to separate co-located and nuclear households. The independent nuclear household form remains the least dominant, especially amongst the poor households. Women across generations have contributed to the reproduction of the extended household, and consequently to the reproduction of the material aspects of poverty. Although women acknowledged the negative effect of the extended household structure on household livelihood and its distribution of resources, they reproduced extended households across generations. This is by no means unrelated to the lack of material alternatives, especially for refugees, but it is also influenced by the gender dimension of women's enactment within the household. In both El-shuja'eya and the Beach camp, women from different generations, demonstrated their interests and desires to keep their married sons socially and emotionally attached to them, as their main source of personal and familial security. Women's struggles to achieve the autonomy of their household unit, during the early years of their marriages, appears to facilitate the reproduction of the cycle of extended family during later phases of women's lives.

Gendered Power Relations in Households Headed by Wage Labourers in Israel

The involvement of Gazan men as wage labourers in the Israeli free market economy during the 1970s and 1980s had a significant effect on gendered relations of power within Gazan households: but these changes were also mediated by age and generation, which played a critical role in the changing power relations. Their work in Israel required Gazan men to be away from home for long hours, sometimes for days at a time. This gave older mothers the authority to assert control over the household resources and decisions, and also to maintain and enhance networks with family and kin relations. This period was primarily experienced by two generations of the research sample: mothers-in-law aged 50 years and over, and daughters-in-law aged in their early 40 and late 30s.

The coding and classification of the 60 women's interviews in relation to their households' gender relations show a remarkable finding with regard to gendered relations of power within the household. I examined a number of categories, including husband-wife, mother-son, mother-daughter-in-law, and mother-father relations of power. The data shows that in El-shuja'eya, for example, 26 out of 30 women stated that they lived in a male-headed household. Fourteen of the twenty six women asserted that their husbands did not actually have a strong say at home in the early phase of their marriages, during the 1970s and 1980s, and in some cases this has remained the status quo during the latter phases of their married lives. They all asserted that their mother-in-law was the actual decision-maker at home. According to the women interviewees, decision-making in this context is confined to the domestic sphere and kin and communal relations: and does not necessarily represent formal mechanisms of decision-making used by men, and associated with authority in the public sphere (Rogers 1975: 728).

The fundamental change in the Gazan economy due to the proletarianisation of men in the Israeli labour market had remarkable effects on the gender order. The power of mothers over their domestic affairs and inter-household relations was socially authorised by the absence of men from domestic life and from the local community. Elderly mothers became responsible for the day-to-day management of households, and the protection of family honour. This allowed them to communicate and to negotiate in public, and to become involved in the local market. Young women, on the other hand, became more domesticated and subordinated by older women. The best expression of these gendered changes based on age, in the Gazan household, was given by Mudallala who has witnessed the changes that have occurred in Palestinian society, especially among non-refugees, since the early 1960s:

> After the Israeli occupation, the men became absent, either getting involved in the resistance against the occupation or they worked in Israel to provide a living for their families. We only saw them either in the evening after the children went to bed, or twice or three times a week when they were not staying overnight in

> Israel. They came back home very exhausted, had their food and went to bed as they had to wake up early the next morning. Women in such situations had to maintain the family and land. Women became responsible for providing for the family and keeping its reputation, because the reputation of the family is the reputation of its women. My mobility was easier whilst my father was working on our land: but when he started working in Israel, my mother began to prevent me from even going to help her on the land, and she only took my brothers. Her life became much harder as she became responsible for the housework as well as the maintenance of our land. She was planting and harvesting the products and selling it in the market to earn more income to support the family. We were a big family of 13 persons and my mother saved my father's money to construct a big house, and used her small income for our daily expenses. My father didn't know anything about the family income as he came back so tired from work and didn't have time to ask.

The narration of women's life stories in El-shuja'eya provides further analysis of the domination of older women, not only over female members of the household, but also over males. Mothers in El-shuja'eya encouraged their sons to join their fathers working in Israel, back in the 1970s, whilst the sons were still teenagers. When the sons began to earn their own income, their mothers were motivated to marry them at an early age, whilst they were aged 18–20. The mothers that I spoke to presented two reasons for this: a) early marriage prevented them from being seduced by the western style of Israeli society, where free sexual relations were not forbidden; b) to keep them accommodated with the extended family where their mothers acted as the managers of the domestic sphere, and the protectors of the family honour. These early marriages had a clear influence on the young men's sense of masculinity. These young boys became husbands and fathers before they had any actual life experiences, because their work in Israel from a very early age had served to isolate them from interactions within their own community and culture. Their sense of manhood and masculinity were basically constructed by their adherence to their mother's values, as opposed to personal day-to-day communications and negotiations with family and kin institutions. Older mothers used to meet the family social obligations, such as weddings and funerals, on behalf of their men during the men's absences. This trend was more obvious amongst non-refugee men who were more involved in the Israeli labour market and less involved in day-to-day local community social and cultural encounters. In the 1970s and 80s, young refugee men were more involved in the national struggle against the Israeli military occupation, and this enhanced their sense of masculinity and their connection to the patriarchal culture of their local communities.

The interview material suggests that men in the Beach camp were less dominated by their mothers, and they were more dominant over their wives than men living in El-shuja'eya (only 8 out of 30 women stated that their husbands didn't have any say at home, or that husbands were controlled by their parents in the 1970s and 1980s). Husband-wife and mother-son relations of power in the

Beach camp appear to have been more 'normative' (i.e. male dominant) than in El-shuja'eya. Um-Fadi is a 56 year-old mother from the Beach camp. She described the difference between women in El-shuja'eya and the Beach camp in terms of gendered relations of power:

> Women in El-shuja'eya were *masnodat*, supported by their land, whether through their fathers and brothers, or husbands. A husband would not think to divorce his wife for any reason, because he gave consideration to her father or brother and their property. We refugee women did not have land: our brothers were as landless and poor as our husbands. We women used to stand beside our husbands. They remained very sensitive to their manhood, even when they had nothing, and they did not accept their women controlling them. We mothers supported our sons, but we did not dominate them. Our dignity has been the dignity of our sons. We used to look after and protect the honour of our sons' wives and sisters and to control their mobility.

In the 1970s and 1980s, the difference between refugee and non-refugee women's practice of power within their households was influenced by the nationalist ethos of the relationship (men were the heroes of national resistance and women were the mothers and wives of heroes), as we will see in the section on the First Intifada. However, the structure of extended households in both El-shuja'eya and the Beach camp, associated as it was with material poverty, was a site of contestation between the women in these households. Daughters-in-law, in particular, were treated as the instruments that mothers-in-law used in order to wield power over their sons and husbands, whilst men were not in daily contact with their wives. Mothers-in-law controlled their daughters-in-law's mobility and decisions, in order for the latter not to influence the sons' loyalty to their mothers. Through this dynamic, mothers maintained their control over the process of family reproduction, through which all brothers remained connected to their mothers rather than their wives. This argument is supported by Henry Rosenfeld's description of changing family relations resulting from Palestinian men's involvement in the Israeli labour market. He stated that during male absences, mothers-in- law acted as the main overseers of their sons' wives' activities and movements. For Rosenfeld, this not only serves in the continuity of the function of the extended family, but also maintains the future relationship between mothers and their sons (Rosenfeld 1968:746). Um-Saed, a 48 year-old woman from El-shuja'eya, described the changes that affected her position as her sons grew up.

> My father-in-law and my husband were working in Israel in the early 1980s. They used to leave home at 3:00 am in the morning and come back at 6:00 or 7:00 pm. I don't remember that I had time to talk with my husband about the troubles his mother caused for me. My father-in-law and my husband used to give money to my mother-in-law to spend on the household daily expenses. I was not able to ask for anything personal, only for what the children needed. She

> used to go shopping and made social visits, and I was responsible for doing all the housework.
>
> [So] I put lots of pressure on my husband to live in a separate house away from my mother-in-law. My husband [eventually] agreed to rent a very small house close to *beit el a'ila*. This unfortunately did not stop my mother-in-law from interfering in my everyday life. I was not allowed to move without her permission. I lived with this situation till the mid-1990s, when my sons grew up and worked together to construct a separate house for us, a little bit far from *beit el a'ila*.

Female heads of household, despite their actual control over the household's affairs and its members, were very careful in the presentation of their power, particularly over their sons. From women's narrations of their everyday experiences, the power of decision-making has two dimensions: the social and cultural recognition of power and authority based on gender; and the capacity to shape decisions without it being associated with public authority. Although it would be more socially accepted for a female head of household to practise control over her sons than a married woman with a male head of household, female heads of household in Gaza act differently. They try to compensate for the absence of the father of their male children by demonstrating the power of their sons, who have been raised solely by their mothers. For a female head of household this is a powerful symbol of her success as a mother. This enactment of power intentionally operates in order to maintain the ideology of male domination: in other words, it is a negotiated form of gendered power decision-making that does not dismantle the gender order (Kandiyoti 1991c, Agarwal 1997).

Although older fathers had a less significant role in implementing this domestic process of the family's reproduction, they benefited from the outcome of this process in the public domain. In only four cases did women describe their husbands as controlled by their father. In both El-shuja'eya and the Beach camp, fathers used to rely on older mothers as the transmitter of the family male lineage, and to protect the honour of the family by maintaining its structural image as male dominated. This process was achieved by mothers being responsible for selecting appropriate brides, '*banat aisha*' (i.e. not rebellious and able to serve all the in-law family members and to satisfy their husbands). The mothers decided about the number of children, especially male, that the wives must have; they influenced the child-rearing, and also managed the ways in which domestic work was carried out, in order to satisfy the male members of the family-in-law. Through this mother-in-law led dynamic, fathers and sons maintained their dominant social status among family and kin relations, without actually being the decision-makers in these processes.

Nucleation of the Household and Women's Autonomy

The expansion of nuclear households in the Gaza Strip, especially in the 1980s, was attributed by some scholars to the flourishing of household income as a result of the involvement of Gazan men in wage labour in the Israeli market economy. It was also attributed to the financial independence of household units headed by wage labourers (Heiberg and Ovensen 1993, Giacaman and Johnson 2002b). Data and analysis of the changing gendered relations of power, as mentioned above, provides another reason for the emergence and the expansion of the development and prioritisation of the nuclear family. Due to the domination of older mothers over members of their extended households, contestation between women within the household increased. This contestation appears to have been the main reason for most young women to struggle to move to a separate house, in order to escape the domination and oppression practised by their mothers-in-law. Despite the economic and financial independence of singular household units within the extended families (i.e. each married son with his wife and young children), many daughters-in-law in the research sample developed a number of strategies to achieve their goal of living as a nuclear family.

Although women's desire for a nuclear household was often provoked by continuous contestation between daughters-in-law and their mothers-in-law, we cannot deny the enabling role of the household's economic capacity. Amongst poorer households, who could not afford the construction of a separate house for each married son with his own wife and children, daughters-in-law often lived in continuous contestation with their mothers-in-law. Almost all of the women who married into extended households in the late 1970s and 1980s, ended this contestation by moving to a separate house. They asserted that they spent around 7 to 10 years struggling with their family-in-law to be able to do so. The lack of income earned by their husbands was not the only reason for this long period of struggle: it was also the family-in-law's control over the husbands' incomes. Wives were not allowed to have control over their husbands' incomes, which were used for the daily expenses of the entire extended household.

From the narrations of the women that I interviewed, it does not appear that any parents-in-law asked their married sons to move to a separate house. It was solely the decision of daughters-in-law to struggle to resist the power of the extended family, in some cases with support from their own natal families. Husbands often realised, however, that their own children were not living in adequate housing conditions, and they were therefore in need of a separate house. In many cases the husbands were acting passively because they did not want to upset their parents, especially their mothers. So they allowed this responsibility to be managed by their wives, as they were the ones most disadvantaged by this extended household structure.

Women's wishes for a nuclear family life do not reveal any specific links with the financial independence or capacity of their husbands. It rather reflects wives' priorities to achieve *Isteqlaliat el a'ila,* their household autonomy.[6] In this context, autonomy for wives does not mean that women seek their individual economic and social independence, but rather that living in a nuclear household in fact returns women to the authority of their husbands, which was presented by all the women that I interviewed as the desirable relationship of power between genders. Most of the women asserted that their social status as wives was determined by being dependent on their husbands' income and social authority, rather than on their family-in-law's authority, particularly that of their mothers-in-law. Women living in a nuclear household perceived themselves as *Set el beit*: literally, the mistress of the house.

Um-Sami, a 43-year-old from El-shuja'eya, described women's autonomy when living in a nuclear household, saying:

> Living under the control of our husbands is much easier than living under the control of [our] mothers-in-law. When the mother-in-law controls her daughter-in-law, everyone in *beit el a'ila* has the right to control [her], including her young sons and daughters. Being under the authority of my husband is, of course, easier because I can at least shame him about his obligations towards his children, without anyone interfering.

The main motives that women usually presented for wanting to move away from the extended family, were not personal. They talked about, for example, the urgent need for more space between brothers and sisters as they grew older. This is a legitimate social reason in a gender-segregated culture which facilitates women's access to a separate house. With regard to personal motives, women described wanting to have more power over their children, and to have greater space in which to negotiate with the husbands, with less interference from their in-law family members. Wives in both El-shuja'eya and the Beach camp used similar strategies to achieve their goal of having their own homes. These strategies included selling their jewellery, borrowing money from relatives, and generating income from agricultural production and trading. They also bargained and compromised with other family members.

Women use jewellery received from dowry and gifts received when they give birth. Women in Gaza often save any money they earn by purchasing jewellery because hard cash is easily spent. A woman's jewellery is her own property, and she most commonly uses it to invest in her family's housing and her children's education and marriage.[7] Women in Gaza do not sell their jewellery when their

6 'Autonomy' is translated in Arabic as '*isteqlaliat el a'ila*'. It means that a wife and her children live in a separate house away from the daily contestation with, and dependence on, the family-in-law members, especially mothers-in-law.

7 See Annalies Moors' study (1990) on 'Countrywomen in the West Bank: A Study of the Gender and Economic Division of Labor', *Afaq Filastiniyya*, pp. 130–145. Moors points out that Palestinian women, from the early phase of marriage, were keen to keep

husbands are in paid work. None of the wives that I spoke to had sold, or would sell, any of their pieces of jewellery to pay for the daily expenses of the extended family. They each stated that they had kept their jewellery for the day they would have their own home, or else for their children's education and marriage. Some of the women mentioned that they used to ask their mothers to keep their jewellery for them so that they would not be asked, or forced, by mothers-in-law to spend it on any of the expenses of the extended family. All the women who had lived in contestation with the extended household had sold their jewellery to contribute to buying or constructing a small separate house. As the proceeds were not sufficient to pay for the new house in entirety, they were forced to use additional strategies. Many women mentioned that they borrowed from close relatives in addition to selling their jewellery. These women then lived in debt for years, as illustrated in this account from Um-Iyad, aged 48, who is from the Beach camp.

> I sold my jewellery, used all my savings and also borrowed lots of money from my parents and brothers, in order to buy a very small house in the camp. I put myself into serious debt. You know, my eldest sons and I have been struggling to repay the debt to my brothers since 1992. I did not care about debt or money at that time: I just wanted to get out of the misery of living in *beit el a'ila*. My husband only shared $3,000 with me when my parents shamed him into doing so. But my eldest son and I paid the rest, which was around $5,000. My husband was not sure that I would be able to manage the rest of the money to buy the house. He wanted my children and I to stay under his mother and sisters' control, and he behaved like he was the master. It was the relief of my life when I paid all the money for the new house and moved in with my children.

Most of the women, who at the time of this research were aged 40 and over (29 out of 60), asserted that they became involved in income-generating activities basically to save money for housing improvements. These women can be divided into two generations: the first generation was older mothers who had been in their 40s and above during the early 1980s, and had struggled to extend their houses in order to marry their adult sons. The second generation had been daughters-in-law in their late 20s, and had struggled to leave their mothers-in-law's houses during the 1980s and early 1990s. It was more socially accepted for the older group of women to become involved in trading activities in the local market, but I found that some of the younger women in urgent need of separate housing arrangements had also felt compelled to leave their homes in order to work as traders selling their agricultural products in the local market.

These younger women faced troubles from their families-in-law as well as their natal families, because it was not socially acceptable for them to work in the local market. They managed these social constraints through bargaining and

---

their dowry to be invested in the building of their own house and in productive property for the husband.

compromising. Um Sufian and Um Haitham, for example, who were both in their early 30s, when they started trading in the local market, made it a condition that their husbands save some of their income for house construction, if they would not allow their wives to trade and insisted that they stayed at home. The result of their bargaining was that their mothers-in-law stopped restricting their daughters-in-law from trading, because this meant the mothers-in-law could retain control over their sons' incomes. Young wives, particularly in the Beach camp, also became heavily involved in paid home-based work, through sewing workshops that offered sub-contracts, or through family businesses.

Um-Ahmad from the Beach camp described how she worked for more than six hours a day at her husband's sewing workshop, in order to save money to construct a second floor extension for her own children. Um-Jehad also became involved in local trading to earn money to extend the house for her adult sons. All female heads of households embarked on trading activities, basically to provide their sons with better housing. These strategies were also associated with the re-prioritisation of household expenditure and consumption. Mothers told me that, whilst saving money in order to construct a separate house, they reduced their household expenditure and consumption to a minimum, depriving all household members of good quality food and clothing.

These accounts illustrate how women who lived in extended Gazan families developed a number of strategies over time in order to achieve their goal of housing autonomy, either for themselves or for their own married sons. Wives' resistance to the extended family is a phase of women's lives that actually facilitates the new generation of mothers in the reproduction of the extended family. This form of autonomy involving separate housing for newly married couples is supported by the text of Islamic family law, which states that married women have the right to a separate home. Whilst the topic of women's rights in Islamic family law (Shari'a) is not the focus of this research, it is important to note that the deprivation of a separate home for young married couples, in the Palestinian context, is not a problem regarding application of Shari'a. It has been attributed to parents' needs for their children's long-term social care and support, especially in a situation in which other formal sources of support for the elderly are lacking (Abu-Nahla 2003, Johnson 2006, Shehada 2009[8]).

8 Shehada in her article (2009) on 'House of Obedience: Social Norms, Individual Agency, and Historical Contingency' studied the relationship between the textual family law and its social practice in the everyday life of people in Gaza. During her fieldwork, she found that women, and Gazans in general, are less responsive to 'fixed' texts of Shari'a law than to their priorities. Shehada's framework of analysis of the family law in Gaza is relevant to the overall analysis of this book, by which she sees that women's agency is not statically determined by the text of Islam or by Shari'a. Rather, women and people's interaction with the legal framework is both manipulative and instrumental. They exploit the law's fixity when it suits them and utilise its indeterminacy when it serves their interest to do so.

Um-Ibrahim, a 57-year-old from the Beach camp, struggled to have a separate house for her dependent children in the early 1980s, before her husband died. She also struggled to reproduce the extended family through her married sons in the late 1990s. Her account provides insights into what women value in reproducing the extended family.

> Do you think it is easy for me after all these years of tiredness and suffering to accept my sons to go and live somewhere else? No, it would be shameful of them to do so. I spent years depriving myself to feed them and to make them *rejal*, men. I made them marry early in order to ensure that they are going to stay with their wives and children around me. My real happiness is when I see my grand-children. All my daughters-in-law are obedient. They don't talk with their husbands about their problems, but they come to me. My sons too, they don't do anything without consulting me. They follow my advice because they know that I have much more experience than they have. I encourage my sons to join in *el-deywan*[9] in order to show other male family members they are more men who have been raised by a woman. Thank God, I produced real men who have a strong say.

The discourse that Um-Ibrahim and other mothers in Gaza use to describe the process of household configuration is gendered. Women intentionally produce and reproduce their household composition to achieve strategic goals in life. They develop multiple strategies to move from one form of household to another, tactics which change their positions, and enable them to wield their actual power in the household and also to be recognised and valued by the community as ideal mothers. They endure suffering and self-sacrifice in early phases of their lives because they know that this will lead to social and emotional rewards later. From their perspective, their role as the producers of real men in their society should be rewarded by the moral loyalty of their sons. One example of this moral loyalty is for their sons to live with their mothers in an extended household. Anything else would be shameful for both mothers and their sons.

The formation of household structure in Gaza is a non-linear developmental process. During the course of almost two decades, women in the research sample experienced multiple gender identities: moving from their position as daughters-in-law to the relative independence of being wives and mothers, and then becoming mothers-in-law themselves when they reached their mid-40s. Women's autonomy in relation to housing or household composition is an essential instrument for reproducing family hierarchy based on gender and age. The dynamic of family

9 A site where each clan resolves family disputes or discusses collective issues related to family and kin interests. El-dywan is only for males, and is usually located in the house of the family or the clan leader, *Mukhtar*. El-dywan is a site where power relations between men are shaped and reshaped based on age and life experience, but not necessarily on wealth or class.

formation has been reproduced across generations of women, from extended to co-located, to nuclear households, before reverting back to the model of the extended household.

The First Palestinian Intifada and Changing Gender Relations

The First Palestinian Intifada erupted in the West Bank and Gaza Strip in December 1987, after two decades of Palestinian grassroots political and social struggle against Israeli military occupation. The ensuing massive civilian involvement in, and support of, the First Intifada, especially in the camps, affected the entire Palestinian social order, embodied in age, class and gender hierarchies. In Gaza differences in age, class and gender ceased to be of importance, as almost the entire population embarked on activism. The massive involvement of young men in national resistance against the Israeli military, and their subsequent exposure to torture, imprisonment and death, affected mothers' relationships with their sons. Mothers' concerns shifted from having control over their sons' working as wage labourers in Israel, to being the self-sacrificing protectors of their sons who had become significant figures of national resistance. Mother-son relationships extended beyond domestic boundaries to take on a wider national and political dimension.[10]

Neither home nor the domestic sphere has ever been private in the Palestinian historical context. Each has always been the site for processing and reproducing the public (Peteet 1997, Jean-Klein 2000). The difference in mothering between the pre-Intifada period and during the First Intifada, according to Julie Peteet, was related to a mother's sense of belonging. During the First Intifada, mothering enhanced women's sense of belonging more to the nation, as women were called the mothers of all *shebab*, or Palestinian young men. Before the intifada, mothering was more about belonging to the narrower micro scale of the family unit and kin relations (Peteet 1997: 123–127). At this point, the household was headed by the elder father who was responsible for family provision and the protection of family members, and as described in the previous section, mothers' control over the household was concentrated within the domestic sphere, aimed at transmitting and maintaining the honour of the family. The practical function of motherhood during the First Intifada transcended domestic limits to serve national political resistance. As the relative power of fathers shrank, so the power of mothers shifted its focus towards their sons who were involved in national resistance and struggles. This was a generational change, because the discourse of male domination shifted its focus from fathers to sons.

The changing position of young men during the First Intifada, from a marginal to a leading role, contributed to the reproduction of a changed masculine identity. This was especially the case with men in their early 20s. Most of these young sons

10 See Julie Peteet (1994 and 1997) in her articles on 'Mothering in the danger zones', and 'Male gender and rituals of resistance in the first Palestinian Intifada'.

used to be under their mothers' control while they were working in Israel, with their income, social decisions, wives and children all managed by their mothers. During the First Intifada, young men returned to act as leading figures in the local community, as well as in their families. Their involvement in resistance revived their masculinity in addition to their authority within the family. Although the father-son relation of power has not been described in depth in this research, as my focus is on the mother-son relationship, the interviews and life story narratives illustrate that the actual practice of power by fathers with adult sons was insignificant. This does not mean that the adult sons wielded the actual power within households, but it was the changing position of mothers that obscured the father-son power relations. However, in this context, the father remained labelled as the head of the family, even when he lived with sons who were married and employed. Fathers' positions of power were more symbolic of the patriarchal family, but the actual dynamic of power within the household took a different direction. The sons' adulthood was the moment when fathers' actual power shrank, and mothers' power expanded, without the symbolic image of patriarchy being distorted in the process. The distinctive change during the First Intifada was the breaking down of the patriarchal image of the family, by which young sons transcended the symbolic moral boundaries of patriarchy by not responding to their fathers' orders (Peteet 1997, Jean-Klein 2000). While fathers lost their powerful position in public and were replaced by their young sons, mothers were presented in public as the symbolic agents of sacrifice for the nation, by emerging as the mothers of '*shabab el watan*', the young men of the nation.

The agentive nature of mothers during the First Intifada, as 'a nationalist project', as described by Peteet, remained tied in with the moral aspects of the mother-son relationship. The Palestinian mother sacrificed herself for *shabab el watan* as if they were all her sons. The life story of Um-Mahmoud from the Beach camp illustrates this, and reflects the multiple roles of mothers during the First Intifada, especially amongst refugees. Her life story represents poor refugee families who have associated their struggle for household survival with their struggle against the Israeli military occupation. Um-Mahmoud is 61 years old and has witnessed and reflected upon the different political contexts of Palestinian contemporary history. She said:

> By the start-up of the First Intifada, my two adult sons were not yet married. They got involved in the resistance. I couldn't of course stop them; it would have been a scandal if I had done so, and even if I had asked them to stop, they would not have responded to me. Although I, as other mothers, wanted my sons to finish their education and to have good jobs so that I would be able to rest, this didn't work. I was responsible for the family's survival. My husband was sick and my sons were working in the camp. None of them were working in Israel. I was selling clothes in the Israeli market and earned good income for the family, while my daughters were responsible for looking after their father and the domestic work.

> My two eldest sons (aged 22 and 25) were imprisoned in the second year of the intifada. At the same time, the Israelis stopped me from crossing the border to sell in the Israeli market because I was a mother of prisoners. I moved to trading in the local market. It was okay, but I did not earn the same money as before. We lived under curfew most of the time, and my trading was not working well. For the sake of our family survival, I decided to get out of the camp during the curfew to earn some money, by selling my products out of the camp. That was really dangerous, but I had no other options.
>
> After the imprisonment of my sons, I was encouraged by the activists of the women's committees, and others, to participate in the intifada. I was solely responsible for my family survival, and my participation in women's committees made me feel proud of my sons, and myself. I became very active. I used to go out with other mothers to visit the families of prisoners, martyrs and the injured. I also participated in demonstrations and in clashes with the Israelis. My sons were proud of what I was doing and they encouraged me. In the beginning, my husband tried to make some troubles for me because I spent most of my time outside the home. But I was supported by my imprisoned sons. When he said "no" to me, I just told him that what I did was at the request of his imprisoned sons. Then he stopped making any troubles [for me].

Um-Mahmoud's life story is also supported by my own personal experiences. For the first three years of the First Intifada I was living in the Beach camp. My husband and my two young brothers-in-law were in Israeli prisons and my mother-in-law, like the majority of other Palestinian refugee mothers, was proud of her son's involvement in the national resistance to the Israeli military occupation. My mother-in-law participated in public demonstrations, and daily clashes with Israeli soldiers, attempting to save other young Palestinians from being injured or imprisoned. My mother-in-law also spent long periods of time each day visiting the families of prisoners, and those who had been injured, as an expression of collective solidarity. We younger wives and daughters used to stay at home, mostly with our father, to look after the young children. My father-in-law was earning an income, and he was very authoritative with his wife and daughters: but during the First Intifada, he was not really able to dominate his wife and daughters, because he did not want to be challenged or humiliated by his own sons.

In her research, Julie Peteet points out that young husbands and brothers became more authoritarian as a result of their involvement in the Palestinian national resistance during the First Intifada. Their authoritarianism was expressed in attempts to assert control over the mobility of their wives and sisters (Peteet 1997). However, the experiences recounted by wives and sisters of prisoners, and those who were injured during the First Intifada, have a specific interpretation of male authoritarianism. These women considered the authoritarianism of their young husbands and brothers to be a positive change, compared to the period before the intifada, as it implied increasing male concern for the honour of wives and sisters, who were facing continuous harassment and violence from the Israeli military. These women did not, however, accept authority from their mothers-in-law during the First Intifada, interpreting it as a dynamic used by mothers to benefit from their sons elevated status as activists resisting the Israeli military occupation. The public power that mothers gained through their son's status was reflected in their increased domination over other family members, including their husbands.

The women of the Beach camp experienced the First Intifada as wives, sisters and mothers. Sisters and wives assert that they were proud of their husbands and brothers during that period. Um-Sameh (35 years old), Salma (36 years old) and Um-Abed (37 years old) from the Beach camp, each experienced the injury and imprisonment of their brothers and husbands during the First Intifada. They asserted that their husbands and brothers were authoritarian, but regarded this positively, as a revival of the men's sense of personal and national masculinity.

The difference in gender relation dynamics between the First Intifada period and the period before the intifada suggests consideration of the debate on the gender impact of the First Intifada. Some literature argues that mothers played a critical role in resisting patriarchy and male domination in the Palestinian family (Peteet 1997, Sayigh 1998, Jean-Klein 2000). Others argue that mothers had not transcended attitudes towards women that are 'profoundly traditional, patriarchal and condescending' (Hilterman 1991: 201–202). I believe that neither of these two positions is supported by enough empirical evidence from data collected during the First Intifada. A father's loss of power within the household for the benefit of his sons was a result of changes in family dynamics between one generation and another. This change in turn enhanced the discourse of male domination at a wider national level, as younger men were given more power and authority. Mothers, on the other hand, maintained and accumulated power, in both the public and domestic spheres, through the enhancement of their sons' public power. The fluidity in gendered relations of power within the household and in public during the First Intifada was more situational, reflecting the dominant national discourse but not undermining the ideology of male domination. I would therefore argue that the ideology of male domination was well utilised by mothers to facilitate their own status as the mothers of the nation's heroes.

The Establishment of the Palestinian Authority and the Re-Stabilisation of Gender Relations

The First Intifada was ended by the signing of the Oslo agreement between the Palestinians and Israelis in August 1993. The Oslo agreement committed the new Palestinian National Authority (PNA) and Israel to a series of actions and interim measures that included partial Israeli military withdrawal from Gaza. For the first time in their contemporary history, Palestinians had the opportunity to experience some national governance. This created an environment of national optimism amongst Palestinians, for whom the most important post-Oslo change was life without the militarised existence of the Israeli occupation, and the opportunity to become more responsible for their own political affairs. Palestinians had aspirations for their economy, and high hopes for their liberation from economic dependence on Israel. However, these aspirations floundered due to Israel's continuing control over Palestine's natural, economic and human resources. Israel used its borders to restrict the movement of Palestinian goods, and its 1994 security policy also heavily restricted the movement of Palestinian wage labourers into Israel (Roy 1999).

The post-Oslo period (1993–2000) also raised Gazan women's expectations of increased access to education and employment opportunities. Relative economic and institutional stability during these seven years did indeed improve opportunities for women in Gaza. Women's participation in the formal labour force increased from 1.7 per cent in 1992 to 8.8 per cent in 1999 (PCBS 1999e, 2000d). More than half of these women worked in the health and education sectors. The private sector also flourished through the relative stabilisation of the Palestinian economy and absorbed an increasing number of women, especially in the service industry. Large numbers of highly educated young women in Gaza became involved in the formal labour force during this period: however, the majority of poor middle aged and old women, who had less education, remained confined to unpaid labour at home, or else worked in the informal sector that served cross-border trading with neighbouring Egypt.

The seven years of the post-Oslo period did not add up to any real structural improvements in the overall situation of Palestinian women, the vast majority of whom remained poor and remained in the informal sector. A comprehensive study by FAFO[11] on living conditions in the Occupied Palestinian Territories (OPT) during the First Intifada, shows that 60.6 per cent of women in Gaza were involved in the informal economy, and 85.7 per cent of them were active in household domestic economy (Ovensen 1994). These statistics are also supported by Reema Hammami's study of gender segmentation in the Palestinian economy (Hammami 2001). She argues that women's involvement in the informal sector continued to be substantial under the PNA, because jobs in the formal sector were not available for women (ibid.). Those jobs that were provided to women under the PNA were concentrated in the service sector, relevant only to a small number of women of a certain age, and with a certain level of education. Married women with responsibilities for childcare have always been economically, socially and culturally restricted from participating in the formal work sector in Palestine. The informal sector, comprised almost entirely of home-based activities, has turned out to be an inherited generational tradition amongst poor and less educated Gazan women, who are taught traditional skills from an early age by their mothers, in order to be able to participate in informal economic activities throughout their working lives.

11 FAFO is the Institute for Applied International Studies in Oslo.

The establishment of PN institutions was associated with Israel's policy of permit restrictions, which prevented large numbers of Gazan men, and a much smaller number of women, from taking up paid wage labour in Israel. The majority of unemployed Palestinian men who had been former wage labourers in Israel were absorbed into the Palestinian public sector, especially in the national security forces. However, senior and middle management positions were allocated to those considered loyal to the ruling Fatah political party. Tens of thousands of young men in their early and late 20s who were prevented from entering the Israeli labour market for security reasons (for example, men who were politically active, or who had been imprisoned by Israel during the First Intifada) became involved in low income employment in the security apparatuses of the new PNA. The majority of these men came from poor refugee camps and urban neighbourhoods in the Gaza Strip. Their absorption into the public sector during a period of relative calm between Israel and Palestine meant that they also spent more time in the vicinity of their own households. The men went to their jobs at 8:00 am and came back home at approximately 2:00 pm. They spent most of the rest of their time at home or in the local community, becoming involved in the day-to-day affairs of their households and kin relations. Women stated that their households were re-stabilised after long years of conflict against the Israeli military occupation. Young husbands and fathers spent time with their wives and young children, and provided them with a welcome sense of security.

My research does not include any employed women, as I purposely selected poor housewives for this sample. These women described their experiences during the initial period of the PNA, referring to the system of job-distribution and allocations amongst men and women in that period. They asserted that many job opportunities were offered to women, regardless of their age and education, but based on *wasta* (political and kin networks). The women in my sample group were deprived of these opportunities because they did not have *wasta*, especially with relatives who enjoyed political influence. Women in El-shuja'eya and the Beach camp mentioned that they knew many women who gained jobs and regular income without actually attending their work places at all. These women acquired these jobs by virtue of their strong social networks with senior male officers, or through their kin and family networks. The women that I interviewed pointed out that most of the wives and daughters of political activists, whether martyrs or injured men, and the members of women's committees, were given job opportunities, whilst destitute women with no network but in actual need of jobs, remained disadvantaged.

From the early years of the PNA in Gaza, there were widespread tensions amongst poor women, who often had to overwork in order to gain the necessary social and political networks to facilitate their access to jobs. According to some of the interviewees, some women resorted to borrowing money to bribe senior officials, or offered sexual services to some corrupt government officers, in order to gain jobs in the formal sector. The widespread phenomenon of corruption in employment in the PNA was one of the reasons women shifted from the informal sector, or from being housewives, to consider working in the formal sector. Parents' preferences for their daughters working outside the home in the public sector also increased, in order to utilise these employment opportunities. Many of the interviewees who experienced chronic economic vulnerability during the Second Intifada, especially from the Beach camp, regretted that they did not apply for a job in the PNA – even in fields that were not socially accepted, such as the police and the security service sector. One middle aged woman from the Beach camp said:

> There was nothing shameful about women working in the police. It was office work. When my husband worked in Israel, I was staying at home doing nothing. I only took care of the children. I thought Israel would last forever. Some relatives showed their interest in helping me to get a job in the police. I refused because I thought it was shameful for me to work in the police. I regret it now. I wish I had accepted the job at that time.

A further gender issue that my research participants identified during this initial period of the PNA was that the corruption of Gazan men was increasingly supported by their wives. For example, the wives of senior officers in the PNA utilised their husbands' positions in order to support their relatives. Um-Haitham from El-shuja'eya attempted to secure a permanent job in the Ministry of Social Affairs. She contacted the wife of a member of the Palestinian Legislative Council (PLC) who lived in El-shuja'eya, hoping that this woman might assist her because Um-Haitham was supporting her husband's election campaign. However, this woman did not respond to her request, although she assisted other women who were her relatives to secure similar positions. Um-Na'eem, a 37-year-old from the Beach camp, also narrated her experience of how wives of senior PNA officers came to be influential figures during this period, saying:

> I was actively involved in the Fatah women's committee during the First Intifada. I thought it was my right to get a permanent job in the government. I contacted the wives of Fatah leaders who I used to work with in the women's committee, and asked them to ask their husbands to help me to get a job. They did not do anything. As a result, I decided to leave them and to get involved in another women's committee, hoping that they would be of more help.

The main gender implication of this period is the shift from the centrality of the mother-son relationship to the husband-wife relationship. This shift began with families of middle to senior public employees, and expanded to encompass low-income employees. The wives of middle and senior security officers, who mostly belonged to the ruling Fatah party, wielded power as a result of their husbands' positions. This power was enhanced when many of these officers generated money, in relatively short periods of time, and were able to purchase separate houses and live in nuclear families. Wives, as opposed to mothers, and regardless of their education, were perceived as powerful potential networkers. Wives started to act as intermediaries between women in need of help and PNA government officials.

Families with no public employees remained the most disadvantaged. Low-income employees, who constitute the majority of the labour force in the public sector, benefited from the establishment of the PNA to a certain extent.[12] Many young couples with young children became involved in a new PNA housing improvement scheme, and were subsequently able to move away from the extended family to live in nuclear households. The housing improvement policy contributed to a rapid nucleation of households, and as a result young wives exerted greater control over their household resources and their own movements.

The empirical data on household nucleation during the period 1993–2000 has mainly been gathered from the participants of the El-shuja'eya and Beach camp focus groups, with whom I had discussions during the first half of 2008. These groups were comprised of women who were living in nuclear households headed by low-income public employees. Women who shifted from extended to nuclear households during the PNA period emphasised that it was much easier for wives to achieve their social autonomy and freedom by living in nuclear households under the sole authority of their husbands, rather than in a household under the authority of their mothers-in-law.

Almost one third of the women I interviewed were in their early 30s, and they lived in nuclear families during the period 1993–2000. They asserted that their family atmosphere was calm, and their relationships with their families-in-law were very cooperative. They considered their dependence on their husbands' income not to contradict their self-respect and their ability to share in family decision-making. Living in a nuclear family gave them greater spaces within which to negotiate family decisions with their husbands. Some young wives stated that, since moving to their new homes, their relationship with their husbands had improved. Although the nuclear household, in this context, remained male dominated, it was not purely patriarchal. This gender relational change was perceived by young wives as a fairer relationship. Domination in a nuclear household includes negotiation of gender roles and responsibilities. Whilst husbands were the main breadwinners, their wives were happy to be responsible for the domestic sphere, including their children's education, management of the household resources and decision-making about domestic affairs.

In the focus groups that I conducted with men in both the Beach camp and El-shuja'eya, most of the young low-income employed men emphasised that their wives and children had benefited from moving away from the extended family. Some of them described how the household budget was managed, asserting that part of their salary was spent on paying their mortgage, and that they handed the rest over to their wives, who were responsible for managing the daily family

12 According to the PCBS labour force surveys 1995–1999, 25–28 per cent of the labour force worked in the service sector, and 19 per cent of them worked in the public sector, as low and middle income earners (see FAFO Report 2007, No. 41).

expenses. These men acknowledged that their wives were much better at household budgeting than they were themselves, and that it is not shameful for a man to leave his wife controlling the household expenses whilst he busied himself earning income for the family.

The changing household structure and the stability of men's incomes also had an effect on marriage patterns. Men felt encouraged to transcend marriages within the extended family. As described earlier, this pattern of kin marriage was common in the Palestinian family before the establishment of the PNA. It functioned as a means of securing marriage within the extended family, and was based on the supportive nature of kin relations (Johnson 2006). Kin marriage began to weaken with the establishment of the PNA, as men began to feel secure in their employment. Young single men with a regular income became more self-reliant. This widened their choices in marriage beyond the restrictions of kin relations. Among poor families, although mothers continued to select brides for their sons, they too became less confined by kin marriage. They considered their sons' ownership of a separate house, and being employed with a regular income, as an advantage and a basis for a secure marriage for a bride from any family.

The shift in family gender relations, due to the nucleation of the family and the stability of husbands' incomes, was a positive advantage for young wives, who became mistresses of their own homes. The relationship between mothers and sons developed into one based on moral rather than socio-economic factors. In such contexts, mothers' domination, associated with the extended and co-located family structure, lost its basic socio-economic function, but its cultural moral basis remained intact, as a symbolic feature of Palestinian cultural identity.

It is also noticeable from the focus group discussions, that the nucleation of the family, and the shift in gendered relations of power in the domestic sphere from mothers to wives, weakened family contestations, reducing conflicts of interest between mothers and daughters-in-law. Relations between mothers and their daughters-in-law became more tolerant and cooperative. Family relations were re-stabilised and operated on a more complementary basis. Adult married sons fulfilled their moral obligations to their mothers and family members, but at the same time, fulfilled their social and economic obligations to their wives and children. It was the same with daughters-in-law, who offered respect to their husbands' families, especially to their mothers-in-law, but also controlled their own household domestic affairs. By this division of social, economic and moral responsibilities, gender relations within the household were re-stabilised, and wives were able to reproduce their power within the domestic sphere, based on their gender identity as wives and mothers.

Conclusion

The overall empirical analysis of this chapter emphasises that gender relations in the Palestinian family have always been fluid and adaptive, even as gendered relations of power have remained configured within the ideological boundaries of male domination. Two main interlinked elements played a critical role in the process of women's wielding of power within the household and in the local community in Gaza: women's stages of life; and the changing socio-economic and political structures in the historical context of Gazan society.

Throughout generations in Gazan society, women have contributed to the reproduction of the extended household, as a strategy to wield personal power through their positions as wives and mothers. The first generation of married women in the post-1948 period was more dominated by their fathers and husbands than by older women. This was because men were physically present in the vicinity of the household, and controlled the production of household resources, although women participated in agricultural production. Men exerted control over the household, and over public decisions. Older women practised their power as the transmitters of family wealth and honour, through family and kin relations, and through the arrangements of kin marriages. This was the stereotypical form of gender relations in the patriarchal traditional peasant family in Gaza before the 1967 Israeli military occupation.

The second generation of married women, who were wives of wage labourers in Israel, came to be more dominated by older women, especially mothers-in-law, than by men. This was a direct result of men being absent from the domestic sphere. During this period (1970s until the late 1980s) mothers-in-law acquired social authority from their men during the men's absence whilst working in Israel. The older women took responsibility for managing all household resources and decisions, a shift which facilitated their involvement in economic activities, agriculture and trading. This form of household gender relations broke down the patriarchal traditional structure of Gazan households, even though the image of patriarchy remained a dominant discourse in society. Young men and women (sons, daughters and daughters-in-law) were all dominated by the older mothers, whilst the power of older fathers was obscured by their physical absence due to their wage labour in Israel.

The third generation of women mostly married in the early to mid-1990s. For them, the early phases of their marriages witnessed the relative political and economic stability of Gazan society that followed the establishment of the Palestinian National Authority. It seems that third generation of women continued to be housewives, but also enjoyed higher levels of autonomy compared with women from previous periods. The autonomy that women sought in all periods was to exercise control over their own household unit, and over their own children. This autonomy was largely achieved by the nucleation of households that took place under the PNA during the period 1993–2000. This group of women was, however, dependent on their husbands' incomes as the only source of livelihood.

Gender relations throughout the three generations have taken different forms, and the gender order has stabilised, destabilised and re-stabilised over time. Gender relations during the First Intifada, for example, were destabilised by the domination of the nationalist discourse. Within the specific national and political context of the First Intifada, mothers were empowered by the power of their sons, whilst fathers lost power. Younger women were disempowered by the increasing authority of their mothers-in-law, but they felt morally empowered by the increasing authority of their young husbands and brothers as the leading figures of the national Palestinian struggle.

This chapter also gave emphasis to the effect of household composition on gender relational dynamics over time and in each historical period. Before the establishment of the PNA, when the extended and, to a lesser extent, the separate co-located household were the dominant forms, mothers-in-law were often in a position of power. The shift from an extended household to a nuclear household that occurred among low-income employees during early to mid-1990s meant that young wives had a wider space to act as the mistresses of the household, and to negotiate domestic affairs with their husbands. Nevertheless, the majority of the individually interviewed women in my sample group did not become mistresses of a nucleated household, but remained living in extended or separate co-located households even during the PNA period. Some of these women continued to be controlled by their mothers-in-law. They were negotiating conflict and contestation within their extended households in order to achieve their familial and personal goals. This leads to an overall conclusion that it is hard to generalise about gender relational dynamics within households, even within the same historical period. Women are continually placed in different positions given the different structures of households. These differences are negotiated and renegotiated over time, and at the same historical moment they produce different gender relational dynamics.

Chapter 4
The Impact of the Second Intifada on the Economics of Everyday Life

Introduction: The Destruction of the Gaza Economy during the Second Intifada

The Second Intifada resulted in economic hardship across Palestine, marked by loss of employment, particularly loss of access to wage labour in the Israeli market for Palestinian men. This has been devastating for low-income households. Work in Israel used to constitute 23 per cent of the total employment for Palestinians in Gaza and the West Bank (PCBS 2000d), however, when Hamas began to govern Gaza in 2006, wage labourers were prevented from crossing into Israel. Unemployment subsequently reached an unprecedented level of 44.8 per cent during the second quarter of 2008 (PCBS 2007). The Labour Force Survey of January–March 2009 stated that 48.3 per cent of the employed labour force in Gaza was working in the Palestinian public sector, mostly as low-income earners, while the PCBS survey of 2009 highlighted that unemployment was highest amongst Palestinian youth aged 15–29; in the Gaza Strip it reached 58.6 per cent.[1]

Israel's closure of the Gaza Strip continued to strangle the industrial backbone of Gaza. Prior to the 2006 closure, over 54 per cent of employment in Gaza was private sector-driven. Gazan manufacturers imported 95 per cent of goods from the Israeli market. As a result of the closure, according to the 2008 records of the Palestinian Federation of Industries (PFI), of 3,900 industries in Gaza, only 23 were still operational. The PFI records also show that around 40,000 farmers in the agricultural sector, and more than 70,000 workers in other sectors (including 34,000 in the industrial sector) had lost their jobs (World Bank 2008).[2]

The closure also led to a significant increase in poverty. The official poverty rate for 2007 was 51.8 per cent, compared to 47.9 per cent in 2006. The percentage of Gazans in extreme poverty increased from 33.2 per cent in 2006 to 35 per cent in 2007 (UNDP 2007).[3] However, since family remittances and humanitarian food aid provided for poor families by formal and informal institutions were

1 See PCBS press release on Labour Force Survey Results (January–March, 2009).

2 See World Bank report 2008 on 'Recent Developments and Prospects in the Occupied Palestinian Territories'.

3 According to UNDP report of Development Times, issue no. 1, July (2007), extreme poverty in Palestinian society is when a household of two adults and four children live on NIS 1,000 (US$250.6) per month or less: about NIS 5.5 (US$1.38) a day per person.

excluded from the official measurement of poverty, it probably underestimated the reality. According to the World Bank, the poverty rate in Gaza reached 79.4 per cent in 2008.

Increasing poverty has led to increasing vulnerability. Amongst Palestinian households classified as extremely poor, 83 per cent said they did not have enough to live on, and thus depended on humanitarian food assistance (UNDP 2007). A World Food Program survey conducted in 2008 found that food insecurity had continued to rise, affecting 56 per cent of households in Gaza. Approximately 66 per cent of income earned in Gaza is spent on food: however, the WFP survey also revealed that Palestinians are now eating less: 75 per cent of Palestinians have reduced the quantity of food they buy, and 89 per cent have reduced the quality of their food. Due to the lack of basic public health services, poor households increased their spending on health services from 5.5 per cent to 12.1 per cent of their income (ibid.). Continuous Israeli restrictions on the mobility of goods in and out of Gaza, and the subsequent loss of local income sources, destroyed all means of self-reliance and threatened the capacity of households to survive. In 2007 UNDP reported that 39 per cent of households/families in the Occupied Palestinian Territories (OPT) did not have the means to extricate themselves from poverty. The report asserts that Palestinian households, predominantly in Gaza, have increasingly lost their capacity to cope, as their income was mainly dependent on the Israeli market (UNDP 2007).

This chapter discusses different coping strategies used by Gazan households during the livelihood crisis of the Second Intifada, and how gender and generational dynamics within the household affect, and are affected by, these coping strategies. These dynamics are important as they illuminate the intersectional structural and institutional factors which shape women's agency within the households. However, the outcomes of this model of agency are not sufficient to argue about the constitution of gendered selfhood which appears to be multiple and contradictory, as will be analysed in Chapter 5. In this chapter I provide empirical evidence that coping strategies have, from a material perspective, the potential to produce positive outcomes (such as challenging household poverty and vulnerability, developing individual capacity and enhancing individual autonomy). However, these outcomes remain controlled by the factors of contingencies and uncertainty in the specific economic and political context of Gaza, where both women and men refer to interpersonal relations based on gender, class, political loyalty, and patriarchy, in order to achieve personal and familial security. In this chapter, I will focus on three key themes:

First, the gender differentiated basis of household livelihood during the Second Intifada, and the ways in which gender and age link to how household poverty and vulnerability are categorised. I will examine how changing sources of livelihood are used by the research participants to typologise the winners and the losers of the Second Intifada. Although the typologies of poor and vulnerable households as identified by the research participants reflect their own experiences and their knowledge and observation of other households in their local communities, these typologies represent types of household that match the official definition of extreme poverty, i.e. those who live on $1.38 or less per day (UNDP 2007). Households in the two research sites have been classified, and named, in three typologies named by the research interviewees as: a) households with low-income earners (*mastoreen*); b) households in debt (*makshofeen or madyoneen*); and c) female heads of household (*ghalbaneen*). Each category has different characteristics of poverty and vulnerability based on multiple socio-economic, political and subjective moral factors.

Second, I explore the coping strategies for household survival, and how these create enabling and disabling environments for both men and women from different generations. This section will focus on three main coping strategies used by poor households in Gaza: the adoption of new household production and income-generating activities; dependence on humanitarian aid; and changing gender preferences in education and formal employment.

In the third theme, I discuss the gendered and generational effects of these coping strategies, by examining: youth taking a leading role in family survival; liberation of women's mobility and the feminisation of humanitarian aid; and changes in patterns of marriage.

Changing Livelihood Economics

Household poverty and vulnerability have become collective features of Gazan society during the Second Intifada. In order to categorise the households of the research participants, and other households in the two research sites, I used individual interviews and focus groups to ask the participants an open question: 'in your opinion, which households are the most disadvantaged by the closure and siege of Gaza?'

Although women's categorisation of poor and vulnerable households does not cover all potential diversities, it does reflect the majority of households considered as extremely poor, including households with incomes below the national measure of extreme poverty.[4] The difference in women's categorisation of poor and vulnerable households in this research is that women do not only use the common economic measures of poverty and vulnerability, but also consider the moral and gendered dimensions of their understanding of poverty and vulnerability in Gaza. The women used Arabic terms to define and describe three categories of poor households, which, from their viewpoint, represent the majority of households in the two research sites.

First, *mastoreen* refers to households that are able to manage with limited sources of income, and do not expose their needs to anyone beyond their immediate

4 See Hasselknippe and Tveit, FAFO Report No. 41 (2007) section on coping strategies pp. 58–98. The report in this section describes the diversity of household categories in Gaza and the West Bank. The overall description in this section supports the classification of poor and vulnerable households as defined by women in this research.

family members or kin. Although most of these households rely on an income below the national definition of poverty, in most cases it is regular and to a large extent secure, such as public sector employment income. The term '*mastoreen*' also has a gendered dimension, as it is used to describe a housewife who is able to sustain her household whilst depending on the low income earned by her husband or adult son. In this case, if she is forced to borrow money from a stranger, it is not the woman who is dishonoured but her husband or son, because his income is not enough to provide for his family.

Second, *makshofeen* or *madyoneen* is defined as 'vulnerable', and usually refers to a male-headed household that is unable to provide for the basic needs for its members because of the absence of sources of income, from either formal or informal economic activities. These households are often forced to borrow money from others and subsequently fall into debt. They borrow money from relatives, and are then forced to borrow from non-family members, such as retailers and neighbours. Households in debt are threatened economically and socially because they cannot depend on borrowing from strangers whilst they have no method of paying the money back.

Third, *ghalbaneen* is the Arabic translation of the English word 'helpless'. This term is commonly used to describe households headed by chronically sick men or women. For example, a household headed by a widow with dependent children is called '*a'ila ghalbana*', a 'helpless' household. This type of household is not necessarily vulnerable, as these families are considered eligible for regular cash and food assistance from the Ministry of Social Affairs (MOSA) and from UNRWA. *A'ila ghalbana* is a gendered term which means the absence of able-bodied adult men responsible for family provision: its use reflects the assumption that women without male breadwinners should be the subjects of compassion and support from social institutions, even if they are able to manage the livelihood of their households economically and socially.

The women interviewed for this research stated that the second term, *makshofeen* or *madyoneen*, is rarely used to describe female heads of households, because it is considered shameful for a woman to be in debt and subsequently forced to borrow money from strangers. It is part of the social construction of gender that women, especially heads of households, learn how to manage their household budget with minimum resources to avoid borrowing from strangers. During discussions, many of the research participant female heads of household described themselves as *mastoreen*, even though their livelihoods are very different from the type of *mastoreen* households which generally rely on sources of regular low income.

The frequent use of the word '*mastoreen*' as opposed to '*makshofeen*' by the female research participants also implies that the critical element of household disadvantage during the second intifada is more the moral than the economic aspect of their poverty. The participants defined a household as vulnerable when its members are forced, by the absence of sources of livelihood, to admit their inability to cope to strangers, whether individuals or institutions. One woman from the Beach camp in her late 40s said:

> I have been living in poverty all my married life with bad housing and little income. My husband worked for one week, and spent the rest of the month without work. We managed our life with the little money we earned, but no one around us knew what we were eating. I never asked strangers to help.

Women categorised households in Gaza by reflecting on their inter-household and intra-household relations and networks, as well as on their perception of the normative gender enactment within the household. The following are the three main types of households named and defined by the women in my research sample: low-income earner households, households in debt, and female-headed households.

Low-income earner households – Mastooreen This socio-economic group was considered by the research participants to be better off than others during the Second Intifada, because they have been able to manage their household needs without exposing their poverty to people outside their family circle. Amongst the participants, all of these households consist of one or two adult sons who earn a low income (except in one case where three sons were working as low-income employees in the national security forces). The majority of these households are extended families with unemployed or sick older fathers. The vast majority do not own land and rely on their income to maintain their family livelihood. Some of the men were previously wage labourers in Israel until the border closed in 1995, and have now been absorbed into the Gazan public sector. A few of the participants mentioned remittances from brothers or close relatives who work in other Arab countries, or from their parents or brothers residing in Gaza. The amount of money these households receive from their relatives, in the form of assistance, is estimated to be around NIS 100–300 ($25 – $75) per month.

This group of households would have been considered either poor or very poor before the closure of Gaza during the Second Intifada, if their current income were compared with that of former wage labourers in Israel before the closure. Research participants with one to three low-income earners in their household calculated an average monthly income ranging from NIS 1,000 to 3,000 ($250 to $750).[5] The PCBS considers this lower level to be the line of extreme poverty ($250.60 per month) for a household of two adults and four children (PCBS 2007). The participants generally had much larger households: more than half of the women (35 out of 60 women) had 7 to 12 children in addition to other members of their

5 Women who have one to three sons working as soldiers with the national security forces earn a monthly income of NIS 800 to NIS1000 ($200 to $250) from each employee. This is the basic salary of soldiers in the national security forces. At the time of the field research, $1 was equivalent to approximately NIS 4.

extended households. In larger extended families, sons were usually the income earners. Fathers had been made unemployed by the closure, or were older and in ill health. Families with low-income wage earners were not eligible for regular humanitarian aid. Refugees used to receive food assistance once every three months, but this ceased after the decrease of funds for UNRWA's food assistance as a result of the international community's boycott of the Hamas government in 2007.[6] Women living with low-income earners were criticised by other women if seen asking for coupons, or other forms of humanitarian assistance. Some of the women within this group, therefore, tried to conceal the fact of any of their sons or spouses working with the PNA institutions.

Many of these households have, directly or indirectly, belonged to mainstream political factions and had acquired their income, often through jobs in the security forces, either through family and kinship connections, or through patronage and clientelism. Some men had belonged to Fatah (the previous ruling party in Gaza) and received jobs with the PNA government before Hamas took control of Gaza in 2006. Others had more recently become involved with Hamas' executive forces through family networks, for the sake of having regular jobs. Most income earners in these households were the sons of unemployed wage labourers who formerly worked in Israel. Since 1995, parents started to search for kin channels and connections with political factions in order to find a regular job for their adult sons. Other sons had not finished their education, but would have quit for the sake of a regular job.

For those in extended families, the income of these sons was used for the entire extended family's expenses. In extended families from El-shuja'eya and the Beach camp mothers usually controlled their sons' income, because wives were mostly very young and given few responsibilities. Most of the young wives in this group had been recently married, and therefore had to accept that their husbands' income being used by the whole family, including married and unmarried brothers who were jobless. This illustrates how women are, from an early age, socially nurtured as to gender and moral obligations within the extended family. Income is distributed according to the priorities of the extended family's needs, and the wage earner's wives and young children, in some cases receive the least, depending on the decisions of mothers-in-law. Fathers-in-law in this group did not interfere in household domestic affairs or expenses because they were all unemployed or ageing and sick.

The dominant assumption amongst the women of this group was that, as long as a married woman has an able-bodied husband or adult son, she does not feel vulnerable. Women of this group emphasised that it is not significant how much money their husbands or sons earned, but the regularity of this income, as an indication of certainty. Women in this group are expected to be responsible for managing the household expenditures and consumption according to the monthly

6 See details available at: http://cnpublications.net/2007/04/29/economic-disaster-in-gaza/.

regular salary received, and not to borrow money from strangers. During the Beach camp focus group, a woman called Majda said:

> We get used to this situation. My husband receives NIS 1200 (around $300) at the end of the month, and more than half of it is spent in the first week: paying the shop keeper, and our bills, and for the children's education. I have to manage the rest of the month with the remaining money. In fact, most of the time, I don't know how to manage. But at least I know that there is a salary coming at the end of the month.

Housewives of this group emphasised the presence of male income earners as both enabling and disabling for women. It maintained their social status among family members and in the local community as wives and mothers of income earners. This meant that they were still *musatatat* (i.e. reliant on their husband's income and not forced to leave home to search for coupons to feed their children).

Although the majority of housewives with low-income earners did not regularly join community associations that provide humanitarian assistance, a few educated women from El-shuja'eya and the Beach camp volunteered at women's associations in order to provide support to vulnerable families, and to develop their experience and knowledge. Um-Ashraf from El-shuja'eya, who is married to a low-income Hamas government employee, mentioned that she joined the women's association because she liked the idea of supporting local families in need. She was doing administrative work and was not considered a beneficiary of this association. Nevertheless, she was rewarded on her volunteering by having access to coupons, although not on a regular basis.

Households in debt – Makshofeen or Madyouneen[7] This social group has increased considerably since 2006. They include households with small and medium businesses that were forced to close during the siege of Gaza: metal workers, carpenters, construction workers and small traders with business in Israel and/or Egypt. The households of former Gazan wage labourers, formerly employed in Israel, both skilled and unskilled, make up the largest proportion of this group. Many of these households have large numbers of dependent children, including university students. Many of them have spent their savings and sold personal and household assets, especially women's jewellery, in the first few years of the intifada (2000 to 2004). These households subsequently became resourceless, and fully dependent on humanitarian aid. In this group, skilled labourers considered themselves to be worse off than unskilled labourers, as unskilled labourers would accept any temporary job, no matter how menial. Skilled labourers, however, considered these jobs as humiliatingly low status. It also appears that, since

7 According to FAFO Survey of Palestinian opinions (March 2008), 68 per cent of Gazan households rely on borrowing from others. Available at: http://www.fafo.no/ais/middeast/opt/opinionpolls/2008-4%20Household%20economy.pdf.

the closure, skilled labourers have become more indebted than those who are unskilled. According to men and women in the focus groups this can be attributed to the inability of skilled labourers and their families to adapt their household expenditure and consumption to their current financially deficient situation.

Kawther, the wife of a former construction contractor in Israel, is from El-shuja'eya. She described how her husband has been forced to change his lifestyle:

> My husband used to earn around NIS 200 ($50) a day from working in construction in Israel. He spent all his money on good food and on buying himself cigarettes, nice clothes, and spending money on his friends. He is now trying to stop smoking and reduces his expenses, as we are in serious debt. But he seems to find it so hard. Whenever he receives a little money he buys silly things, instead of what the children need. [But] I understand that it is hard for him to manage on such little money, when he used to earn thousands.

Suad, a 43-year-old mother from El-shuja'eya, said:

> I have never thought that one day we would come to live in such poverty and deprivation. Before the intifada, I used to spend at least 100 NIS a day on meat and chicken to cook for my family. Today, I spend just 200 NIS in a whole month. My husband accepts whatever I cook, [but] If I had known that we would face this situation, I would have saved all the money I spent on food [in order] to buy jewellery. The jewellery of women has rescued many families from hunger, but it cannot last forever.

Falling into debt has affected the social relations and networks of most jobless households. Many of the female focus group participants in both El-shuja'eya and the Beach camp asserted they had stopped visiting siblings and other relatives, because neither they nor their husbands have been able to repay debts. Some family members are now in conflict with others because of their inability to repay debts.

The livelihood crisis has also clearly affected women's sense of self-respect. The focus group participants said they felt sad about being forced to sell their own jewellery to pay for household expenses, when they had wanted to use it to fund their children's university education. Psychologically they found it easier to borrow money from relatives, friends and neighbours, as opposed to searching for coupons in public institutions. It was only when this borrowing mechanism reached its limit that they searched for alternatives, outside of their families. These young and middle aged housewives stressed they had never previously experienced such humiliation.

Female heads of household – Ghalbaneen According to the Palestinian Ministry of Planning the female head of a household is defined as a woman who has lost her adult male bread-winner through widowhood, divorce, or chronic sickness, and who has thus become solely responsible for providing for her family (Ministry of Planning 1998). These women are entitled to regular cash and in-kind assistance from the Ministry of Social Affairs and UNRWA social welfare schemes. The 1997 national census stated that female heads of household constituted 8 per cent of total households in Gaza (Giacaman and Johnson 2002a). During the Second Intifada this number rose to 12 per cent, as a result of increasing male imprisonment, death and injury (ibid.). Besides the limited financial support they receive from the social security system, many of these middle aged and older women also take part in home-based economic activities, such as food production and small-scale trading, in order to supplement their income. Although female heads of household were perceived as the poorest and most vulnerable social group before the Second Intifada (Johnson 2002: 6), research suggested that during the intifada they were not any more at risk of poverty than other households (Jacabsen 2004: 19).

In this research female heads of household were all classified as housewives, whether they participated in economic activities or not.[8] During the fieldwork it was observed that many women referred to themselves as the 'head of household' if and when their husbands became chronically ill during the Second Intifada (the majority of chronic illnesses were described as 'mental illness').[9] I observed that many of the husbands who had worked in Israel before the border closure, had become physically or mentally ill after the closure due to chronic stress.

According to the measure of income used by the PCBS, female-headed households are classified as the poorest due to the combined assistance they receive from MOSA and UNRWA being less than the income of extremely poor households ($250.60 per month for six persons). However, female headed households also have access to humanitarian assistance from informal, family and community institutions, and are not forced to search for coupons like the wives of jobless husbands. The qualitative data for the period of closure and siege on Gaza in the years 2007–2009 reveals that female heads of households responded to their income-poverty in different ways, according to certain socio-cultural and moral dimensions. Nevertheless, this is not a homogeneous social group. Some are more disadvantaged than others, economically, socially and morally. The field data shows that female heads of household can be divided into two sub-groups.

Wives and mothers of martyrs, injured men and prisoners[10] This sub-group is perceived as better off than others, and even classified by some participants

8 This group constitutes 11 out of 60 women in the research sample, and around 10 out of 50 participants of the focus groups conducted for the purpose of this research in both El-shuja'eya and the Beach camp.

9 See the Near East Consulting report on 'Depression in the Occupied Palestinian Territories' September 2006.

10 'Martyr' is somebody who is prepared to die in the course of his/her submission to the will of God. Defined as *Shaheed* in Arabic, it appears in a variety of contexts in the Qur'an and in the hadith (sayings of Mohammed). *Shaheed* in Islam is one who struggles

as better-off than low-income earners' households. This classification does not, however, contradict the definition of these women as '*ghalbaneen*'. These women are not blamed for living without a husband, like divorced women. Rather, they are treated with more compassion because their widowhood, or equivalent, is beyond their control. This sub-group also has a particular positionality following the national resistance discourse (Peteet 1997). There are three reasons why they have greater social and moral advantages than other female heads of household:

First: they are officially entitled to regular support from formal and informal institutions, and not so exposed to vulnerability or food insecurity. Although the monthly allowance these women receive from the PNA is much lower than the minimum income paid to public employees (NIS 600–800, or $150 to $200 per month, according to the research participants),[11] they are also compensated with food and financial assistance from charities and informal institutions.

Second: they do not need to humiliate themselves by searching for a source of livelihood. The mothers or wives of martyrs who go in search of paid work are considered to be devaluing the martyrs who struggled for their nation and their God. The mothers of martyrs are more appreciated than wives, as a mother from the Beach camp explained: 'for me to sacrifice my son to be a martyr is never compensated for in ordinary life. My real reward is in heaven. A young wife who lost her husband still has an opportunity to marry again and to be compensated by having sons'. Women in this position are more socially and morally valued than other women while they are perceived as contributors to the national struggle and in '*El Jehad*'.[12]

Third: wives of martyrs, injured men or prisoners who belong to Hamas currently have more advantages in Gaza than wives and mothers of other martyrs, and feel empowered by belonging to the political party of their martyrs. The majority of mothers and wives of Hamas martyrs have become deeply involved in Hamas community-based organisations and mosque activities. They feel proud of their involvement, are respected by others and their mobility is socially accepted and valued.

Widowed, divorced women and wives of sick husbands Female heads of household used to receive economic and social support from social institutions before the Second Intifada, but it was also more acceptable for them to be involved

---

and gives up his life in the cause of Allah (Jihad), see *The Concept of Martyrdom in Islam*, A. Ezzati, Tehran University, Al-Serat, Vol. XII, 1986, available at: http://www.al-islam.org/al-serat/concept-ezzati.htm. In the context of Gaza, all men who are labelled 'martyrs' gave up their lives in their struggle against the Israeli occupation, which is considered by most Muslim Palestinians as the enemy of Islam.

11 According to Penny Johnson (2002), the Ministry of Social Affairs offers only 96 Israeli shekels (around $25) per individual per month. This has become more irregular in the circumstances of the Second Intifada.

12 *El jehad* means holy fighting or struggle for the sake of God.

in income generating activities than it was for married women. Older female heads of households asserted that they have largely been involved in home-based economic activities and cross-border trading, and have passed these skills onto their daughters-in-law. Women of this sub-group have large families and mainly live in extended families. With the rapid deterioration of Gaza's economy after the closure, many mothers preferred their sons to marry at an early age (18–20 years old) in order to maintain their eligibility for regular humanitarian assistance (*Shu'un* marriage as it is described by poor people in Gaza).[13] Their sons' individual households are also entitled to aid coupons. In 6 cases out of 11 female heads who participated in the research, married sons with three or four young children, each lived in one room, and they were all mainly dependent on regular food and cash assistance from UNRWA and/or the Ministry of Social Affairs. They also received support from informal institutions, such as relatives, neighbours and mosques.

In both El-shuja'eya and the Beach camp, female heads of household age 40 and over did not mention being in serious debt to local grocery shops, or to relatives. These women were extremely careful with money and able to manage their household expenditures and consumption. They did not regard the quality of their basic livelihood as being significantly different now as opposed to before the closure of Gaza. This was due to their livelihoods being relatively secured by regular financial and food assistance from formal institutions. In addition, they benefited from *ad hoc* humanitarian aid by civil society organisations.

The collective impoverishment of all segments of Gazan society has undermined the efficacy of people whose coping strategies rely on domestic resources and family relations. This has placed women in a moral dilemma as their efforts to sustain the family's basic needs may jeopardise the reputation of their household. Basically, it is very difficult to obtain outside assistance without anybody else knowing. Poor vulnerable women in Gaza are forced to publicise the vulnerability of their households and the hopelessness of their men to strangers, for the sake of humanitarian assistance.

Gender-Differentiated Coping Strategies

Palestinian women's methods of coping with absolute poverty and pervasive crises in family livelihoods during the Second Intifada have been a matter of concern for national and international scholars and institutions. A review of the available literature reveals that the coping strategies adopted during the Second Intifada owe their form and nature to a strong legacy that emerged from the history of

13 According to the Ministry of Social Affairs policy of social welfare, humanitarian assistance is curtailed when any of the household male children reach the age of 18. This age-limit was raised to 20 years during the Second Intifada as a result of the massive increase of unemployment amongst young men (Ministry of Social Affairs 2008).

the traditional Palestinian family.[14] The persistence and depth of this economic crisis has, however, undermined the efficacy of traditional coping strategies, and exaggerated dependence on institutional humanitarian aid. Nonetheless, despite the declining economic powers of family and kin relations as a result of collective impoverishment in Gaza, women have maintained the social and moral aspects of household and family connectedness as a long-term resource of personal and familial security. During the Second Intifada, as argued by Liza Taraki, 'women developed multiple strategies that entail accommodation, resistance and negotiation of patriarchy' (Taraki 2006: xviii).

What has distinguished households' coping strategies during the Second Intifada is their expansion from a narrow to a wider definition of coping. During the first two years of the intifada most coping strategies were domestically based, using the household's resources and assets and interpersonal household relations. Coping strategies in the latter years have forced a dependence on formal institutional humanitarian aid. Poor uneducated women in particular have had to learn new languages of communication and negotiation with public institutions for the sake of obtaining humanitarian aid. In order to cope with, and resist, long term Israeli policies of collective punishment, households and families in Gaza have utilised various different mechanisms.

This sub-section will focus on three main coping strategies that have been widely used by Gazan households, and led by women in particular (one coping strategy that is purposively not included here, is that of borrowing from relatives and neighbours, because it can be sufficiently understood from the description of the typology of households in debt which has already been presented, and is also sufficiently covered by secondary resources).[15] These three strategies are described and analysed through the lens of gender differences.

Promoting household production and income-generating activities As noted in Chapter 1, generations of poor Gazan housewives have historically been involved in home-based income-generating activities which are almost an extension of their domestic gender roles. In both nuclearised and extended households, women's involvement in activities such as food processing, making clothes, keeping

---

14 See Hammami PhD thesis (1994) on women's coping strategies in the post 1948 period, entitled 'Between Heaven and Earth: Transformation in religiosity and labour among southern Palestinian peasant and refugee women, 1920–1993'. Also see research by Lang and Muhanna on refugee women coping during the First Intifada (1992), and Liza Taraki's edited book (2006) *Living Palestine: Family Survival*. See Sletten, P. and Pedersen, J. (2003), FAFO Report No. 408, and FAFO Report No. 41 (2007) written by Hasselknippe, G. and Tviet, M. (2007). See also Oxfam Assessment report, 'Resistance, and Mobility under Occupation' (September 2006).

15 See Sletten, P. and Pedersen, J. (2003), FAFO Report No. 408, and FAFO Report No. 41 (2007) written by Hasselknippe, G. and Tviet, M. (2007). See also Oxfam Assessment report (September 2006).

chickens and other forms of household production has largely involved housewives, regardless of age or social background. However, household production is not only a strategy used during livelihood crises: it continues during times of relative economic stability as well, for economic and cultural reasons: a) to manage the household budget by balancing income, consumption and expenditure; and b) to maintain the authentic culture of the peasant family (Sayigh 1979, Lang and Muhanna 1992, Hammami 1994). During the Second Intifada, household production was used extensively by women to compensate for the scarcity of cash. Women used traditional skills of agriculture and food processing, as well as creating handicrafts. This is the reason why women find the management of household food and clothes items much easier than the management of other essential items requiring cash.

I selected three common narratives that represent the discourse of most women who have used similar means of household production, aimed at reducing their need for cash. Amira, 37 years old from El-shuja'eya, living in an extended family, said:

> Since cash became scarce, I have returned to producing cheese and yoghurt, using the milk powder I receive from coupons to make them. I can't afford to buy them. I also built a "*furun tena*" in front of my house to reduce the expense of gas.[16]

Manal, 32 years old, from El-shuja'eya and living in a nuclear family, said:

> Before the intifada, I never cooked without meat or chicken. Now I cook chicken once a week, sometimes once every two weeks. Of course, we also don't buy fruits as before. How do you think I manage food for the big family? I pay as little as possible for my children's meals in order to save the little money we have for other important things.

Um Husam, 32 years old from the Beach camp and living in an extended family, said:

> We are 12 persons living in one house, most of them young children. How can we survive? When my children ask for new clothes, I either borrow from my sisters who have children of the same age, or I re-tailor the old clothes to make them fit. I learnt sewing a long time ago, but I didn't practise it. Now I use an old manual sewing machine to sew clothes for my children. I manage food like other women in the camp: one day I cook lentils, another day beans, and the third day I fry potatoes and tomatoes. My children get fed up from the routine of food

16 A traditional oven used in Palestinian peasant families, made from clay or mud used for bread-baking and for cooking. It relies on firewood.

> they have, but what to do? We have no other options. I basically rely on the food items I receive from UNRWA and other charity associations to feed the children.

These narratives illustrate how middle aged women (the mothers of young children) have returned to traditional skills of household economy, as a strategy to meet their children's needs for food and clothing. This clearly reduces household expenditures, but is not sufficient to sustain their households. Women spend a great deal of time producing food at home from the scarce resources available. Most women assert they have to do so, as they are unable to buy enough basic food items from the market, citing steep increases in food costs, sometimes up to 300 per cent.[17]

Um-Abed, a 37-year-old woman from the Beach camp, explained how changing household expenditure and consumption patterns have affected her daily routine:

> In the past, I used to get up at 6:00 am, in order to make sure my children went to school at 6:30. Now I have to get up one hour earlier in order to make breakfast for them. My washing machine is broken, so I hand wash clothes, which takes three times as long. Because of the electricity cuts, I have to help my children with their homework either in the morning or the afternoon, depending on their shifts at school, and so I put off my house work until the evening, when there is no electricity.[18] Don't forget the time for shopping and the visits I make to search for coupons from here and there. I don't allow my husband to go shopping because he doesn't know how to buy the cheapest items. This is how my daily routine goes, God bless me.

In addition to producing their own food, women have also become involved in income-generating activities in the informal sector. Before the Second Intifada some of these women were involved in agriculture and trading activities. They continued their income-generating activities after the Second Intifada, as the households' need for money increased. Some women mentioned that their jobless sons worked with them. None of the women in the research sample mentioned starting a new business alone (i.e. without her husband) after the Second Intifada.

---

17 After 2006, the prices of food items rapidly increased because the Israeli government stopped the passage of food trucks from Israel. The scarcity of food items made grocery shops raise the prices without any control from the government.

18 Since mid-2006, Israel reduced the electricity supplies to Gaza to a minimum rate. Fuel and gas were also restricted which forced Gazan households to live without electricity for two-thirds of their daytime. The shortage of cooking gas made its price unaffordable, even for middle-income earners. Most households returned to using firewood for cooking, including refugees. See details on the fuel crisis caused by the Israeli policy of closure in OCHA report, with a particular focus on August 2009, available at: http://www.ochaopt.org/documents/Ocha_opt_Gaza_impact_of_two_years_of_blockade_August_2009_english.pdf.

A few of the younger female participants of the focus groups had started shared businesses with their jobless husbands. Although their involvement in the informal economy was irregular, invisible and insecure, it had an important effect on household survival, especially during the Second Intifada when most families lost their regular sources of income (Kuttab 2006: 285–263). Women's involvement in these income-generating activities, and in household production, has become the most common coping strategies they utilise when their men lose their jobs.

The field data shows that (out of the research sample of 60) 21 women aged 40 and over, and 5 aged 30 and over, stated that they were involved in income-generating activities before the Second Intifada. Most of them continued these activities, to a lesser extent, until the siege of Gaza in 2006. They worked in trading, grocery stores, sewing workshops, food processing, farming and livestock production. The majority of these women are married and living in extended families with their married sons, and the rest are female heads of household, because they are either widowed or else have chronically sick husbands.

The majority of women who owned a business stated that they were not encouraged to take micro-loans from women's organisations or from UNRWA before the Second Intifada. They emphasised that they managed their businesses well and made reasonable profits. When Gazan men realised they had no hope of returning to work in Israel, they encouraged their wives to apply for loans from women's micro-credit programmes to set up home gardens, poultry farms or grocery shops. Throughout this process, the gender division of labour had not changed. Men were basically involved in marketing and managing the money, whilst women were running the actual business. Suad, a 45-year-old from Al El-shuja'eya, described her business:

> I used to manage my trading when my husband was working in Israel, and it was going very well. Now he is jobless and has nothing to do. He has control over the money and he does the marketing, but in fact I don't really feel secure about the business being handled by him, but what to do? I don't want any conflict with him. He is not careful about managing the money, and I am responsible for repaying the loan.

In many cases the loans were received by women, but this was not actually their preference. They were pressured by their husbands to obtain loans in their own name from women's credit institutions. The new business ideas were men's ideas, but the women were doing the hard work from home. Many of the new businesses initiated by men and funded by loans received by women failed, and instead of generating income, generated serious debt.

Men's involvement in women's business domain put the women in a dilemma with credit associations. Some men decided to sell the business assets in order to repay the loan. Nevertheless, both men and women insisted that business failures were caused by the lack of raw materials, or lack of demand, not by bad management. Many couples are still repaying their loans today, at the expense of their children's basic needs. Some of them borrowed money from close relatives to repay the loans. Because of these women's experiences of the impact of the destruction of the local market system in Gaza, there has been widespread rejection of micro-credit programmes and ideas of starting a new business. Some women admit that they don't consider taking out loans while their husbands remain jobless, in order to avoid their interference in the loan process. Women's rejections of loans are reflected in the official records of one of the biggest women's credit institutions in Gaza (UNRWA).[19] The number of loans given to women declined from 12,685 in 2005 to 3,112 in 2008 (UNRWA 2008).

Since June 2007, the Israeli government reduced the amount of industrial fuel allowed entry to Gaza, resulting in enormous increases to the cost of public transport and its accessibility.[20] Many women traders have become home-based workers in order to reduce transport costs. Other women stated that they changed the type of products they traded in order to cater only for the demands of their neighbours. A few women, especially older women, replaced their market-based trading with a small *basta* in front of their homes.[21] Women in El-shuja'eya saw their sales from agricultural production reduced, particularly those women whose land was located close to the Israeli border. They increasingly used their seasonal agricultural products to feed their families. The transport crisis caused by the shortage of fuel meant that women who lived far from the local market, and who did not own a donkey or horse cart, were forced to concentrate on selling their products to neighbours.

Other women described the termination of their income-generating activities due to the closure:

> I used to go to Egypt three times a month, and brought food, clothes, cigarettes and other stuff. I made good money, and I built my house from the profits of my trading, while my husband was working in Israel. Since the closure, I stopped trading. My brothers encourage me to continue through the illegal tunnels[22] at the Egyptian border but I am very hesitant as this is a risky step. I am now doing some trading from home, and only deal with local traders who sell me goods at

19 UNRWA, Micro Finance Department's annual report 2008, supported with an interview conducted with the head of the department in June 2008.

20 See footnote 20.

21 *Basta* is a tiny place located in the road in front of women's houses. Usually managed by old women or teenage children, it is like a middle sized table 1.5 x 1.5 metres square, where sweets, crisps, and other children's items are sold. Sometimes, women use *basta* to sell clothes, especially if they live close to the local market. The *basta* does not cost anything and is not subject to market regulations.

22 After Hamas took control of Gaza, and Israel tightened its siege, many merchants built tunnels through the Rafah border for smuggling – to bring goods from Egypt. These tunnels are not secure, as they are always exposed to explosions by the Egyptian or Israeli military forces.

> higher prices. The profit I earn is not even enough to buy basic food. (A woman from the Beach camp)

These narratives show that women's income-generating activities failed to be sustainable. Instead, they have made many households more vulnerable by creating serious debt. In the later years of the Second Intifada, especially after Israel began its siege of Gaza in June 2007, most of the women in my research sample either stopped their businesses, or reduced them to a minimum scale. Husbands lost interest in sharing income-generating activities with their wives. Women reflected on the failure of these particular survival strategies as being due to Israel's blockade of Gaza and its devastating impact on the capacity of the informal economy and people's purchasing power. The latter, in particular, made income generating activities operate at a loss, while no alternative economic sources were available for poor households.

Household reliance on humanitarian aid Gazan household reliance on humanitarian aid has gradually increased to reach an unprecedented level. A December 2007 report by OCHA states that 80 per cent of households in Gaza became dependent on humanitarian aid (OCHA, 2007).[23] All of the women interviewed for this research asserted that they often visit government and community-based charitable associations, particularly those managed by women (*el jami'at*), to ask for coupons, or to search for temporary jobs for their husbands, sons or for themselves.[24] Whilst socialising in *el jami'at*, women listen to each other's stories, and have developed a specific language and techniques to support their common purpose of obtaining aid coupons. In El-shuja'eya and the Beach camp people began to differentiate between good and bad 'coupon collectors' based on women's skills of bargaining and manoeuvring with *el jami'at*. Um-Hasan, a 32-year-old from the Beach camp, said:

> There are a number of women in the camp who became well known as good "coupon collectors". In the beginning, I used to go ask them where to go to get coupons. We used to tell each other about how to receive coupons, but now we don't. Now, most women have learned how to collect coupons for their families. We don't leave any association without at least one visit to register our name, as not every association always has enough coupons.

Um-Sufian is a 48-year-old from El-shuja'eya and only finished her elementary school education. All her knowledge has been accumulated through her domestic

23 OCHA is the United Nations Office for the Coordination of Humanitarian Affairs.

24 Temporary job-creation programmes are mostly implemented through community-based organisations (CBOs). They are somehow attached to the local poor, and responsible for selecting the beneficiaries based on criteria identified by the international agencies like UNRWA, WFP, UNDP, and CHF … etc.

life and to some extent from the local market. She had never had any experience with formal and community institutions, until her family's vulnerability forced her into this realm. Um-Sufian has succeeded in using the language of formal institutions in order to become closer to the heads of women's community-based organisations that she approached to search for humanitarian support.

I noticed a clear difference between the language Um-Sufian used in group meetings in the association, and the language she used during my home visits. In group meetings, Um-Sufian used women's institutional discourse: she talked about women's need to work on their self-esteem and to participate in community activities, their need to work for the association not only to receive coupons, but also to change their lives for the better; she discussed encouraging mothers not to marry their daughters at an early age … and so on. In our individual meetings, however, she used her normal language, learnt from her actual life experience. These bargaining tactics used by poor women are similar to those described by Emma Crewe and Elizabeth Harrison, who describe the changing bargaining techniques of the poor, aimed at obtaining humanitarian assistance for their basic needs. The two authors argue that the poor 'learn to adopt their behaviour in anticipation and they can predict potential benefit … some become adept at manipulating … through the adoption of particular aspects of language' (Crewe and Harrison, 1998: 157–160). Women in Gaza used several bargaining techniques including deception within the family and in community institutions, when their normal stereotypical strategies were not sufficient to sustain their families' livelihood.

Women's socialisation through their wide participation in *el jami'at* has, to some extent, replaced the traditional forms of family and neighbour socialisation. The family, kin and neighbourhood networks and connections remain as a form of social and moral obligation, but are not so frequently drawn on as they were before the Second Intifada. With the collective impoverishment of Gazan households, family, kin and neighbourhood socialisation has become an additional economic burden. This situation confines traditional forms of kin and neighbourhood relations and networks to necessary social obligations like weddings, funerals, or giving birth.

Other poor women act and interact with *el jami'at* in different ways. The scarcity of resources, and the irregularity of the distribution of coupons, has made some poor women – especially those who do not have a strong relational network – more hesitant about informing their closest women relatives and neighbours of the availability of resources, assuming that this will reduce their own share. This has led to poor women concealing their limited resources, to avoid sharing them with close relatives and neighbours, as they themselves do not feel certain and secure about the future. In addition, it was repeatedly noted during the interviews that many women cannot make ends meet in spite of the coupons they obtain. They resort to deception to obtain more coupons from other associations, especially for food staples. These women try to secure food resources for the future, regardless of the needs of others. The lack of coordination between the local Community-Based

Organisations (CBOs) has reinforced individualism and opportunism among poor women as a strategy for survival.

Women experienced another complication regarding the expansion of humanitarian aid provided by CBOs. The provision of food coupons to women is almost always conditional upon membership of, and participation in, organised social, cultural and religious activities. Through the domination of the Islamist discourse in Gaza during the Second Intifada, most CBOs – both Islamic and secular – as well as mosques, increased their religious mobilisation, especially religious lectures and counselling. Women, mainly those who were younger with no childcare responsibilities, and older women, became more interested in religious lectures about Islamic laws and principles. This is in addition to social activities, such as lectures and training in women's reproductive health and childcare. Poor women perceive all these activities as obligatory, fearing they will otherwise be deprived of aid coupons. Women's participation in CBOs has affected their behaviour and attitudes: many of them have used their newly accumulated religious knowledge and interpretations to judge their daily life, and the lives of others. The increased religiosity of women also reflects their personal desires to be more knowledgeable of Islam, as well as it being an instrument to access humanitarian assistance. From conversations with these women, it seems their increasing religiosity does not undermine the strategies they use in order to achieve their goal of accessing assistance.

Um-Sufian is a strong example of poor women's abilities to bargain within the institutional discourse, whether Islamist or secular. The mother of a Hamas martyr, she has been involved in many associations – first with Hamas institutions and then with Fatah institutions, and in public she wears the *niqab*.[25] She admits that her main motive in participating in CBOs is her household need for coupons. But she has also become more religious in her daily life and is now committed to praying, fasting and full veiling. Her religiosity does not, however, prevent her from contacting men in institutions, or from communicating with strangers, and it allows her to bargain with charitable associations and even employ mild deception for the sake of receiving more coupons to sustain her large family.

Um-Sufian has used several coping strategies. She has sold her jewellery, reduced her household expenditures and consumption greatly, sold clothes in the market and borrowed from relatives. None of these were enough for her 14-member household to survive. After her son was martyred in 2003, she joined a Hamas women's organisation, and participated in demonstrations, food distribution, and social visits to families of men who had been injured and martyred. She also expanded her activities within secular women's associations.

25 The *niqab* or full face veil, was not common amongst veiled Gazan women before the Second Intifada. It is one interpretation of Islam for women to cover like this, but it is not obligatory or socially or culturally encouraged. During the Second Intifada, women increasingly used the *niqab* to facilitate their frequent mobility without being recognised by neighbours or relatives.

Um-Sufian eventually became less concerned about political or religious loyalty, and more attracted to the material and social rewards that she gained from charity associations.

Um-Sufian discovered from her own experience that interpersonal relations within, and networking with, humanitarian associations are critical. Thus, she tried to please the heads of different associations by following their orders without comment. After three interviews, Um-Sufian, felt relaxed enough to speak openly about her actual feelings towards CBOs:

> To tell you the truth, I sometimes felt humiliated by *el jami'at*. They only use me to do boring work, but if there is anything serious, they don't call me. Sometimes I think about stopping visiting them and just going back to my sewing which I used to do all day. But when I think about my family, I change my mind and keep compromising. My family depends on the coupons I receive from *el jami'at*. I suppress my feelings and try to ignore the crushing behaviour of the head of the association to which I am now committed. I believe they benefit from leading these associations. But so do I.

Changing gendered education and employment preferences From the early 1970s, education, especially for refugees, came to be seen as an important precursor of a sustainable family, as well as the critical means of social reproduction and the accomplishment of better social positioning (Rosenfeld 2002, Jacobsen 2004). Therefore, one of the priorities of Gazan women has been to educate their sons, in order for them to find employment with UNRWA, for the sake of securing an income and also enhancing their mothers' social status. Educating daughters has become important too, as it maximises their opportunities of finding better husbands, thereby securing their own lives (Johnson 2006). These gendered attitudes towards education and employment emerged and expanded before the Second Intifada, and were more common amongst low and middle-income families who prioritised their household budgets to fund their children's education. Very poor households used to take their sons out of school to work and support the family, and to marry their daughters at a young age to reduce their economic burdens.

The closure of Gaza, and the subsequent collective loss of sources of sustainable income, led to poor and vulnerable households returning to education. Um-Sami, the 43-year-old from El-shuja'eya, represents the views of many of her research participant peers:

> I sacrifice food for my family, to save money for my children's education. I don't want them to have the same future as their father, who has been jobless for years [now]. After university he decided to work in Israel, to earn better wages. He thought that work in Israel would last forever. If he had used his degree to work as a government employee, our situation would be stable now. I sell vegetables in the local market, but my work has never been secure.

Women over 40 years old who did not send their sons to university said they now regretted their decision, as they feel more vulnerable than other families who have at least one child who is a graduate. Educating children has become a vehicle for securing formal employment and regular income. Most women admitted they had borrowed money from relatives, neighbours and friends to pay their children's education fees.

This trend, particularly regarding daughters, has been influenced by the remarkable increase in job creation schemes provided within the framework of humanitarian assistance programmes. These programmes claim to be gender sensitive and concerned with shifting the emphasis from relief to development, by providing poor women with job opportunities.[26] The temporary jobs provided are distributed in cycles – three months for example – with salaries ranging from $200–$300 a month. Equal opportunity policies mean individuals rarely have access to more than one temporary job a year.

In the female focus groups most of the young educated participants stated they had been volunteering with community-based associations for years, in order to receive one or two temporary jobs (two being the maximum available per individual per year). Nadia, a 23-year-old from the Beach camp, studies IT at Gaza Islamic University, and also volunteers with a women's association in the camp. She said:

> The $600 I received from my previous two [temporary] jobs sustained my family for six months. I finished my [second] contract three months ago, and continued volunteering with the association, for the opportunity to get another job. I am just helping them with some computer work. I am not really learning a lot, but it is fine, as long as I can earn some money for my family. Since my father stopped working in Israel he has not been able to find a job. I got very good results at university, and got a full scholarship. I am no longer a burden on my family: now they rely on my efforts to earn income. (From a focus group conducted in the Beach camp in April 2008)

Jobless young men, whether educated or uneducated, reflected on their sense of responsibility for the survival of their households in a different way. Many became more interested in joining militant resistance groups, saying there were no other opportunities for them to secure their households' survival. However, a few educated men began volunteering with community youth institutions, for the sake of trying to secure a job, and have developed their work skills in order to maximise future job opportunities. Young males with family responsibilities in households with no male breadwinners were less concerned about their future than men of low and middle-income families: they tended to view family responsibilities as an obligation that restricts their future. Some educated men accepted temporary jobs as street cleaners, guards, agricultural labourers, members of the executive forces,

26 See UNRWA job creation report (2007).

or militant resistance groups. Young single men were usually more flexible than their fathers about accepting low status jobs in order to support their families.

Daughters, on the other hand, have benefited from culturally derived gender divisions of labour and taken up paid opportunities in the public domain. During the Second Intifada traditionally male dominated sectors of Gaza's economy, particularly in the private sector, were decimated and the informal female work sector shrank. The only expanding sectors are the public sector and the voluntary sector of charitable associations. Jobs provided in the voluntary sector – mainly in education, health, social work and administration – are most available to educated young women. Nevertheless, parents' ambitions for their daughters' education remain restricted by their wish not to jeopardise their marriage opportunities.

Temporary job-creation programmes have facilitated an environment in which women, in particular, can develop their skills and have increasing access to paid employment, as most of these jobs are concentrated in pre-configured female-focused areas and gender-segregated institutions. In some individual cases women have succeeded in challenging their domestication as well as stereotypical divisions of labour. However, these changes have been concentrated amongst small numbers of highly educated women, whilst uneducated women have remained disadvantaged.

Generational and Gender Effects of the Second Intifada

Households in Gaza, especially the poor, have historically relied on the economic efforts of adult sons to sustain the household and to reproduce the gender order. The structure of power relations has, despite its fluidity, remained patriarchal. Fathers are publicly empowered by the numbers of adult sons who maintain the family's male lineage, whilst mothers are domestically empowered by the reproduction of this ideology. This gender and generational structure of households/families, is ideological, and resilient in the face of changing contexts.

In Palestinian society, this gender and generational structure has always been negotiated and contested under Israeli military occupation (Taraki 2006). The context of the Second Intifada has generated unprecedented fluidity in practices of gender and age within households regarding their responses to livelihood crises and insecurity. This following section will describe the gendered and generational effects of coping strategies used by men and women to sustain their households. This includes progressive and regressive changes occurring in the practice of gender and age.

Shifting the power of responsibility from the older to the younger generation Young sons and daughters were formerly reliant on their able-bodied fathers to provide for the family, until sons either graduated or started to earn income, and daughters married. During the Second Intifada, when their fathers lost their sources of income and their mothers became dependent on humanitarian aid, young men and women were forced to search for ways of supporting their households before they reached the socially sanctioned age of adulthood (i.e. having graduated, being employed and married). All the young men and women interviewed in the focus groups (age 18–28) asserted they were economically dependent on their parents before the Second Intifada. The majority of them stressed that during the last few years of the intifada they either left university education to search for paid work, or else took on temporary jobs in order to finish their university education and support their families.

Uneducated single young women were encouraged by their parents to search for temporary jobs, and for aid coupons. But job opportunities were rare, as most of those offered by community-based associations prioritised university graduates. Some uneducated young women were forced to accept socially and culturally low status jobs, such as cleaning or hairdressing that may jeopardise their reputation, and as a result reduce their marriage opportunities.

It was noticeable in the male focus groups that young men were less committed to volunteering with CBOs than young women. The young men explained that they could not volunteer long term because they needed to support their families. Some of the men commented that temporary jobs were mainly given to women because they were more 'feminine' roles, such as food distribution, childcare, education and food production. Others asserted they had left community associations and joined Hamas executive forces in order to have a regular income. Young women, on the other hand, displayed high levels of commitment to CBOs, tending to volunteer for one to three years, but sometimes as long as five years. These organisations are the only sources of socially accepted job opportunities for young women, as the government and private work sectors have lost their capacity to absorb any more labour.

Although young women usually graduated from university in order to secure a job to support their families, their attitudes towards work have begun to change. Young female graduates in their early 20s, especially from the Beach camp, asserted that their university education, and work experience with CBOs, are ways for them to achieve economic and social autonomy regarding their future work, and marriage, opportunities. This change has, however, placed them in a quandary between marriage, as the traditional social determinant of their status, and their new interests and desires to be autonomous and empowered through their education, employment and public participation.

In the Beach camp female focus groups, a 24-year-old woman from the Beach camp described searching for a job:

> I insisted on graduating from university in a shorter period than is usual, to find a job to support my family. But I also had to volunteer for a long time, with the SHAREK youth association, [or] I wouldn't have been able to find a good job. All the training courses I attained and the voluntary work I have done eventually gave me the opportunity to get a good job in the association. I have now been a project coordinator for 6 months. I get a salary of $700 a month [and] pay my

> whole salary to my parents, except $100 for my transport and personal expenses. This is fine for me. I am enjoying the progress that I've made.

Within the specific context of Gaza during the Second Intifada a number of gender-based socio-cultural and institutional reasons have facilitated the commitment of young educated and uneducated women to CBOs. These include: a) the inclusion of gender mainstreaming in international humanitarian aid policies, in order to create equal opportunities for men and women; b) the available jobs being more socially relevant to women's educational and professional skills; c) the implementation of job creation and humanitarian aid projects being mainly administered by women's community-based organisations, in which men are rarely involved; d) the physical locations of community-based associations being easily accessible to women; e) the Islamicisation of many community-based associations having enabled parents to feel secure about their daughters visiting and participating in community-based activities.

Young women's involvement in CBOs has exaggerated gender segregation in Gazan society compared to the period before the Second Intifada, whilst at the same time enhancing their participation in community activities. The Islamicisation of CBOs, including associations that were secular before the Second Intifada, has allowed young women to develop new attitudes towards their education and employment, and to be mobilised as agentive actors in new ways, whilst not restricting them from resisting some stereotypical gender norms. Some stated they volunteered as teachers of young children in mosques, where they also attended religious lectures which reaffirmed their commitment to Islamic codes and principles. Nevertheless, these women presented some examples of challenging traditional patriarchal norms and customs based on gender and age.

The first example concerns the engagement of young women in training and awareness activities provided by CBOs, which contributes to their development of life skills, communication and negotiation skills, as noted by a female staff member of one of the largest youth association in Gaza:

> I went through 200 CVs, to select a list of job interviewees. We did not mean to prioritise men over women or vice versa. The job advertised was a 'group facilitator' which is appropriate for both. I found around two thirds of the CVs were from women. What surprised me is that most women's CVs are filled with experiences of volunteering, and training courses in different subjects. We selected the best for interviews, and they were all women. We decided to add the two best male CVs, in order not to be seen as biased.

A second example is of young women challenging obstacles to their education. During the fuel and transport crisis in Gaza, especially during the months of March – May 2008, all the female university students interviewed asserted that they made tremendous effort not to miss lectures, or exams. Those living relatively close to university walked to their studies, whilst those living further away either waited for transport, or borrowed money for taxis in order not to miss their classes. They also stressed that despite the electricity cuts they managed to study and passed their exams.

The third example of agentive transformative actions taken by these young educated women is their attempts to transcend gender divisions of labour by entering fields of work that are historically male dominated. Some stated they searched for jobs in media production and IT. Others emphasised that substantial numbers of university graduates volunteered or worked as correspondents in digital TV stations, including those belonging to Hamas. Other young women challenged stereotypes that discriminate against those working in menial jobs, like cleaning, asserting that they knew young female graduates who were working either as cleaners in private houses, or CBOs. The focus group participants stated that, in addition to the urgent need to support their families, some of these young women wanted to complete their university education without being a burden on their households. Others considered these menial jobs as a means to develop their skills, or to network with CBOs, in order to obtain better jobs in future.

These examples appear to be the main reasons for which young women have had better access to temporary and permanent jobs than both educated and uneducated young men. This context, however, is perceived differently by young men, many of whom assume that job distribution within civil society organisations and to a lesser extent government institutions, is gender-biased in favour of women. They believe job creation programmes should prioritise men, who are the 'natural' family breadwinners, and are reticent about applying for these kinds of jobs, which they believe are not appropriate for men.

In arguing for gender transformation, the changing distribution of jobs cannot be taken as the only factor. However, in a situation of male breadwinner crisis, young men may be forced to accept jobs that are considered female-focused. In time, this practice will most likely become socially legitimised (but amongst the male research participants it applied to just two cases). One man from the Beach camp in his mid-20s stated that he had accepted a cleaning job in a women's organisation. A second man, from El-shuja'eya and in his early 20s, accepted a temporary job managed by a women's organisation, distributing food to families in need.

Among the research participants, only a few households acknowledged their dependence on their daughters' income. This dependence is not presented as desirable, especially by men, who, regardless of their ages, found it difficult to discuss their attitudes towards being dependent on the income of a young daughter. Only one father was willing to talk about this. His daughter – Ne'ema – works as a hairdresser to support her family. Her father said:

> Do you think it is easy for me to accept that my daughter is the one who feeds us although I am still in my *afiati* (able-bodied). This in fact makes me feel that I am 90 years old. But what other choices do I have?

The father's anxiety about his daughter's work as a hairdresser reflected his own fears of being seen as inferior by other men in the focus group. His daughter, Ne'ema (one of the Beach camp research participants) is 23 years old. She graduated from high school at the beginning of the Second Intifada, but her family was not able to afford to send her to university. Ne'ema does not want to work as a hairdresser, but said she has no option because she needs to support her family:

> I feel proud of being responsible for my family. My mother waits for my income to go shopping for the family. But my mother is worried because no suitors are asking to marry me. My younger sister got married before me. At first my parents refused to marry her before me, until I put pressure on them [to do so]. This is my fate and I have to accept it. Maybe one day I can finish my university education and get a better job. Then I would have the chance to marry a good husband. (Ne'ema participated in a focus group in February 2008)

Young brothers are also influenced by their household dependence on their young sisters' temporary jobs, and their spending long hours outside the home. In the female focus groups, young women were asked about their brothers' reactions to their involvement in CBOs. Most young women replied that some of their brothers became involved in resistance groups, while others became apathetic. Young women described their brothers' reactions as resistant to feelings of inferiority. Some young females, however, refused to discuss their personal experiences with their brothers, for cultural and/or security reasons. For young men these reactions are linked with stereotypical and historical understandings of male power and authority. In a situation of national resistance, young men's involvement in militant 'resistance' groups is a means of reproducing their masculinity (Peteet 1994, Jean-Klein 2000).

Although these empirical findings show that the patriarchal structure of Gazan households has broken down, and the power of responsibility has shifted from the older parents to younger sons and daughters, it is still early to argue whether these changes will have long-term sustained effects on the dominant gender ideology. Rather they can be seen as a situational reaction to the destruction of traditional male sectors of employment. The criterion of power distribution here is not only the sexual division of labour. It is rather the dysfunction of the gender order, by which men are not able to practice what they see as their basic social responsibility of family provision, while young women are doing so. The issue of gender and generational change cannot be sufficient evidence to argue about gender transformation, unless the dysfunction of male gender remains.

The liberation of women's mobility and the feminisation of humanitarian aid The Second Intifada also led to the liberation of Gazan women's social mobility. This fundamental change, however, is an indication of the need for women to access a greater space for communicating and negotiating with the public world beyond their limited domestic spheres. This change has presented an overt challenge to the patriarchal features of Palestinian social institutions (Walby 1996).[27] Indeed, most Palestinian development scholars and planners consider that women's increased mobility during the Second Intifada is an indicator of their autonomy and empowerment.[28] Nonetheless, it would be a simplification, within the specific context of Gaza, to make a proportional link between this increased mobility and women's increasing autonomy and empowerment, by which, for example, they have control over domestic and public decisions.[29]

The majority of the female research participants interpreted this mobility beyond domestic boundaries as a necessity imposed on them by the destruction of their household economics. Lamis Abu Nahla explains that poor Gazan women have taken up the role of primary provider, whilst their men 'employ the strategy of isolation, avoidance, aggression, and assistance refusal and striving to maintain their status as heads of household' (Abu-Nahla 2006: 181). The social realities of Gazan women reveal that their increased mobility is, amongst other things, a reflection of men's loss of their 'normal' traditional role as the primary household providers. As a result, women are forced to search for resources in both domestic and public domains. The emergence and expansion of humanitarian aid provided by public institutions to poor families has extended women's social mobility to incorporate certain public spaces.

All of the female research participants interviewed in both the Beach camp and El-shuja'eya stressed that their mobility has increased as a direct consequence of the inability of men in their households to provide sources of income, and the exhaustion of household savings and other resources. All of the married participants considered themselves eligible for humanitarian assistance, and felt obliged to visit various institutions several times a week in order not to lose any opportunities for assistance. The changing trend of women's mobility suggests that Gazan women have been more flexible in adjusting to this new context than men (Hammami 1998: 308–309). This is most likely related to the types of available coping strategies, which are still perceived as an extension of the domain of women. Men's support of women's mobility in order to search for coupons is directly linked to gender-biased assumptions: most men argue that women are more able to play a role in charitable associations, as they have the innate skills of being able to focus their compassion. Gazan men also assume that women

27 See Sylvia Walby's definition of patriarchy in relation to women's domestication and lack of participation in the public social institutions, in 'The Declining Significance or the Changing Forms of Patriarchy' in V.M. Moghadam (ed.) (1996) *Patriarchy and Economic Development: Women's Positions at the End of the Twentieth Century*.

28 See the Palestinian Human Development Report (2003–2004), Oxfam briefing paper no. 28 (2002) in 'Forgotten Villages: Struggling to Survive under Closure in the West Bank', and the IWS report (December 2008) on the gender impact of the second Intifada.

29 Naila Kabeer's definition of women's autonomy and empowerment in her article 'Resources, Agency, Achievements: Reflections on the Measurement of Women's Empowerment', *Development and Change* (1999) Vol. 30, 435–464.

are more capable of acting as beggars for humanitarian aid, for the sake of their children. One young mother from El-shuja'eya, aged 34 and with 5 children, said:

> I never imagined that a day would come when I would be in this situation, having to go out to search for coupons. I lived as a respected housewife all my married life, [but] my sister-in-law convinced me to go to visit *el jami'at* (a local CBO). I agreed because my husband had no money. I was very shy of showing myself to be helpless. My shyness about showing off my urgent need for assistance made the head of the association think that I did not really need coupons.

Women's views of their mobility are divergent. Most of the wives interviewed for this research expressed dissatisfaction with their increased mobility, citing that the material benefits are much less than the social costs they incur. A few said that the livelihood crisis, and the necessity of spending more time outside the home, have opened up opportunities for them to get to know the world around them, and to develop a network with other people in their community. But they also asserted that their increased mobility would not continue if it did not result in material benefits to sustain their households. In many conversations, poor women who participated in charitable institutions, expressed a preference to return to their traditional life, that is, a life where they stay at home and men work to provide for the household. The majority of women interviewed for this research did not present the extension of their mobility as a free choice, especially middle aged women with childcare responsibilities. But for them, mobility is the only option in order to fulfil their households' minimum survival needs. Um-Sufian from El-shuja'eya, said:

> I was very satisfied with my life around my children, while my husband and sons were selling products in the market. I never complained. Our life was stable. Now I visit every institution in the neighbourhood, and even further away. Since my son died as a martyr in 2003, my husband and my eldest married son became jobless [and] life has become unbearable. I decided to veil my face because my martyred son was from Hamas. But I found later that the veil made my mobility much easier, as people cannot easily recognise me. I do not only visit Hamas' associations, I participate in the activities of all associations that support me with coupons. How [else] do you think my family survives? I hope to go back to my previous life, when I was sewing at home and the men went out doing to their work. I just want to have a rest, I really feel tired and sometimes humiliated by these associations.

Only three women from the Beach camp and none of the women from El-shuja'eya mentioned that they had been involved in women's institutional activities, or had heard about their existence, before the current economic crisis. Women's associations have taken a leading role in humanitarian aid distribution. These associations are community based, and often rely on poor women's membership fees, alongside food and money donations from wealthy people and/or formal institutions. Hundreds of poor women in both El-shuja'eya and the Beach camp pay fees of NIS 20 or 30 ($5–7) for their annual membership. These women develop an assumption that their eligibility for humanitarian assistance is conditional on their payment of membership fees. During the individual research interviews, many women stated that they borrowed money to pay for their membership, in order to ensure they regularly received aid.

The empirical data shows that increasing humanitarian support, and the increased number of women's charity associations responsible for the distribution of aid, has encouraged many women, regardless of their age and education, to become involved in social and cultural activities as well as political demonstrations.[30] Gazan women and men both perceive the task of food distribution as the domain of women. This has encouraged the involvement of middle aged women in particular, and poor middle aged women have been encouraged to establish their own CBOs. During the field work, three of the female research participants were managing women's community-based organisations. These three women asserted that the motive behind them establishing their own organisations, and the work they did, was to sustain their households through receiving coupons and obtaining temporary jobs.

Um-Iyad, who leads a women's CBO in the Beach camp, had three temporary jobs in the space of three years (each lasted three months, with a monthly salary of $300). Um-Ashraf, who manages humanitarian aid in the *Zakher* association in El-shuja'eya, had two temporary jobs within one year.[31] The main tasks these women carry out in their organisations is preparing lists of local families in need, visiting homes to check the families' eligibility for support, monitoring families' use of the support provided, and informing women in the neighbourhood about the association's activities. These tasks have made these women well known and, to a certain extent, respected by their local community.

Although these women's CBOs are officially registered with the Hamas government, during the period of research they were not accountable to any official body. These associations also operate in the absence of law enforcement, especially after the Hamas-Fatah split in 2007, and the subsequent Hamas takeover of Gaza. These associations also operate on minimal levels of institutionalisation (Oxfam 2006). Board members of these CBOs are poor women from the local community, the majority of whom have no experience of institutional work. They are all managed by one person who is registered as the head of the board, and the other women involved are classified as volunteers.

During the fieldwork, the three CBOs were all located in empty apartments, or a basement of one of the women's homes. The three women running these

30 According to recent statistics from the Palestinian Interior Ministry, the number of registered CBOs – or charitable associations, as they were classified by the Ministry – increased from 227 in 2000, to 535 in 2005. There were 938 in 2008 (August 2008).

31 *Zakher* is the name of a women's community-based organisation in El-shuja'eya.

organisations are middle aged and married. They have developed a strong network with formal and informal institutions at local level, and have used this network to register their association with the local government and to receive government support. One of the women pointed out that establishing a CBO is easier than opening a business because the former does not need capital, but still brings in money for the head of the association, and others. She said:

> It becomes a fashion now, for poor women to establish community organisations, with the shifting of most institutional funds to immediate humanitarian assistance. It does not require high education or qualifications, only a woman who knows her local community. Hamas women are also doing the same. If you have a strong social network with official figures in your family, or neighbours, it is easy to manage an organisation. It just needs a woman who is brave enough to collect donations from here and there. I thought, if it works then it will be good for me and for other poor families. If not, I would search for another association to join.

Involvement in CBOs has become largely feminised, and socially accepted as such by local communities in Gaza. The majority of women interviewed, especially middle aged women, reported that they did not face obstruction from their families when they wanted to visit local community organisations. Their jobless husbands encouraged them to visit these organisations, and to become involved, so long as they could obtain benefits from doing so.

Changes in Patterns of Marriage

Hania Shalkomy (2003) and Penny Johnson (2006) suggest that patterns of marriage in Arab societies have also changed in response to the situation of persistent public insecurity. In the specific situation of Palestinian society – which is heavily scarred by dispossession, dispersal, military occupation, colonial modernity and national resistance – the everyday practice of marriage and kin relation, as stated by Johnson, 'is not only a response to the hostile Israeli rule that threatens Palestinian identity, but also a response to the absence of a Palestinian state' (Johnson 2006: 52–53).

As argued earlier, within this context of insecurity, kin marriage has played a key role in maintaining the survival of individuals, families and national identity. The harshness of life during the Second Intifada and the socio-political fragmentation of Palestinian society have contributed to a dismantling of the patriarchal basis of marriage. The historical pattern of consolidating family connectedness through marriage within a situation of collective impoverishment and vulnerability has gradually lost its socio-economic, political and symbolic function.

Marriage shifts to become an economic project The most striking aspect of changes in marriage in Gaza is a male shift in preference towards marrying employed women, regardless of their kin connection. This preference reflects the immediate need for livelihood resources. Marriage decisions go beyond traditional cultural norms, where the bride is at least five years younger than the groom, and conforms to expectations of beauty and appropriate family and kin lineage. Men and women realised that neither family, kin relations, nor public institutions have the capacity to achieve household security in the short or long term. Thus, they have attempted to find alternative marriage patterns that contribute to their households' economic survival.

During the interviews and focus groups with men and women, the participants emphasised that kin marriage was encouraged during the first three years of the intifada, as a source of social and cultural capital. Many participants attributed the subsequent reduction in kin marriage, and the increase of non-kin marriage, to increased employment opportunities for young women, especially in the voluntary sector. In contemporary Palestinian history, marriage has become a socio-economic and cultural institution (Moors 1990). During the years of livelihood crisis in Gaza marriage has become an economic project for the survival of the whole family. This implies an undermining of the dominant patriarchal family norms. The harshness of the economic situation and the vulnerability of the family during the Second Intifada have undermined the symbolic and cultural function of kin marriage 'to inherit the cultural identity of kinship patriarchal systems' (Barakat 1985: 28).

Since the beginning of the livelihood crisis in Gaza, marriage patterns have diversified, reflecting changing realities of living and the increasing diversity of men and women's desires. It appears that some young women are conflicted between wanting to marry better-off husbands, and their parents' desire to secure their daughters' marriages. The majority of parents feel more secure about their daughter marrying someone they know and trust, as opposed to a stranger (Johnson 2006). In the first years of the Second Intifada, the decision as to whom the daughter would marry was not dictated by the financial capacity of her suitors: her parents were more concerned with the reputation of his family, and their livelihood resources. For some parents, the security of marriage, and its likelihood to last, was more important than the immediate economic benefits. Educated and employed Gazan women usually prefer men with a university degree, even if they are jobless. This is attributed to the perception that the current crisis will not last forever, and to their belief in male education as a sustainable source of livelihood. It is therefore seen as the promise of a sustainable marriage.

The preference for marriage security over household economic survival can also be attributed to the historical experience of the Palestinian household. Some parents want to secure their daughter's marriage, even if it will result in poverty. Daughters are expected to adapt to their husbands material circumstances. In the focus groups, some parents were dissatisfied with their sons' decisions to marry employed women for the sake of their income. Mothers, in particular, were concerned that these employed wives would create controversy by earning income when their husbands were jobless.

Another aspect of marriage also revealed during the individual interviews and focus group discussions was polygamy, which appears to have increased during the later years of the Second Intifada. Middle aged married men have become more interested in marrying a second wife, and occasionally a third, especially women who work as teachers and nurses. One jobless man in his 40s from El-shuja'eya admitted that he was seriously considering marrying a teacher or a nurse, in order to financially assist his family. He described this as both legitimate and rewarding for women who are '*awanes*', spinsters. He said:

> Islam gives me the right to marry a second wife. My first wife does not care. There are a number of women who are in their 30s and don't have any possibility to marry a single man. To marry at this age would be an advantage for [her]. At least she would be able to have a child. We would both benefit from this marriage: I can't understand why, at this time, it would be a scandal [for me] to marry a second wife.

As none of the female research participants was in a polygamous marriage, I relied for my analysis of polygamy on their local knowledge and experience. During interviews the participants confirmed that an increasing number of single women aged 30 and over, especially those working as teachers, nurses and secretaries, have recently married men close to their age or even younger, who have an existing spouse. The research participants, including younger women, supported the Islamic point of view that this kind of marriage is also rewarding for women, because employed women who marry in their late 20s or early 30s improve their social status. The women went on to argue that a single teacher in her early 30s would accept to become a second wife out of her desire to be a wife and mother, even if this marriage would compromise her control over her income, which she knew to be her new husband main motive in marrying her. This new polygamous trend has implications for daughters' families, resulting in some mothers being more guarded about the marriage decisions of their employed daughters.

The empirical data shows that the majority of marriage decisions operate according to a number of factors. Households try to meet the immediate goal of livelihood survival. They also try to minimise the risk of long-term marriage insecurity by negotiating patriarchy. This is illustrated, for example, with the preference of kin marriage for uneducated young women because they have less opportunities to marry based on their education or employment potential. In this situation, parents consider kin marriage more secure for their daughters. However, non-kin marriage is encouraged for educated women. If the educated employed women get divorced, they, at least, have their education and employment to secure their future. The patriarchal culture of marriage remains vital when other sources of livelihood survival and security are unavailable. This is why non-kin marriage in Gaza is not a substitute for kin marriage. Marriage decisions taken by Gazan families have become more rational, as opposed to ideologised by patriarchy. The following conversation that I had with Um-Haitham, a 48-year-old woman from

El-shuja'eya, gives a clear example of how the decision to marry a son is calculated amongst poor vulnerable families, based on the situation of each household.

Researcher:

> Why did you make the decision to marry your son (Haitham) at this particular time, when you are in debt?

Um-Haitham:

> Abu-Haitham (the father of Haitham) is increasingly sick, and the children have almost left home. I can't stop my voluntary work with the women's association, as it is our family's only income. If I get sick and I cannot manage the household tasks by myself, what would happen [then]? My son is restless and uncertain about his future. No one knows how long I will be here for them. [So] I want him to marry now, not only to please him, but also to bring a woman to support me at home, and to look after my husband while I am out.

Researcher:

> Who is the bride you selected?

Um-Haitham:

> I chose his cousin. She is 17 years old and her family is very similar to ours. I know her very well and she likes me, she used to come to help me with my domestic work. Her family is very poor and she has five sisters. Her parents want the older daughters to marry to reduce their burden. I don't think I can find a better bride to care for my sick husband. She is very polite and obedient, and her mother is not a troublemaker. This girl knows our life and she can cope with it. Do you think I am able to choose an educated bride to marry my son? She definitely would make troubles that we would not be able to manage.

Researcher:

> How are you going to cover the marriage expenses this summer?

Um-Haitham:

> God has not forgotten me. Throughout my volunteering with the women's association, I made many friends, who all know my family situation. I also have a good relationship with the head of the association, and she won't hesitate to help [me]. I will borrow from my friends and my mother has also promised to give me some money. The bride's mother doesn't care about the dower. She just wants her daughter to have a stable marriage. So we may agree to pay only 2000

> Jordanian Dinars (around $3,500 (while the normal dower paid now is minimum 3000 JD around $4500). Everything is getting expensive after the closure, but I can manage. I just need some money to paint my son's room and to buy a bed. But God will help me!

The age of marriage There are now slight differences between the ages that Gazan men marry. The men's focus groups revealed that some men, especially educated men, remain unmarried until just under the age of 30, because they have refused to accept their marriage merely as an economic project for the survival of their family. These young men still prefer the traditional pattern of marriage that enhances their sense of manhood (i.e. to marry a woman who is a few years younger than her husband, and has less education than him). Some families, in both neighbourhoods and in the camps, have tried to avoid the effects of the livelihood crisis on their sons' marrying ages, by placing themselves in debt. Some mothers borrow money for their sons' weddings, as in the case of Um-Haitham. For Gazan families, marriage is a sign of adulthood and manhood, where the collective sense of family responsibility is created.

The Second Intifada has had two different effects on the age of young women marrying. Uneducated women are marrying younger, because this is their only means of security: but university educated women are marrying later. However, some mothers (in El-shuja'eya more than in the Beach camp) prioritise marriage over education for their daughters, feeling that university is important, but not at the expense of their daughters marrying at an appropriate age.

Young women and men demonstrate slight differences in their preferences regarding the appropriate age for marriage. During the focus groups with men and women in their 20s, many asserted that the bride should, ideally, be the same age, or a few years younger, than the groom. Most young men, regardless of their education, appeared to be more conservative in their opinions of this matter than their parents. In focus groups with older men, some of them criticised stereotypical patterns of marriage that reinforced ideas about a groom being older and more educated than his bride. These criticisms may be a reflection of the number of jobless fathers who attend to justify their sons' marriages for the sake of sustaining their families. They may also reflect feelings of guilt amongst fathers who have lost their capacity to facilitate an ideal marriage for their sons. One man, in his mid-40s from the Beach camp, who used to work as a wage labourer in Israel, described his son's experience:

> Youth are different today. My son finished his university and married a university graduate. They were both 27 years old. Young uneducated girls do not have experience of life: women's education and work with institutions is making them more able to manage their families now; they behave better with their husbands, educate the children, and know how to look after themselves. I see my son's wife – she looks after her husband, and knows how to behave with us.

> So what is wrong with a young man marrying a woman of his age, or even few years older, if she will make his life better?

Uneducated young women prefer to marry whilst they are young, because marriage is their main source of personal security. Educated women, however, especially those who are active in institutions or have temporary jobs, stay single until the ages of 25–28. This is probably one reason why educated men are also marrying later. Another reason is related to women's changing attitudes towards themselves, and their increasing social and economic autonomy. Most of the university educated women in the research, including those who belong to Hamas and *Jehad* Islamist parties asserted that now they control their own marriage decisions, and some have postponed marriages in order to support their families economically. Educated men, however, mainly leave the decision of selecting their bride to their mother.

The rise in marriage age, especially amongst educated young people, has also been influenced by an increasing trend of newly married couples living in extended households, for economic or social security purposes. Um-Iyad from the Beach camp, who lives in absolute poverty and with a violent husband, presented this assessment of selecting a potential bride for her university educated son, who would join their extended family:

> It is so hard nowadays to find an educated woman who can also find a job, and would accept to live in our miserable house with a miserable father-in-law. To avoid shame, I am going to find *bent aisha* – a sober, uneducated young woman – for him; there are many like this in the camp. I will also pay less dower for her.

Dower[32] *and marriage arrangements* In a society with peasant roots, a woman's dower, as stated by Annelies Moors (1995), is a sign of family social status and honour. In Gaza, the dower stabilised at around 2,500 Jordanian Dinar (JD), on average, but it increased to JD 4,000, including *el Shabka* (the gold given to brides at their wedding party) during the years 2007–2009. This increase was caused by

32 Dower or *maher* in the Muslim Arab region, refers to the Qur'an; '*Give to the women a free gift of their marriage portions*' (Surah an-Nisa, 4: 4). The dower belongs to women exclusively, and is a gift to be paid directly to them. According to Shari'a law, dower is part of the contractual marriage agreement and is divided in two: 'prompt dower' which is payable immediately on demand by the wife and 'deferred dower' which is payable only on dissolution of a marriage by death or divorce. The former is used by women for their *shabka* and trousseau. From a Shari'a perspective, dower is the sum of money, or other items, which the wife is entitled to receive from her husband. The amount of a dower may, or may not, be fixed either before, during or after the marriage. Nevertheless, the social and cultural rituals of using dower in marriage arrangements is not the same in all Arab Muslim societies (see the detailed difference between Palestine and Egypt for example in Diana Singerman (1995) *Avenues of Participation: Family, Politics and Network in Urban Quarters of Cairo* and in Islah Jad (2009) *The Politics of Group Wedding in Palestine: Political and Gender Tension.*

the increase in the price of gold as a result of its scarcity during the years of border closure. With the huge hike in both the price of gold, and the items for a bride's trousseau, some families prefer to separate *el Shabka* from the total dower, in order to ensure their daughters have sufficient money to purchase their marriage trousseau, especially the gold.

Men's focus groups conducted in different areas of the Gaza Strip revealed that families have formulated new forms of marriage contracts, in order to manage dower payments. Two contracts are signed: one in the Shari'a court that includes the total dower agreed upon between the two families; a second is signed with a public notary, stating that the groom's family will pay a portion of the total dower before marriage, with the rest being paid after the marriage. This second contract is also binding, and has caused problems for some women after marriage, particularly if they have not married a kin relative. In one case in the town of Beit Hanoun, in the northern Gaza Strip, there was considerable conflict between two families due to the inability of the husband to commit to paying the second portion of the dower, as explained by a local middle aged male resident:

> When couples have problems, the bride's natal family asks the husband to pay the remaining dower for their daughter, and if he fails to pay, the bride's family might take them to court. This type of contractual arrangement only occurred amongst close relatives, but it is so shameful to encourage it among non-kin marriage.

This may be a reason why kin marriages have not been widely replaced by the new forms of non-kin marriage mentioned earlier. When a young man fails to find a bride who is employed, he then prefers to marry a relative, particularly from his mother's family lineage. Mothers who are closely related, especially sisters or cousins, are able to negotiate dower openly with each other, and may accept a lower dower for their daughters. The total dower is less among kin marriages, where marriage expenses are usually negotiated between mothers. Some mothers assert that they borrow gold from close siblings, just for the wedding party. However, some educated women from the Beach camp mentioned that many marriages have broken down since these new arrangements emerged during the second intifada.

The livelihood crisis has also reduced the traditional extravagance of weddings. In the past parents had many wedding party expenses, including the venue, food, music and gifts. Cancelling the wedding lunch, or staging the wedding at home, reduces expenses significantly. Before the Second Intifada the groom was obliged to buy presents for his sisters, and in many cases to new parents-in-law and the sisters of his bride, but this is no longer the case. Women borrow wedding dresses from each other, or from neighbours. Another fashion that has emerged during the Second Intifada is of collective Islamic weddings, some of which are completely financed by Hamas and other religious groups, whilst others are paid for by the family, but cost significantly less. During the Second Intifada weddings have also become sexually segregated. The Islamicisation of marriage rituals has occurred for two interlinked reasons: the increasing religiosity of Gazan families, and their inability to cover the cost of modern Western-style marriages. In many cases, the former reason legitimises the latter, and also minimises tensions commonly created between families regarding the rituals and arrangements that used to signal families' social and economic status.

A further impact of the Gazan livelihood crisis is that most individual households are now making marriage decisions and arrangements without consulting other family and kin members as they used to do in the past. Families reject or accept new patterns of marriage, or shape their own, based on their calculation of the benefits or advantages of doing so. This suggests the liberal notion that individuals shape their actions and decisions based on a calculation of advantages (Kaplan 1973). The difference here is that rational choices of marriage taken by Gazan families reflect the absence of individual and familial freedom and dignity.

These changing patterns of marriage during the Second Intifada also contradict Bourdieu's concept of '*habitus*', which suggests that people always return to the past, or to their embodied history, in order to determine the dynamics of their action for the recognition of social identity, or more broadly to achieve 'social importance and reasons of living' (Bourdieu 1998: 241). Gazan parents, who are less educated and less immersed in modernity, have transcended their previous ideology of marriage as a reason for being. They shape decisions regarding their children's marriages according to calculations of material and social advantages, where the recognition of patriarchal identity and ideology is not an immediate priority.

Conclusion

Despite a chronic scarcity of resources, households in Gaza have developed coping strategies to survive the hardships of the Second Intifada. Family and kin relations, and the traditional household economy, have been efficiently utilised for household survival. Other coping strategies have had a transformative dimension, which has entailed relational changes based on gender and age, and may have long term-effects on the gender order in Gazan society. During the first phase of the economic crisis, households relied on their assets and savings, and also promoted their traditional skills of household production by raising poultry and cultivating small allotments around their homes. After their savings ran out, households began to borrow from relatives and neighbours, and later from shop-keepers. However, most of these coping strategies had only short-term impacts on family survival. Many households were forced to look for more long-term and sustainable solutions. The persistence of the economic crisis also pushed many households to prioritise their children's education at the expense of their own basic needs. They shifted their efforts towards education for the sake of its potential to secure paid employment, and better marriage opportunities for their daughters. Households also changed their marriage patterns, by increasing or decreasing the age of marriage according to whichever option was better for achieving marriage security and sustaining the household.

Whether the effect has been to resist or accommodate the gender order, these coping strategies have been instrumental in meeting families' basic material needs. From the experiences presented in this chapter, it appears that gender and age expectations have become more fluid in adapting to these coping strategies. Women were encouraged to reconfigure their gender roles, re-allocating material and social resources as they became the primary family providers and men lost their economic sources of power.

These changes were more a response to sustaining families during the livelihood crisis than a deliberate effort towards gender empowerment. The material data does not provide sufficient evidence to show significant changes regarding men and women's images of gender. Most of the women interviewed displayed an interest in returning to their traditional domestic lifestyle, if their men could obtain jobs. Being at home and fulfilling her domestic role and responsibilities remains the normal respected position for the majority of Gazan women.

Households' decisions regarding marriage are also a good example of the calculus required for gender and age negotiation during this livelihood crisis. The rejection and acceptance of new patterns of marriage has not been significantly influenced by the social gender order. In marriage, for example, structural constraints such as the absence of livelihood resources, make families more dependent on their own initiatives as opposed to dominant ideological boundaries. The patriarchal norm of marriage, based on family and kin connectedness, is no longer the singular element of marriage security, but only one means of obtaining marriage security applicable to certain households. Collective impoverishment and massive levels of insecurity and uncertainty mean that poor vulnerable families are less anxious about being stigmatised when and if they transcend dominant cultural norms of marriage. Their priority is rather to choose a bride who either contributes to the survival of the family, whether a close relative or not, or to secure the continuity of the marriage.

The empirical analysis in this chapter shows that the model of women's agency constructed during the livelihood crisis is situational and provisional, but not transformative. This is illustrated in women's perceptions of their liberated mobility as an undesired change. The majority say they would prefer to return to their previous status, where their time was mainly spent in and around their home. This finding raises a question about the link between changes to women's physical mobility and their satisfaction with a form of agency constructed during a situation of chronic need.

Through a gendered and generational analysis, I have found clear examples of the transformative effects of coping strategies: but these remain concentrated amongst a small proportion of highly educated women, and do not affect the majority of poor vulnerable Gazan women. The empirical analysis revealed that resistance to the existing gender and generational structure does not only rely on individual interests and the desire of women to make transformative change, but also on the evaluative capacity of women to calculate the effects of resistance.

The findings of this chapter raise a number of questions that will be discussed in the next chapter: why do the reconfiguration of gender roles and the liberation of women's mobility not change women's and men's images of their gendered selfhood? Why do Gazan women struggle to preserve, but not to resist, the dominant image of masculinity and femininity despite the structural gender and generational changes that occurred during the livelihood crisis? What are the threats that both women and men may encounter if they challenge the dominant image of their gender, and what are the rewards they may gain by maintaining this image?

Chapter 5
Gender Dynamics and the Crisis of Masculinity during the Second Intifada

Introduction

The prolonged livelihood crisis has led to individual and familial insecurities in Gaza that have heavily impacted on daily life for both women and men, and have also deeply affected their senses of self. Six decades of Israeli military occupation has influenced how Gazans understand themselves in both nationalistic and cultural senses. Losing their capacity for self-help and mutual sanction, as well as being forced into aid dependency, has had long term negative effects on men and women's subjectivities. Men, in particular, have claimed this extended crisis is akin to '*yom el Qiyama*', 'the day of judgement'.[1] Gazan men and women have never in their contemporary history experienced such fundamental changes within the family and across their wider society. Many men feel they have become valueless, with no role in life, whilst their women, in a fundamental reversal of traditional Gazan family gender norms, have been forced to work or volunteer outside the home as they search for sources of household survival. Described by Taraki as a crisis of male bread-winners (2006), this critical distortion of embodied masculine and feminine roles inside Gaza needs to be analysed and understood: the Second Intifada has repositioned both men and women's selfhood in crisis. They have been forced to act in ways contradictory to their moral perceptions of their gendered selves.

Another critical differentiating element of the Second Intifada, adding to the complexity of the crisis of gender roles, has been the changing dynamics of Gazan national resistance. Men's participation in the national resistance is no longer as publicly visible as it used to be.[2] Men who are frequently seen in and around their homes and their local community are generally perceived as not being

1 *Yom El Qiyama* is an Islamic Arabic term meaning 'the day of judgement, when ordinary life ends, and people are revitalised to be distributed between heaven and hell'. People in Gaza use it to express unexpected and disastrous changes in their daily lives.

2 Before the establishment of the Palestinian National Authority in 1994, national resistance against the Israeli military occupation was activated inside the camps and villages, and was recognised and valued by the local community. After the Oslo Peace Agreement and the withdrawal of Israeli soldiers from inside populated areas in the Gaza Strip, resistance shifted from inside the camps and villages to the borders with Israel. This has continued in the Second Intifada, and resistance activists are little known by ordinary

involved in resistance activities. Their public participation in the resistance used to be perceived as a signifier of their masculinity, whilst women's femininity was perceived as their ability to reproduce and enhance men's participation in the resistance for the liberation of their nation (Peteet 1997, Jean-Klein 2000). Now the invisibility of men's resistance, linked with the crisis of their joblessness, has forced both sexes to reactivate symbolic historic presentational aspects of masculinity and femininity.

Although gender relations within the Palestinian family have been historically and contextually shaped and reshaped in order to operate within the political economy, they have never taken just one form of domination or subordination (Hammami 1994). They have, instead, been fluid, always interweaving between different forms of domination and subordination, following changing socio-economic and political contexts of patriarchy and hegemony. Throughout contemporary Palestinian history gender relations have been the outcome of actions and interactions taken by men and women in response to their immediate needs, as well as to the discourse of national resistance against the Israeli military occupation (Johnson and Kuttab 2001, Taraki 2006).

They continue to be portrayed as patriarchal, in order to maintain cultural and moral boundaries and to uphold the distinctiveness of Palestinian identity. There is sufficient evidence to show the resilience of class and gender relations in Palestinian history, though these have shifted dramatically in both the domestic and public spheres. This resilience points to the prioritisation of the survival of the Palestinian family, and its maintenance as the central institution feeding the process of national resistance against Israel's military occupation (Swedenburg 1990, Hammami 1995).[3]

Before the Second Intifada, while many men sacrificed themselves for the liberation of their nation, women acted as the main providers for the family (Massad 1995, Peteet 1994, Johnson and Kuttab 2001). Palestinian women have never devalued their domestic roles and responsibilities, because they have been perceived as serving the wider national goal of national liberation. A woman's capacity, and her desire to lead her family and maintain its honour, while men were involved in the national struggle, constituted the moral aspects of feminine and masculine selfhood (Massad 1995). Men struggled to maintain their masculinity through widespread involvement in national resistance, whilst women struggled to maintain their moral sense of femininity by sacrificing themselves for their families and the nation.

Gazan civilians. See Johnson and Kuttab in their article (2001) 'Where have all the women (and men) gone? Reflections on Gender and the Second Intifada'.

3 Also see earlier writings on gender and Palestinian national resistance in Rosenfeld 1968, Sayigh 1984, Peteet 1994 and 1997 that all emphasised Palestinians' preservation of their patriarchal peasant culture based on gender and age for the sake of national resistance against the Israeli military occupation.

This fluidity of gender relationality in both the domestic and the public spheres has, however, been more instrumental than merely moral or ideological. Women's identities have always been a symbolic interweaving of discourses of empowerment – as agents contributing to national resistance – and subordination – as those who maintain the image of male domination within the family. This has restricted the transformative nature of women's exercise of agency, not only during the Second Intifada, but throughout contemporary Palestinian history. The continuous harshness of Palestinians' lives, with no tangible positive economic or political outcomes, has denied them personal and familial security, whilst also undermining reconstitution of any positive self-images. On the contrary, socially constructed images of masculinity and femininity have been used as a coping mechanism to counter Israel's attempts to devastate Palestinian moral subjective sources of power centred on the ideology and culture of patriarchy and kin relations. Contemporary literature on gender in Palestine shows that the fluidity of gender has not been critically enacted against subjective moral meanings of masculinity and femininity (Jean-Klein 2001). This leaves the question of gender transformation in Palestinian society as yet unresolved. The power that women wield in domestic and public spheres is mainly used to reproduce perceptions of male domination.

This chapter will analyse the data and interpretation given by the research participants, comparing arguments regarding gender transformation up to the Second Intifada, with changes that occurred both during the intifada and afterwards. The analytical framework will follow the intersectional feminist approach, where women and men's selfhood is perceived as neither fixed nor defined by a singular characteristic. In my own analysis, I refer to conceptions of masculinity and femininity as they are situationally and socially constructed and reconstructed, in relation to changes in institutions, economies and everyday life experiences (Cornwall and Lindisfarne 1994, Kandiyoti 1994, Moore 1999 and 2007, Connell 2000, Adibi 2006). However, I will focus on how cultural and the interpersonal settings affect both men's and women's self-presentation, which, in this chapter, will be analytically linked with actual enactments of both women and men. This is in order to understand the relationship between the ways in which women practice agency and power and the subjective meanings behind these practices.

Gazan women may present themselves as empowered and subordinated, as superior and inferior, or as both masculine and feminine, in order to create a balance between their exercise of agency as a response to their immediate needs, and the socially constructed and embodied image of their femininity. According to Anthony Giddens, the gender order acts to both facilitate and constrain the shaping of relational dynamics and their subjective meanings (Giddens 1991). The outcome of this process of self-shaping may not necessarily entail resistance to the historical image of male domination, even if there is a material basis for this change.

This chapter will focus on several questions: how have dynamics of gender relations changed in the specific situation of political insecurity and livelihood crisis in Gaza during the Second Intifada? How has the current crisis of masculinity – the inability of men to practise their normative gender, as it is socially and historically constructed, i.e. to provide for their families and children – affected women's exercise of actual power within the household and family?[4] Does women's exercise of power – in the form of undertaking activities that are socially perceived as masculine activities – create a crisis of femininity? Reflecting on these questions will lead to a greater understanding of the complex crisis of masculinity and femininity in Gaza, and how this in turn has affected intra-familial gender dynamics and relations. This will offer a greater understanding and more exact analysis of why Gazan women and men have rejected any resistance of the ideology of male domination, despite dislocation of structural gender arrangements within the family and in wider Gazan society.

This chapter consists of two main sections. The first section focuses on family position, life-cycle and intra-family dynamics: I present a general portrayal of gender relational dynamics within the Gazan family before the Second Intifada. This includes divergent and interrelated factors influencing the dynamics of negotiation among male and female family members – such as age, wifehood, motherhood, single-hood, and fertility. This section also addresses women's perceptions of masculinity in relation to their perceptions of femininity, and how these perceptions are reflected in their presentations of self and of the other.

The second section explores the crisis of masculinity during the Second Intifada and changing gender relational dynamics. It considers two particular relational aspects and compares them to points raised in the first section: those of husband-wife and mother-in-law-daughter-in-law relations. It shows how women's exercise of agency and power based on factors of age, wifehood and motherhood, have been renegotiated to respond to the demands of daily life – without necessarily breaking down fixtures of the overall gender order and its symbolic meanings. It examines men's changing behaviour towards their wives, the centrality of young wives, the marginalisation of mothers-in-law and the shifting of mother-in-law/daughter-in-law relations from contestation to cooperation.

4 'Actual power' here refers to women's capacity to take decisions and shape their choices without necessarily being linked with a recognised and legitimate right in public. This does not specifically denote authority, as women practise different forms of power (power over and power for) within the domestic sphere without gaining authority. See the debate between women's actual power and political authority in Rogers, C.S. (1975), *Female Forms of Power and the Myth of Male Dominance: A Model of Female/Male Interaction in Peasant Society*.

Family Position, Life-Cycle and Intra-Family Dynamics before the Second Intifada

Women's positionality, as wives and mothers, versus men's positionality as husbands and sons, has historically played a critical role in forming gender relational dynamics throughout the life cycle of both women and men in Palestinian society. These positions are determinants of how power within the family is used, with both men and women losing and gaining power at certain times of their life cycles. As their age and position changes, women also change their strategies for negotiating power. While they are still young, wives with dependent children accept their subordination within the family, accumulating power during later phases of their life cycle. They are, as Foucault argues, always in a position of power (Foucault 1985, cf. Sawicki 1991: 25).

But dynamics of power as shaped by women have multiple forms, including: domination over, and the empowerment of, others. During the early phases of their marriages, Gazan women accept their husbands' domination in order to act as empowering agents for their children, particularly their sons. In later phases, women are empowered by their adult sons to resist their husbands' domination and to practise domination over other female members of the family (Allen 1998: 31). Women's power within the family entails their capacity for making decisions, allocating and reallocating economic and social household resources, and participating in public informal institutions. However, all these forms of domestic micro-power allow the continuation of centralised and repressive forms of macro-power operating outside the domestic sphere. They leave the prevailing gender order intact (Sawicki 1991: 21).

The empirical data shows that women's space for manoeuvring increases when they in turn move from wifehood to motherhood. Their power within the family is socially and culturally enhanced as they become older and their sons grow to be men. At a certain age mothers redefine their power through the power of their sons as opposed to their husbands. Men's domestic power, in contrast, gradually reduces as they become older, and is replaced by the power of their sons. Although these two dynamics operate to support the reproduction of a hierarchical structure and culture based on sex and age, women play a central role in its reproduction. They practise their power of motherhood in order to reproduce the domination of their sons and the subordination of their sons' wives. This was acknowledged by most of the mothers interviewed for this research, who nurtured their daughters-in-law to be 'good wives' and their sons to be 'real men'.

Women's stories of married life also reveal they often begin to accumulate their power from the very beginning of their marriages. They start with specific tactics aimed at their husbands and families-in-law, in order to instil their own security and not be exposed to either divorce or polygamy. Women then shift to the critical position of being the mothers of growing sons. Unless it is associated with being a mother, being a wife does not appear as a critical role in the interviewees' narratives. Being married at a socially acceptable age is considered important as a 'marker of a normative female sexuality' (Sa'ar 2004), and a sign of moral integrity (Johnson 2008). Wifehood is the first phase for women to accomplish their social being in the process of gender order reproduction. As confirmed by Johnson, 'singlehood can be configured in the Palestinian society as unnatural and a sign of social ill health' (Johnson 2008: 4).

According to the female interviewees, marriage is the legitimate social umbrella by which they enter public life securely. This was encapsulated by Um-Haitham, who said: 'if you are unmarried, all eyes watch you, but if you are married you are more protected from people's eyes'. Marriage not only functions to meet women's personal sexual desires, and their desire for motherhood – which can only be achieved in a Muslim culture by contractual marriage. It is also the only institution in Gazan society, especially amongst unemployed and less educated women, that provides them with a sense of long term social and personal security. The empirical data of Chapter 3 illustrates that wifehood is a vehicle for activating women's agency to exercise their power in order to build their family's future. The overall experience of poor women reveals that they remain emotionally and/or socially committed to their husbands, or else compromise with their relations and husbands until their sons have become adults. As can be seen in the majority of interviews, wives asserted that they endured daily contestations with their husbands and families-in-law because of their children. The sons, regardless of their age and level of education, appear to be a key element in the shift of domestic gender relational dynamics. Tensions between husbands and wives calm, and the power subsequently shifts towards the relationship between mother and sons.

Few of the married research participants aged 40 or older showed any emotion regarding their relations with their husbands. Middle aged and older women rarely discuss their emotions towards their spouses: intimacy is legitimate, but should not be shown to others as it emasculates masculinity. In Gaza this shames both the wife and her husband, because women's social status in the family and in the local community is based on their husbands' practise of power and authority. Although the wife-husband relationship is a personal one, it is not described to others as such, but clothed in the language of socially constructed relations that function to maintain the reproduction of the image of male domination (Meriwether 1999). One of the most repeated statements of women during the interviews was: 'the husband who shows off about his intimacy (love) with his wife is stigmatised as '*mahkoom*', or 'controlled by his wife'. Men who are in love with their wives sometimes present themselves as tough husbands, to demonstrate their dominant status.

From the birth of her first child, a wife in Gaza has to accept the state of her marriage. If it is good, she enjoys the relationship. If it is bad, she has no option except to compromise and bargain until her sons have grown up and they can support her. Among the research participants, wives of dependent husbands who had been dominated by their mothers and other members of their natal family, had experienced more contestation than wives of independent husbands, who had space to negotiate with their husbands without the interference of other members of their families-in-law, especially their mothers-in-law. This is why young women prefer to be under their husband's authority, as opposed to the domination of their mothers-in-law. The bargaining dynamic that young wives often use to resist the domination of the mothers-in-law while the husbands are unable to protect them, is to leave their marital home (*tehrad*), sometimes in order to put pressure on their families-in-law to treat them better.[5] In a few cases, women mentioned that they complained about their husbands and mothers-in-law to local traditional leaders responsible for overseeing family affairs, in an attempt to resolve their conflicts.

More than half of the women aged 30 and over asserted they had resorted to leaving their husbands' home on half a dozen occasions during their married life, for periods ranging from a few weeks to a few months at a time. None of these departures, however, led to divorce or to improvements in their married lives, except for one woman from the Beach camp who stated she was married to a drug addict, and had divorced him as he posed a violent threat to her and her children. According to the women interviewees, their husbands and families-in-law realised that these departures were an expression of their frustrations, and also that, sooner or later, the wife's own parents would force her to return to her husband. Although the behaviour of their husbands and mothers-in-laws did not usually change, most of the women decided to manage their situation until their children, especially their sons, were old enough to protect them.

In a few cases, women said they succeeded in making their husbands behave more kindly and tolerantly towards them after they had temporarily left the marital home. But the majority of women modified their own behaviour. A common saying, used by women in El-Shujae'ya and the Beach camp, is: '*el mara el shatra* – the adept wife knows how to deceive her husband to gain his support'. Other women referred to another local saying: 'If we satisfy our husbands, they satisfy us'. Mariam, a 43-year-old from El-Shujae'ya, blamed women who complained about their husbands, stating that husbands are: 'easy to manipulate, when a wife knows how to enhance his manhood, even if he does not actually practise it'.

The analysis of these women's interviews and life stories also reveals the significance of the interplay of their positions as wives and mothers. For example, in a situation of a woman's inability to have children for medical reasons, even if her husband is the cause of her infertility, he is socially legitimised to remarry in order to maintain his manhood by fathering children. Across generations, women have developed different strategies to negotiate issues of gender, either by denying their own desires for motherhood (in the case of male infertility) or, if the wife is unable to bear children, enabling her husband to take a second wife in order that he can become a father. This implies women's self-sacrifice, and their exploitation

5 *Tehrad* is a verb referring to a woman leaving her husband's home, whether she lives in a nuclear or extended household, as an expression of her anger. *Tehrad* is not like separation; it's a tactic used by women to reduce their anger and to rest themselves for few days, or few weeks, away from continuous family contestation. Women always *tehrad* to their natal family houses (parents or brothers and less often sisters).

of other women: but, significantly, in neither case do women jeopardise their own position as wives.

In the research sample, only two of the married women had no children: one was a woman in her late 20s from the Beach camp; the second was a woman in her mid-50s from El-Shujae'ya, called Um-Khaleel who was unable to have children because of her infertility, but refused to accept her childless fate.[6] Um-Khaleel is an uneducated woman, originally from a peasant family. As she was medically unable to have children, her husband was, according to Gazan peasant culture, socially and legally justified in remarrying. However, as his first wife, she also had the choice of divorcing him if he did remarry. Um-Khaleel described her situation:

> When the doctor told me it would be very difficult for me to be a mother, I told my father. He asked me if I wanted to get divorced [but] divorce is not a solution, as I would stay divorced and without children and it would bring shame on me. Of course this situation would never happen if my husband was responsible for our not being able to have children. I was young, 27 years old, and I was beautiful. I rejected the idea of divorce because no man will marry a woman who is infertile. Instead, I decided to suggest that my husband marry another wife. He loved me, and in the beginning he refused: but I convinced him, by explaining that I was going to find him a wife just to provide him with children. I selected an older woman called Sadia, who was not really beautiful, and I made all the arrangements for his marriage. I sold my jewellery and borrowed money from my father to pay for a new bedroom. I tried to be nice with Sadia in order to keep my husband calm. I looked after her when she was sick or in need of anything. She is a passive woman, who would not think to argue with me because she knew from the beginning that my husband is in love with me, and that we selected her only to bring us children.
>
> When Sadia gave birth to the first baby, I called him Khaleel. Neighbours and relatives called me Um-Khaleel (the mother of Khaleel). I looked after the baby and treated him as my real son. Sadia had a child every two years and I was responsible for them. We have seven children now, four sons and three daughters. I arranged my daughters' marriages with our relatives at an early age, and they are all happy with their husbands. People always gossip about my husband being controlled by me, but this is not true. It is common here in El-Shujae'ya to characterise the intimate wife-husband relationship as a man being controlled by his wife [but] we have a common understanding. My husband trusts me and respects what I have been doing for him and his seven children. I arranged the marriages of my eldest sons, and they lived in our house. I worked very hard and

6 These two cases are, however, not representative of all motherless wives; their situations are used as an example of contradictory strategies used by women to wield power, even in a situation where the determining social factor of their power to have children is missing.

> saved enough money to build a three storey house, with an apartment for each of my sons. My youngest son lives with us.

Um-Khaleel always used the words 'my sons' and did not link the children to their biological mother, whilst Sadia accepted her situation as the surrogate. Um Khaleel is the socially recognised mother, thus fulfilling her strategic goals of being perceived as a good wife, practising her role as a mother and determining her social status within the dominant cultural ideology of male domination. She used her power to maintain the socially constructed image of masculinity in order for her husband to father sons. Her story confirms that Gazan concepts of masculinity and femininity are not fixed, and do not statically reflect the normative reproductive function of female and male bodies. Their reproductive functions are rather socially and culturally negotiated and strategised to construct and reconstruct multiple and contradictory practice and presentation of masculinity and femininity (Kandiyoti 1994, Ouzgane 2006, Moore 2007).

Um-Khaleel's story exposes how important it is for Gazan women to become mothers. In addition to being a desirable moral aspect of women's femininity (Chodorow 1978), motherhood is an important position in which women have the potential to go through processes of accumulating actual power within the family, the wider kin institution and their local community. Mothers of adult sons have the social legitimacy to take the lead in negotiating and arranging their sons' marriages with other family and kin members. Um-Khaleel and Um-Sufian are representative of other women in El-Shujae'ya and the Beach camp in being solely responsible for selecting their sons' brides, the process of which is not haphazard but based on strategic economic, social, and personal goals. Um-Sufian and Um-Khaleel overtly expressed their personal and familial interests in the selection of their sons' brides, asserting that brides are chosen not only to please their sons, but also to bring young women into the family who have the potential to give their new mothers-in-law some respite. *El kenna*, the new daughter-in-law, is brought to her husband's house to serve everybody, because the husband's family becomes her new family.

Um-Khaleel deliberately selected her nieces to marry her sons in order to maintain her sons' loyalty to her family lineage. She was always careful not to allow her sons marry someone from the family lineage of their biological mother. Another important element that mothers consider when choosing brides, is to select *bent aisha*: a common Gazan term with both class and gender connotations, that refers to a docile young bride coming from a similar socio-economic situation to the groom's family, who will thereby be able to adapt to its level of poverty. She will accept living with his extended family, and be obedient to all family members, especially the mother-in-law.

These examples of negotiations and decision-making also reveal that Gazan mothers of adult sons do not confine themselves to domestic power dynamics. They expand their roles by acting as active agents with family and kin relations and networks, as well as within the local community. In both El-Shujae'ya and the

Beach camp, many older women like Um-Khaleel and Um-Sufian act as *makhateer*, or female traditional kin leaders, in their neighbourhood. Young women come to them in order to resolve marital and familial disputes. These older women spend much of their daytime visiting family and kin members socially, and socialising and worshipping at the local mosque. Through their social connections with other women they contribute to local conflict resolution. Throughout my fieldwork I observed women in their 50s sitting in front of their homes with local men of the same age, discussing disputes amongst families in the local community.

Most of the research participants stated that without these strategies, they would not achieve any of their personal and familial goals and desires, and would not be respected by their neighbours or their local community. Gazan women say that they feel empowered by their capacity to bargain and compromise, in order to ensure the stability of their families as well as to wield power. These women, nevertheless, always present their power as confined within the limits of customary boundaries. These boundaries uphold the prevailing gender order and its ideological meaning of masculinity and femininity. From within this order, women have space to negotiate and adjust relations of power based on gender, class and other dimensions. This is reflected in how Um-Sufian expressed herself:

> I don't consider myself powerless. I know why I do things in a certain way. My goal in life is to stabilise the family, and to gain the respect of others around me. This requires me to give and take. I gave my sons power and they gave me power back. I don't have to resist my husband's domination, as long as I know he won't restrict my mobility and my decisions. He just tries to show off his manhood. I want him to do so, because I don't want him to be seen as *tartoor*, "powerless" at home, or in our neighbourhood. On the contrary, people always say that I am a powerful respected woman. What else do I need? I don't want to be a doctor or a minister. I just want to be happy in my home and not feeling that anybody in the family is in need.

The paradox in Gazan intra-familial gender relational dynamics is exemplified in women's continuous attempts to present the masculinity of their men as consistent with the standardised social image, regardless of the realities within the family. As mentioned in Chapter 3, women are not happy to live with husbands who are socially stigmatised as being controlled by their mothers or wives, for this undermines their own moral sense of femininity. Women who dominate their sons or husbands do not want to display this in public and instead present their husbands as having the final say. In general, Gazan women state their preference to live with a powerful man practising the socially constructed image of masculine domination over his wife and children, even if this exposes them to domestic violence. Just as Henrietta Moore suggests, this form of representation amongst women who suffer from their husbands' inability to be independent, is a dynamic they use to balance the fantasy of masculine identity and the fantasy of their own power and agency. Fantasies here refer to those identified and invested in social values, systems and ideologies, but not to individual's private desires (Moore 1994:66, Moore 2007: 19–20). In a situation where the material sources of the gender order have degenerated, women and men develop symbolic presentational dynamics aimed at stabilising the gender order and its ideological meaning of masculinity and femininity.[7] This appears in women's presentations of both fantastical and practical concepts of manhood.

Sawsan is a 32-year-old from El-Shujae'ya, who lived with her extended family-in-law during the 1990s. For more than seven years she struggled to save money to buy her own home, away from daily contestations with her mother-in-law, who also controlled her husband. Sawsan described her relationship with her husband, saying:

> I don't really need his love or material support, but I do need people to say I have a real husband. This is so important for me and for the children. I want them, especially my sons, to grow up with a strong model of their father as a real man. This makes my sons powerful too, and I become more respected by others. If my husband was strong, I would not have been humiliated for seven years by my mother-in-law and her elder sons. I used to complain to my parents, but they couldn't do anything for me. They used to tell me, 'go to your husband and ask him to be a real man to protect you.

Um-Samir is a 43-year-old and from El-Shujae'ya. Throughout the three interviews that I had with her, she admitted that her husband had a weak character. She also pointed out that most of the troubles she encountered from her family-in-law occurred because her husband was unable to protect her. Um-Samir asserted that she had never received a nice word from her husband, and this was fine with her, but she wanted him to be a strong man with his own opinions in front of his family and in public. She sees her husband only as the father of her children: i.e. not as a desirable partner. She said that she wished she had married a strong man on whom she could depend.

The cases of Sawsan and Um-Samir show they have not only struggled throughout their married lives to provide for their families, which they believed was the responsibility of their husbands, but also to present powerful images of their husbands' masculinity to their children and in public. This has not been a struggle to resist the Gazan gender social order, but rather to stabilise it, regardless of the actualities of gender practices. Although Um-Samir has been practising her gender role as the primary provider for her family, she considers this to be against the natural gender arrangement. Whilst telling her story, she tried to conceal the

7 The use of the term 'symbol' here and in other parts of the book refers to metaphors that act as a mediator between the structure and its institutional values and ideologies. I refer to Henrietta Moore's argument that in a specific context there is a necessity for individuals to have a capacity of symbolisation for the creation and internalisation of social institutions and values (Moore 2007: 26). Otherwise, everything would have been chaotic.

realities of her actual decision-making powers at home and in public several times. She desires a balance between her feminine desires and beliefs whilst maintaining the image of her husband's masculinity.

Um-Samir also commented on the term that is repeatedly used by other women against her – namely that she *hakma jouzha* (controls her husband):

> I hate this saying "*hakma jouzha*". It has become a stigma against wives who struggle to protect their families. Of course, when a man doesn't do what he has to do, women have to manage the family. Perhaps people expect me to await a livelihood from the sky. Since I left my mother-in-law's house, she has not stopped gossiping about me. She told all the neighbourhood women that I control my husband, and I took him from her house. People don't really know how my husband treats me. He has never interfered with my work: I go to the market every morning to trade. I work on the land, and spend long hours sewing, as well as doing all my domestic work. My husband doesn't make any problems for me when it comes to my earning income [but] when I ask him if I may go and visit my parents or my brothers, he says no, and sometimes shouts and insults me with bad words. My silence provokes him: he wants me to raise my voice and to shout back at him. He wants other people to know that he controls me. But I don't care who controls the other. My concern is my children. My husband is not going to change.

Women's views of husband-wife relations are not homogeneous, but depend on the individual personal histories, and how each individual presents his or her gendered self in relation to collective situations and discourses (Moore 1994:50). For example, the husbands of Sawsan and Um-Samir are calm and non-violent compared to those of Um-Sufian and Um-Iyad, who project their powerlessness by continually creating problems for their wives and children, including domestic violence. Sawsan and Um-Samir communicate more openly with their husbands. All of these women, however, wish they were married to a masculine husband with a strong personality, which Gazan women refer to as *rejal haqeeqi*: a real man.

Um-Iyad from the Beach camp is a 48-year-old mother of eight. She is a university graduate and has experienced a turbulent marriage. She said: 'Believe me, I would accept my husband's violence if he were actually a real man respected by his children and others'. But at the same time, Um-Iyad asserted that she didn't see any reason for a real man to be violent towards his wife as long as she fulfilled her obligations to him. She defined the term 'real man' as:

> A man who presents his authority and power: it doesn't matter how much money he earns. His word is listened to and respected by others. This is the authority of a real man. His wife will be pleased to obey him, to accept his authority and to satisfy him. From my own experience, I see that a man uses violence against

> his wife and children when he is unable to meet his obligations to his family and protect them.

The portrayal of intra-family dynamics up until the Second Intifada in 2000 raises a critical point regarding understanding and analysing male dominance and female subordination. The empirical analysis shows that the practice of male domination within the family, and through the various stages of married life, is not always consistent with prevailing imagery of masculinity in Palestinian society. This imagery is, rather, an ideological instrument that Gazan women, at certain times in their lives, used to wield their power and to practise dominance over other family members, both men and women. In these instances, the presentation of male domination becomes the essential dynamic that maintains the appearance of gender stability. This challenges Bourdieu's theory of practice: women in Gaza strategise their intra-familial gender relations based on socially constructed concepts of wifehood and motherhood, not because they misrecognise their gender interests of power or their goals (Bourdieu and Passeron 1977: 5–10). Rather, they use their positions of wifehood and motherhood in order to consciously wield forms of power without disturbing the prevailing gender order, whilst also achieving their goals in life. The prevailing gender order, therefore, facilitates their meeting of their strategic goals, which are intrinsically linked to the domestic sphere. Gazan women act as 'goal setting creatures' (Rogers 1975:733).

The Crisis of Masculinity during the Second Intifada and Changing Gender Relational Dynamics in the Gazan Family

From a broader perspective, masculinity is not defined as a singular concept. Rather, it reflects the functional, political and ideological basis of gender relations of power (Ortner 1974, Gutmann 1997). Masculinity has little meaning if it does not interplay with feminine identities and practices. This means that men's masculinity is relational; i.e. defined by how women practise their femininity. The gender relational character of masculinity has historically been defined in Palestinian society and, most probably, in other Arab Muslim societies, in order to reflect not only gender performativity, but also the ideological image of gender as exemplified in patriarchy, nationalism and in Islam. In his constructionist analysis, Hossein Adibi sees masculinity in the Middle East as fluid and multiple within the social structure of class, patriarchy, culture, economic structure, religion and politics. He points out that the context of the inability of most Middle Eastern governments to secure employment and well-being for men, especially young men, in order for them to practise familiar models of masculinity, has contributed to the reformation of a masculinity with multiple and contradictory characters, both dominant and subordinate (Adibi 2006: 8).

From a nationalist perspective, the concept of the masculine ideal has historically been shaped in order to act as a signifier of nation-state building and national struggle (Massad 1995, Peteet 1997). Joseph Massad (1995), Julie Peteet (1994 and 1997) and Iris Jean-Klein (2000) argue that the Palestinian sense of masculinity has been reinforced under the influence of political conditions induced by the Israeli military occupation. Organised resistance against the Israeli military occupation has opened new arenas of masculinity, not only as part of family and kin relations, but also as part of the discourse of the wider Palestinian national movement (Massad 1995).

Palestine's socio-economic and political context has had a specific influence on the practice of masculinity and, also on its cultural opposite, femininity. Penny Johnson and Eileen Kuttab (2001) explain how, since Israel's policy of closure during the Second Intifada, the Palestinian political situation has created a crisis of masculinity in which men are no longer able to function with their socially constructed gendered roles in the domestic sphere (as they are unable to earn income to provide for their families), nor in the public sphere (due to the diminishing role of male involvement in the national resistance). The Second Intifada has been an unprecedented political event that has dramatically diluted the material, social and psychological basis of both masculinity and femininity – a man is valueless and unable to sustain his family, while a woman is forced to leave her children and her respected position as a housewife and mother, effectively to beg for humanitarian aid in public. The crisis of femininity is not simply a by-product of the crisis of masculinity. These two crises are by-products of the degeneration of the Palestinian political economy, and subsequent dysfunction of both the public and domestic spheres. Thus men and women are both victimised, as each has lost their normative structural basis of gender enactment (Abu-Nahla 2006).

In Gaza, as in other Arab countries, the concept of the 'real man' is a person who is linked to familial and significant community relationships, in which the family or community is valued over and above the person (Joseph 1993). During the Second Intifada, men in Gaza lost their sense of masculinity that used to emerge from their efforts to provide for their families, connect with their kin and local community and protect their nation. The combination of collective impoverishment, and the internal political conflict, have made it difficult for young and middle aged poor men to reproduce the closeness of family and kin relations, and consequently to challenge the crisis of their masculinity. Women, on the other hand, who used to depend on their family and kin relations as an important source of security, have become reluctant to continue to do so, saying: 'God helps each family to manage itself. There is no space to rely on any one [else] at the current time'. A common proverb used by young and middle aged jobless men in the focus groups is '*nemshi janb el hait we ben koul ya sattar* – we walk beside the wall and ask for God's mercy'. This signifies the seclusion of men from daily interactions with the public as a result of the chronic situation of insecurity. Sayings like this are a clear signal of the crisis of masculinity and femininity. Both men and women have lost the social, cultural and moral elements of their gender signification that are centred on familial, kin and community relationships. The gendered crisis is reflected in the presentation of changing gender relational dynamics and the interpretation of that change (Moore 1994:68), as we see in the following analysis.

Husband–Wife Gender Relational Dynamics: Between Tolerance and Violence

Men's inability to challenge the material aspects of their masculinity crisis has been reflected in two contradictory behavioural dynamics: they have become either sympathetic husbands, cooperating with their wives for the sake of the household, or else they become violent, careless or passive. The former group of men appreciates what their wives do in order to provide for, and to protect, the family, and are tolerant of them. The latter group, which is violent, is described by women as responding badly to the crisis of their masculinity, especially those who live in extended families. They have become more violent with their wives and especially their children, and leave their homes, sometimes for extended periods of time. Younger husbands who live with extended families are, according to the research, less cooperative with their wives than middle aged husbands. Some middle aged men in their 30s and early 40s, who used to work in Israel and had not been strongly linked to kin and familial relationships, are also less cooperative. The two groups of younger and middle age husbands are less cooperative because they had previously experienced their mothers being responsible for family affairs, and had become accepting of women's management of household affairs.

Middle aged and relatively uneducated men in both El-Shujae'ya and the Beach camp, on the other hand, are more tolerant and cooperative than young educated men. Education in Gazan society normally enhanced men's sense of masculinity: but jobless educated young men found it difficult to accept their wives acting as the primary family provider because this undermines the social status they had attained from their education. The overall health of a husband also appears to be an influencing factor regarding their wives' perceptions of their cooperation. A husband's sickness may not be serious, but may be symbolically used by his wife in order to justify his helplessness. Wives' presentations of their sick husbands as cooperative and tolerant also enhance their own moral sense of femininity, as they make sacrifices for their husbands and children. Men, on the other hand, present their sickness as a reason for co-operating with their wives, justifying their helplessness in not providing for their families.

As the researcher, I sought to listen to both wives and husbands' interpretations of the changes that had occurred in husband-wife relations. This enables us better to understand methodologically both explicit and implicit gendered meanings of the changes and struggles of men and women. This is based on my own assumption that the performance and perception of masculinity is always influenced by women's performance and perception of femininity, and vice versa.

Husbands become tolerant and cooperative with their wives The empirical data shows that a remarkable number of frequently mobile wives, aged from 20 to 39, asserted that their husbands have become more cooperative and tolerant towards them since they lost their jobs (this group represents 6 out of 15 women in the Beach camp, and 7 out of 16 women of similar ages in Sheja'ia). These 13 women are mostly from nuclear and co-located separated households. One possible interpretation of why wife-husband relations have become more cooperative in nuclear households is that it is easier for men to cooperate with their wives when this is not visible to other family members. Other factors that enhance cooperation amongst couples who live in nuclear families reflect the different individual history of each couple. It is noticeable that men who are described by their wives as more sociable and more connected with their kin and local community, are more cooperative with their wives than men who do not have this network. Wives interpret this as their husbands making an effort to maintain a good masculine image among kin relations and in public, by not displaying conflict within their families. Wives are more than willing to absorb their husbands' anger and the frustration caused by their joblessness in order to maintain their public image as strong powerful men.

I now turn to a comparison of husbands' and wives' presentations of the meaning of the husbands' cooperation. There are many differences in women's presentations of their husbands' cooperation: some women assured me that their husband's tolerance and cooperation was a response to the specific situation inside Gaza, and that in general their husbands were not happy with how their wives now behave. According to the women, their husbands did feel compassionate towards them, knowing that they had to humiliate themselves by searching for aid coupons. The majority of women presented their husbands' cooperation as a response to their wives' appreciation of their manliness – i.e. enhancing their masculinity and not belittling them for their inability to earn income. Only three of the women research participants perceived their husbands' cooperation as recognition of the value of their important and respected role in sustaining the family. These three women asserted that their husbands depended on them to manage the household income, and that this situation had therefore forced them to be cooperative. Only one woman from the Beach camp said that her husband's cooperation had enhanced her freedom and given her the chance to change her lifestyle.

The women also referred to the moral aspect of being an ideal wife who stands beside her husband in hard times, and does not make him feel interior. Samia, in her mid-30s and living in a nuclear family, presented her husband's tolerance and cooperation, saying:

> Despite all I do, the final decisions are still taken by him in consultation with me. The man is the man and the woman is a woman … should we reduce his value because he becomes jobless? Money is not everything. That he is around for me and the children is enough. He treats me well and has never beaten me since he became jobless. He shouts a lot, but I know how to calm him down.

Samia presents her husband as cooperative and tolerant. She does not allow him to do anything at home in order for him not to feel inferior. She asserted that this technique has led to her husband being calm and tolerant towards her. He trusts her and, since he lost his job, has never prevented her from going out.

Salwa, a 35-year-old from El-Shujae'ya, said:

> My husband is not happy to see me leaving home three to four times a week to look for coupons. He tried in the beginning to stop me – but when I asked him to go out to look for work, he stopped interfering in my mobility. I told him, "do you think I am happy with this humiliation, or do you presume I want to leave home to have fun?" Then I cried and he calmed down, because he realised that he is not able to do anything for the family.

Awatif (29 years old), Manal (32 years old) and Randa (35 years old) are housewives from El-Shujae'ya. They each said that their husbands became tolerant and cooperative after becoming sick. These three women considered the cooperative stances of their husbands to be the direct result of their physical powerlessness and their inability to do any work, even if it was available; they do not believe their husbands would be cooperative if they were able-bodied. Awatif and Manal presented their husbands as not only physically sick, but also as having weak characters that made them unable to manage family affairs in a situation of chronic scarcity. Husbands in this position had no other option than to be cooperative with their wives, especially if they were not financially supported by their natal family. Regarding these two cases, two separate psycho-social dynamics can be inferred:

1. Men realise they are in crisis – they are aware not only of lack of jobs, but also of their inability to work and/or to manage the household. They attempt to hide this crisis by avoiding contestation with their wives. As Awatif explained: 'my husband avoids any encounter with me that may make me criticise him as useless'.
2. Husbands use sickness as a legitimate social reason to justify their subjective weakness. This makes them leave all family decisions to their wives. Both sexes, however, describe this relation as cooperative in order to idealise the husband-wife relationship, and to conceal the negative psychological effects of this crisis of masculinity. Men are not expected to act in accordance with their socially constructed gender role, because they are sick. Women are valued for making extra sacrifices in a family headed by a sick husband.

Neither of these responses, however, evaluates the change in gender relations as positive, or transformative. Um-Husam, a 32-year-old from the Beach camp, was the only wife interviewed who presented the current changes in her relation with her husband as transformative, saying: 'Only now do I feel what freedom means'.

Men, on the other hand, present their cooperation with their wives very carefully, in order not to be perceived as diminishing their own masculinity. In the men's focus groups, the majority of participants presented their cooperation as being situational and moral. They spoke of their efforts to neutralise their helplessness by providing moral support to their wives, who also feel victimised by their husbands' joblessness. Abu-Hasan is 29 years old and has six children. He used to work in the Gazan fishing industry. He explained that his wife never left home to visit charitable associations before the Second Intifada, but now he has to encourage her to search for coupons because there are no other options. Abu-Hasan presented himself as a cooperative husband. He does not interfere in his wife's mobility, or in her management of family expenses. He said:

> My wife isn't doing anything wrong by leaving home to search for coupons while we [men] are unable to earn income. I would not let her leave home and humiliate herself in a normal situation, but what can we do? *El umour mesh be Idna* – things are not within our control.

I asked Abu-Hasan what he does while his wife goes out to search for coupons. He replied:

> I don't do anything at home. I do not really want my mother, sisters and wife to see me at home doing nothing. I leave home during the day, but I feel happy to do so, because my mother and sisters are there with the children. If I stay at home, I would shout and maybe beat my children. So it's better to leave home. I spend my day with my friends: we play cards and chat.

Other men in the focus group supported Abu-Hasan, and one added: 'Yes, we [men] all avoid staying at home. It helps us to control our tempers with the children and wives'.

Another man commented:

> Is it not enough to live without work? It is so hard to stay at home like women. My wife understands why I leave home and she encourages me. When I stay at home, I make her nervous. She used to do everything at home, and when I try to help her in making salad or other little things, she refuses. She says to me: "go, leave the kitchen, and when the food is ready I will call you".

In a focus group in El-Shujae'ya, the husband of Sawsan, who had been unsupportive with her, and whose income was controlled by his mother, became more cooperative with his wife after he became jobless. He said:

> I have to admit that my wife is more efficient in managing the family expenses than me. I don't interfere in how she uses the little money we have. In the beginning I was responsible for household expenses, and the money was spent in ten days. I realised that I am not good at managing money. She knows how to buy the cheapest stuff for the family, and feed us. I used to earn lots of money when I was working in Israel, and my wife used to cook the best food, and we

> had meat every day. Now she uses the coupons she brings from associations to cook and feed the family.

Another critical point to add to the analysis of men's cooperation is their realisation of the importance of women's negotiating skills. Women have learned to negotiate for what they want from an early age, through intergenerational relations within their families. Jobless husbands know that their wives have to present themselves as inferior and docile in order to receive humanitarian assistance. They are also aware that their wives have to present them, their husbands, as helpless and unable to provide for the family. With the absence of any other sources of survival, men accept that their wives have to act in ways that also undermine their sense of femininity in order for their families to survive. Women recognise this too. In this context, inferiority and superiority are negotiated instrumentally. This is openly expressed by Awatif and mentioned by many other women in the focus groups:

> Men can't do what we do. They are in general very straightforward in their communication and negotiation with the outside world. This is not worthwhile in the current situation of scarcity we live in. We women are *mudardahat* (subtle): we don't care if we speak with someone from Hamas or Fatah – if they can meet our needs then we give them the respect they are looking for. We are very patient.

Men's presentation of their cooperation with their wives is paradoxical. They explicitly and implicitly assert that what their wives do is inferior, and can only be done by women. At the same time, they present their wives as dedicated, self-sacrificing and determined. Most of the male research participants confirmed that their wives try to meet their children's needs without letting the men know, in order to avoid their anger and to maintain peace within the family. This discourse, as presented by the men, has structural and subjective implications. First, they attempt to assert that their helplessness regarding family provision is not caused by their lack of manliness, but rather by structural constraints beyond their control. Second, they emphasise that, despite their joblessness and helplessness, their wives still respect and appreciate them, and do not transcend the image of male domination. A middle aged man, who used to work in Israel as a contractor, expressed the political and moral effects of the Second Intifada on husband-wife relations, saying:

> What is happening with us as men has never been imagined before. Does anyone of us expect *marato el musatata* (his respected wife), to be begging for aid coupons? We used to see women of our mothers' age trading in the market, we used to accept our wives going out to do the shopping for themselves and for the children; we also used to accept that they could go out to work as teachers and nurses. But we never expected them to humiliate themselves for coupons. But our wives are really determined and they deserve respect. They do not even let

> us feel bad about ourselves. They bear this burden because they know that it is not through lack of manliness that we cannot earn income, but it is the closure which is out of our control. International humanitarian aid has turned us into beggars.

As this statement makes clear, the changes in gender divisions of labour during the livelihood crisis have not affected Gazan men and women's perceptions of masculinity and femininity. In contrast, men and women, as it appears in these narrations, try to enhance the differentiated gendered images of each other. Men's tolerance and cooperation is provisional, in order to meet the challenge of the crisis of masculinity and femininity, and to re-stabilise their gendered image. This argument is supported by many wives' determination not to let their husbands share in housework, or in teaching their children, only wanting their husbands to keep calm and to be kind to the family. Just two of the women mentioned that their husbands share in the housework, and they both live in nuclear families. 37-year-old Um-Na'eem, said: 'Sometimes I get back home to find that my husband has prepared the food and fed the young children'.

None of the women mentioned her husband cooperating in educating their children, because very few husbands are well educated, and their wives do not trust them with this responsibility. Women also asserted that their husbands willingly leave them to manage their household expenses, and rarely interfere with their decisions. For most women, the most important value they gain from their husbands' cooperation is 'self-respect'. The Gazan man who respects his wife is the ideal man, regardless of his inability to practise his gender role as the primary family provider.

Husbands who become violent, depressed and troublesome Common characteristics of husbands described as violent by their wives are laziness, passivity, selfishness and carelessness. The women who were interviewed said that Gazan men who were deemed powerful due to their employment and education status before the Second Intifada, and were more bound by established patriarchal norms and practices, have become the most violent towards their family members during the male-bread winner crisis. Violent reactions are also more common among husbands who had permanent jobs as skilled labourers in Israel for many years, and whose power was formerly shaped by their ability to earn relatively high incomes from this work. For these men, the low-income jobs available through job creation programs in Gaza were humiliating, due to their lower wages and menial status. Their wives, however, complain about them refusing to accept these jobs. Many of these wives, whose standard of living used to be much better before the Second Intifada, described their jobless husbands as becoming more violent. They said that their husbands cannot forget that they are now without any income, having spent years earning so much money that they could 'play with money'. Other groups of women who described their husbands as violent are married to university graduates.

The majority of wives facing violence from their husbands at the time of this research did not experience this violence before the Second Intifada. The majority of these women are middle aged, and they excuse their husbands' violence, saying that their joblessness and helplessness are *nafsian*, or psychologically unbearable. The empirical data also shows that violence among husbands is slightly more frequent in the Beach camp than in El-Shujae'ya. This slight differentiation between the two sites can be attributed to the heightened sense of masculinity amongst refugee men resulting from their mass involvement in national resistance before and during the Second Intifada. This makes it much more difficult for them to tolerate their joblessness and worthlessness in the family and in wider society and they have become socially isolated. The empirical data also reveals that young married women suffer more from their husbands' violence than middle aged married women. Some wives explain that this is because middle aged women rely to some extent on their teenage sons to earn some income, and to protect them from their husbands' violence.

It is important to note that husbands' violence does not affect their wives' mobility to search for coupons, or other sources of family survival. Wives' access to this form of mobility helps to protect them from their husbands' violence, as it means they are not demanding anything from their husband and are sustaining the daily needs of their households by themselves. This argument is supported by many wives, who asserted that their husbands mainly became violent when another family member demanded money from them. Women therefore prefer their husbands to stay outside the home for as long as possible, in order to avoid conflict with their children, tension and domestic violence.

The discussions and analysis during the individual interviews, as well as the focus groups with both men and women, indicate that wives who live in nuclear families are less protected from violence than those living in extended families. Extended family members, especially mothers and fathers-in-law, support young married women with violent jobless husbands. This support does not lead to tangible changes, but nonetheless gives young women emotional support. According to women who have suffered domestic violence during the Second Intifada, their husbands have been more verbally than physically abusive, compared to before the intifada. The verbal violence is continuous – and vented more against children than wives. Some wives asserted this is because jobless husbands feel embarrassed about beating their wives when they are dependent on them to feed the family: hence these men express their anger and frustration against their children. Women who have been hit by their husbands mentioned that this happened whilst they were trying to protect their children from their fathers.

Jamila from El-Shujae'ya is a married 32-year-old, and has seven children. She has been subjected to domestic violence all her married life. After her husband lost his job he became more violent and unbearable. Jamila is the only research participant who attempted to resist her husband's violence.

> My husband used to work more than 12 hours a day for his Israeli employer. He became the boss of 12 unskilled labourers. At that time, he was very powerful, and we were all scared of him. I was busy the whole day, cooking and taking care of the children, and pleasing my husband to avoid his violence. The only thing I thought about was how to make him treat me respectfully, and to stop [him] shouting and beating me for no reason. [But] he looked after our family, and this is what I miss today. Since the Israeli borders closed, he refused to accept any job in Gaza. Friends came and asked him to work as a day labourer, for NIS 30 a day (around $8) because he is skilled in construction. I tried to convince him to work because we did not have any other source of income, but he always refused to work in such low income jobs.
>
> I realised the only option for me was to go out and search for coupons, and to borrow money. He refused in the beginning, and hit me each time I asked him to go out. Later, he became careless, just wanting to find food ready for him. He is lazy and spends the whole day in front of the TV, or makes trouble with me and the children. Two years ago, he got re-married with an employed woman. He wanted her to feed him. I thought of kicking him out of the house – but what will people say about me if I abandon him when he became jobless?

Jamila had put up with her husband's violence because he was providing for the family. When he stopped doing so, she complained about him to her brothers, who have some power in the local neighbourhood. Her brothers warned her husband to stop beating their sister. When he resumed his violence a few months later, Jamila turned to *lajnet el Islah*, the local conciliation committee, and asked the religious committee leaders to help her. In front of the community leaders, her husband swore that he would not be violent towards her, and that he would provide for the family. This also did not work. Jamila's final option was to ask him to leave the family, and not to have any contact with her, especially after he married another woman. Jamila was aware she could not ask for a divorce, because she was living in his house and he had the legal right of custody of his children. She was looking for alternatives that did not involve losing her children. In our last two interviews, Jamila informed me she had applied for a small loan of $2,000 from a local development association to start her own business – a beauty salon at her home – in order to be economically independent and raise her children herself.

The majority of Gazan wives, however, justify their husbands' violence and try to endure it for the sake of their children. They do not perceive their husbands' violence as a matter of gender, and repeatedly describe it as being due to their husbands' joblessness. Although some of the wives said during individual interviews that their husbands were violent before their joblessness, almost all of the women ignored the historical gender aspect of male domestic violence. In this specific context, the women intentionally normalised and undermined their previous experiences of gender-based violence, in order to focus on wider economic and political issues that have been responsible for dislocating the gender order. Women's justification of their jobless husbands' domestic violence is situational, but it also reflects the value of their own self-sacrifice for the sake of sustaining the whole family, including those who are violent towards them.

In this specific context, I argue that masculine violence is not necessarily a sign of masculine power and authority. It is rather, as stated by Henrietta Moore, a reflection of the fact that 'the perpetrator of violence is threatened and experiences thwarting' (Moore 1994: 67). Wives' justification of their husbands' violence as being due to joblessness can probably be interpreted as their psychological need to maintain the ideological image of their husbands' masculinity even as Gazan men have lost their structural sources of masculinity through the destruction of the socio-economic and political system. There are other structural reasons why Gazan women accommodate their husbands' violence: a) the diminishing family and kin social support system means that women do not have anywhere to flee from violent husbands (Johnson 2006); b) the deinstitutionalisation of Gazan society and the absence of the enforcement of law mean they have little recourse to justice (IWS 2008); and c) if they resist domestic violence, they are criticised as bad wives who do not stand beside their husbands during their crisis. Women in this situation do not, at the very least, want to lose the ideological gender image of being a good wife.

The Centrality of Young Wives and the Marginalisation of Mothers-in-Law

As mentioned earlier in this chapter, a woman's age and stage in life cycle have historically been critical elements in the process of production and reproduction of power relations within the family. The crisis of male bread-winners during the Second Intifada has had a clear influence on destabilising this gendered cycle of power based on age. The central position of young and middle aged wives with young dependent children is an unprecedented trend in the history of Palestinian intra-family relations, especially the extended family. The increased and regular mobility of young Gazan wives has developed their skills in dealing with family members and the public, whilst mothers-in-law have left at home, looking after the young children. This new context during the Second Intifada has presented young Gazan wives with a dual challenge: they are forced to reconfigure their gender performance in order to feed their children, while their family and kin networks lose their economic value. In addition, as their mothers-in-law get older and stop working as traders, the wives' borrowing from relatives reaches its limit. For many young and middle-aged wives their crisis of femininity is triggered by a loss of self-respect. They are no longer economically, socially and psychologically dependent on able-bodied powerful husbands, and are instead living with husbands who wield little or no authority. Gazan women have not undertaken their emerging role of being the primary family provider and leading family decision-maker as willing feminine subjects. For them, these new positions are rather seen as humiliating and exploitative. Women's rejection of their new central position in the family, while their husbands are still able-bodied, is reflected particularly well by Um-Muhammad, the 29-year-old from the Beach camp, who commented:

> It would be *irhram law Ana armala* (a mercy for me if I were a widow), and not seeing my husband with all his *afiato* (physical well-being), unable to do anything.

The centrality of young women's positions during the Second Intifada has been perceived differently by women based on their age and their position in the family. Older women in their position as mothers-in-law consider the moral meaning of young wives' central role in family provision. They feel more secure that their daughters-in-law have become capable of managing their sons' household and family affairs, as the mothers became older and began to lose their capacity for contributing towards the family's survival. Um-Mahmoud, a 61-year-old from the Beach camp, said:

> I always say to my daughter-in-law that if a wife doesn't stand beside her husband in a harsh situation like this, she won't be *bent nas* (an honourable daughter of the family). I have done my work and I wish I could do more, but I am getting older. I raised my son to be a real man, but who expects this situation? Do you imagine an able-bodied man to spend years without work? This situation is out of his control: his wife has to excuse him, and he will find a job when the situation changes.

Um-Mahmoud reflected on her personal experience in life, adding:

> A husband doesn't usually complain to his mother because he doesn't want to upset her, but he can do this with his wife. The husband can [also] be angry with his wife but not against his mother or in public, and she has to manage this too. If she wants to maintain her husband's reputation, she has to absorb his anger and to maintain his name as a man. One day, he will appreciate her standing beside him. Believe me, I feel so sad about these young wives who have not enjoyed their marriages: life has humiliated them from an early age.

Young wives, on the other hand, evaluate their central role differently. Most show their dissatisfaction and unhappiness with the centrality of their position. In both El-Shujae'ya and the Beach camp, 20 out of 31 women in their 30s and below asserted that as young wives and mothers with young dependent children, the central role imposed on them in their families' survival is humiliating. The remaining 11 women, in contrast, asserted their happiness regarding their central role. The wives in the second group were mainly older, with teenage children, and more experience of negotiating their positions than younger wives. There did not appear to be any link between the history of gender oppression within a family and wives' overall views of their central role as the family provider.

For example, Gazan women who were prevented from leaving their homes, and oppressed by both their mothers-in-law and their husbands, did not respond at all positively to emerging opportunities to liberate their mobility. Interpersonal relations based on family, kin and political loyalties appear to have the greatest influence on them. Wives with strong personal relations with the heads of humanitarian associations, and those who have a relation in a powerful political faction, appeared to feel more empowered by their central position in the family. Wives with poor kin and political networks, in contrast, feel more exploited by bearing the main responsibility for family provision. Some women explained this by arguing that women with powerful connections did not feel humiliated by their relations with the public institutions, as they are supported by, and benefit from, their family and political networks. These well connected women do not need to show inferiority in order to gain assistance. The latter group, however, has to resort to deception and deference, and to display their inferiority, in order to gain minimum support for their families' survival. This helps to explain why many young and middle aged wives who are economically and socially destitute, do not place any moral value on their central role as family provider, and more often present it as an undesirable burden.

Awatif, from El-Shujae'ya, expressed how she has been exploited by her responsibility for her family's survival.

> In order to get regular support from the association, I have to accept doing everything the head of the association asks of me. I cannot deal with this [because] I am not part of her kin, or loyal to her political party. She, of course, gives priority to distributing coupons to people who show her loyalty. My mother-in-law and my husband don't know all these details: they just care about how much assistance I receive. Although I was not allowed to go out of my house in the past, and had to get permission to do anything for myself and my children, I was more respected back then. This is why I always pray for my husband to find a job in order to get rid of this humiliating position.

Manal, 32 and from El-Shujae'ya, commented:

> Who said that I want to go out of my home and to make myself valuable, as those women in the associations tell us in their lectures? I had a value and self-respect in the past, but not now.

I asked young and middle aged women how they compared their previous experiences of being suppressed by their mothers-in-law to their position today, when they act as the primary provider of their families, and therefore have relatively more opportunities for freedom and decision-making. Many of them asserted that their previous position as a housewife was a blessing compared to their position today. The most common response was well expressed by Um-Muhammad, a 29-year-old from the Beach camp:

> Our life today is totally dehumanising. In the past, we used to have daily problems, but no one heard or saw us. I used to fight with my husband and my mother-in-law one day, and then our lives together went on with dignity.

Mother-in-Law / Daughter-in-Law Relations: From Contestation to Cooperation

The changing basis for livelihoods, and the exposure of small family units to economic and social vulnerability, has reconfigured wives' priorities and preferences. Wives who, after years of contestation with their mothers-in-law, had moved into separate households, chose to return to living with the extended family, or to share meals and daily expenses with their family-in-law. In situations of chronic livelihood crises and political insecurity, young wives have learnt from the experiences of older women that living within the extended family is the only viable source of security for themselves and their children. Moving back to the extended family has become common among married sons of female heads of household, and also amongst young couples who lived in rented houses. In most cases the decision to move back to the extended family has been taken by the husband, but their wives agreed for the sake of the children. Young wives whose mobility had been formerly restricted whilst living as part of the extended family used the move to negotiate more mobility, for their role as the primary family provider.

In the context of Gaza during the Second Intifada, the extended family structure may appear, on the surface at least, to no longer be patriarchal: men have lost their main source of domestic power, and the central position of older women has been replaced by that of younger and middle aged women. Nevertheless, the extended family has maintained the symbolic meaning and values of patriarchy, exemplified in connectedness and collectiveness. The majority of female interviewees asserted that their return to the extended family has contributed to the survival of the household, but more importantly, it has for them created a sense of personal security that comes from close connection with other family members.

As I emphasised in Chapter 3, familial cooperation and contestation have always existed, and have been transferred across generations of women in Gazan families. The major form of contestation is between mothers and their daughters-in-law. Gaza's changing socio-political context has affected the positionality of both mothers-in-law and daughters-in-law: mothers-in-law have lost their main source of seniority through their sons' joblessness and helplessness, whilst young daughters-in-law have recognised the significance of remaining physically and socially connected to their mothers-in-law. It appears that the majority of mothers-in-law from the research sample have lost their capacity to earn income and to support their sons, whilst young and middle aged wives who used to depend on their husbands' incomes, and on their mothers-in-law to manage the daily household affairs, have been forced to spend time outside the home in search of coupons and temporary jobs. This changing context has reversed the cycle of power circulation between mothers-in-law and daughters-in-law from contestation to cooperation.

The life story of Sawsan, a 32-year-old from El-Shujae'ya, represents a good example of how the loss of male sources of income has contributed to halting the cycle of power circulation for the benefit of young wives, and shifted the mother-in-law/daughter-in-law relations from contestation to cooperation. Sawsan explained:

> I got married when I was sixteen. My husband was twenty, and he was working in Israel as a wage labourer. I lived in one room of the house of my new family-in-law. A month after my marriage, tensions started between my mother-in-law and me. She was sewing and trading in the local market, and wanted me to do all the housework for 15 members of the family. I was very young and didn't know how to do [these] things. My husband's personality was weak, and his mother controlled everything.
>
> The troubles with my mother-in-law continued for around seven years, until I was able to move to a separate house. But in 2005 my house was demolished during an incursion by the Israeli military, so we moved back to live with my mother-in-law for a year. Since my husband lost his work in Israel, he has become lazy and careless, and left me to do everything. Now I raise rabbits and chickens and continue to sew with my mother-in-law, but it is not enough to provide for my children's basic needs.
>
> [But] the increasing harshness of our life made my mother-in-law more compassionate during the last two years. She sees her son without work, and being careless with his children, and she also noticed how much work I do to feed her grandchildren. She started to send me food from time to time; she encouraged me to sew for myself, and to use the income from my sewing on my children. She also told me where to go to receive food coupons, and does not interfere in my mobility. I have also become much nicer to her! I ask for her advice and even join her in some social visits. We are now working together, and we both earn money from sewing. She does not interfere with me as before. She knows that if she doesn't support us, then people will criticise her, because she is still earning.
>
> Despite all these problems with my mother-in-law, I have learned a lot from her. I am now doing what she has done, sewing and selling clothes in the local market. I bought my own sewing machine. My husband has become more responsive to my decisions, and he does not depend on his mother as before.

The narrations of other mothers, and their interpretations of their relations with their daughters-in-law, confirm Sawsan's views. Um-Ahmad, a 59-year-old, from the Beach camp, has five sons and five daughters-in-law. Three of her daughters-in-law live in a separate unit, each made up of one room and tiny kitchen, and all located next to the extended family house. The other two live in the extended household with their mother-in-law. One of Um-Ahmad's sons died as a martyr, a second was injured by the Israeli military, another is a low-income employee with the government, and the youngest two sons are married but jobless.

Um-Ahmad described her daughters-in-law, saying:

> Before the Second Intifada, my married sons used to provide for their children despite their low incomes. They were fishermen; but since the Israelis started restricting their fishing my sons have almost stopped working.[8] We have become dependent on the small income of my older son, and on the monthly allowances we receive for my martyred son and my son who was injured. The total income of our family is NIS 1,700 (around $450 per month). This is not enough for 17 persons living in the house. So, I thought to ask my daughters-in-law to live with us, and share our meals together, so we can all reduce our daily expenses and food consumption. My daughters-in-law did not reject the idea; they are happy to cooperate with me.

Um-Ahmad admitted she used to be very harsh with her daughters-in-law, but explained she wanted them to learn quickly, because they had married very young.

> Yes I used to be *se'ba* (tough), with my daughters-in-law, in the early years of their marriage – but that was to teach them how to manage their families. Now, they are all raising their children and they know what to do, and how to satisfy their husbands and children. I will not be here for them forever.

As a Palestinian researcher from Gaza, I initially found it difficult to analyse the complexity of these changing gender relations. How did these women, who spent years being dominated by their mothers-in-law, turn their situations round so dramatically, and become so close to their mothers-in-law? The way in which the research participants interpreted their own life stories helped me understand how women's agency in Gaza acts to accommodate the tensions between their individual autonomy and their connectedness with close family members. I realised the potential of the use of life story narratives, because these narratives helped me to connect present changes in gender relations with how these gender relations have been strategised by women in the past. It appears that gender relations between mothers and daughters-in-law, have remained connected despite day-to-

8 Starting from 25 June 2006, Israel has been restricting Gazan fishermen's access to the Mediterranean Sea. The fishermen were originally designated access to 20 nautical miles, as stated in the 1993 Oslo Accords; however this was reduced to six nautical miles in 2006. During the Israeli attack against Gaza in December 2008 – January 2009, fishing ceased entirely due to the massive presence of Israeli naval forces. In 2009, fishing resumed but the distance allowed for fishermen was reduced by the Israeli naval forces once again, to approximately three nautical miles. See B'Tselem report January 2011, 'Restrictions on Fishing in Gaza', available at: http://www.btselem.org/gaza_strip/restrictions_on_fishing.

day contestations, for the purpose of serving any future possibilities. This analysis is supported by Gabriele Rosenthal who argues that 'as the past is constituted out of the present and the anticipated future, so the present arises out of the past and the future' (Rosenthal 2006: 14).

The empirical analysis of life story narratives shows that the prolonged joblessness of husbands has made some of them apathetic with regard to their involvement in family, social and moral obligations. Wives, on the other hand, have turned to depending on the social and moral support of their mothers-in-law. Young wives also realised that their increasing mobility required the support of their families-in-law for the protection and care of the children. Young wives described their mothers-in-law as a source of personal and familial security as opposed to being a threat to them. This relation is a reversal of the past, when daughters-in-law were expected to provide complete domestic care, under the supervision of their new mothers-in-law.

I have attempted to explore whether this changing dynamic between young wives and their mothers-in-law is merely a tactic in response to living conditions inside Gaza, or whether it is also part of their historical knowledge and values regarding how family and kin relations should operate and be collectively arranged to challenge threats against the family. This changing dynamic also raises the issue of the relationship between women's personal interests and preferences regarding the subjective meanings of their gender. Young wives showed their preference, at a certain age and within a relatively stable context, to live in a nuclear family and achieve the autonomy of their wifehood and motherhood based on the conception of power fluctuations in women's life cycles.

Before the Second Intifada many Gazan women also mentioned that, since living in a nuclear family their connectedness with their family-in-law had increased, while contestation between mothers-in-law and daughters-in-law had declined. Throughout the contemporary history of Palestinian society under Israeli military occupation, Gazan women have been brought up to perceive family and kin relations as their strategic source of personal security, and the importance of maintaining the connectedness of interpersonal familial relations, regardless of the day-to-day realities of gender-based contestations. Generations of Gazan women repeat the same mantra:

> In hard times, close relatives cannot abandon their obligations. They will be shamed. Who knows what will happen tomorrow; we have nothing to rely on except our family and close relatives.

The specific Palestinian context of prolonged insecurity and uncertainty has taught Gazan women how to shape their gender relationality based on connectedness with family members without jeopardising their individual autonomy. Wives compromise and sometimes tolerate the oppression of their mothers-in-law because they believe that one day they will need their social and moral support, in the case of their husbands' joblessness, sickness or death or any other personal crisis. This does not mean to deny the contestation Gazan women encounter in their life cycles; gendered contestation within the household is not stable, but fluctuates according to the level of threat confronting the collective unit of the family. This may explain why, throughout their married lives, women bargain and compromise, but would be unlikely to instigate a serious conflict with their mothers-in-law, or other in-law family members that could create long-term hostility.

According to Suad Joseph (1993), family connectedness is not always tied to a specific form of gender identity. It is also found in relatively egalitarian and in hierarchal societies. Family connectivity, for Joseph, means that 'a person feels a part of significant others', and where 'persons don't consider themselves autonomous' (Joseph 1993: 453). When family connectedness is the main interest and goal in life, women interpret the act of domination based on sex and age as an act of empowerment. This argument can be understood when we contextualise and historicise the nature of the empowering goal beyond the act of domination. Domination based on gender is not always practised as a singular form of exploitative power relation. It is also practised as a form of nurturing to produce social and ideological values. In the specific historical context of Gaza, although domination of mothers-in-law over their sons and their daughters-in-law reproduces the gender order, it also reproduces care and love, or in other words emotional connectedness, amongst family members. Care and love are critical moral values that provide the sense of personal and familial security in situations that lack other sources of security. This can be understood from the narration of both Sawsan and Um-Ahmad. Um-Ahmad describes her toughness with her daughters-in-law as a way to better nurture good wives and mothers, who are then able to reproduce the connective patriarchy of the family (i.e. to satisfy their husbands and raise their sons to be 'real men'). For Um-Ahmad, keeping her daughters-in-law under her control during their early years of marriage is a means of keeping her sons socially and emotionally connected with their parents and their extended family and kin lineage. Sawsan, on the other hand, who struggled to resist her mother-in-law's oppression for seven years, asserted that despite the prolonged tension with her mother-in-law, she learned from her how to manage her family. Sawsan went beyond her experience of oppression based on her gender, to bolster her connectedness with her mother-in-law as a long-term source of familial security.

Conclusion

This chapter has attempted to understand and analyse the complexity of intra-familial gender relational dynamics in Gaza. The analysis of these dynamics up until to the Second Intifada shows that gender relations within the Palestinian family have been historically fluid in meeting two strategic goals: to reproduce the public image of male domination, and to facilitate women's achievement of their personal interests and desires, as wives and mothers. Throughout the process of achieving these goals, women have used various dynamics of subordination and resistance, acting as both oppressed and oppressor in order to stabilise their wifehood and motherhood. These have become the determinant positions from which they wield power within the perceptions of their gendered self, or as described by Saba Mahmood, in order to achieve their status as 'willing subject' (Mahmood 2001: 210), but consciously not threatening the prevailing gender order. The first section of this chapter showed that women are always in a position of power, but that this power has taken apparently contradictory forms throughout the cycle of their lives: the power to empower others, especially their sons, in the early phase of marriage, and the power to dominate others, especially their daughters-in-law, during later phases of marriage.

The second section of the chapter attempted to capture the changing gender relational dynamics that occurred during the Second Intifada and their effects on gender subjectivity. It demonstrated that the Second Intifada has not only created a crisis of masculinity, but also a crisis of femininity. While men have struggled with their inability to fulfil their family obligations, and to protect their family members, women have been forced to lose their feminine self-respect by their intensive mobility in public to search for coupons. These two forms of gender crisis have reversed two main gender relational aspects based on sex and age: some husbands became cooperative with their wives; and young wives came to occupy a central position in the family, resulting in the increasing marginalisation of mothers-in-law.

This reversal in the actual practice of gender power, however, has not significantly affected the subjective meaning of both masculinity and femininity in Gaza. Through the interplay of these two crises, men and women have struggled to challenge the consequences, with each trying to defend the moral symbolic aspect of the other, and to present the ideology of male domination intact. In this context, masculinity and femininity have been fragmented by the dislocated gender structure, but not by the distortion of ideology. Men and women have attempted to keep the ideology of male domination intact by the presentation of ideological values, beliefs and morals through symbols or means of expression. Symbols act as mediators between the dislocated structure and its ideology in order for people to maintain a meaning for their social existence (Ghouas 2004: 39, Laclau 1996, Moore 2007).

Women, for example, tended to present their jobless able-bodied husbands as still practising their authority in the family in order to maintain their masculine image in public. The analysis has shown that women's maintenance of their husbands' masculinity is the only way for them to reproduce their sense of femininity as ideal wives. Women in Gaza still see their social status as determined by their dependence on a powerful man who practises his masculine authority, without necessarily resorting to domestic violence. This is also reflected in the ways in which women justify their husbands' violence during their joblessness, coupled with their desire to stand beside their husbands in order to maintain their moral image of self as being a good wife.

Husbands, on the other hand, tended to demonstrate compassion towards their wives, on the basis that their wives have been forced to humiliate themselves for the sake of the family. This compassion is reflected in two contradictory aspects of behaviour: either they are tolerant and cooperative with their wives, in order to reduce their humiliation; or else they become violent, passive or careless – symbolising their own senses of helplessness and loss of value. Husbands also tended to emphasise the moral feminine aspects of their wives as dedicated, self-sacrificing and determined. Through this form of presentation, men serve several purposes: a) to reassure us that their joblessness and helplessness is structural rather than personal, and beyond their control; b) to psychologically reduce their sense of responsibility for being the direct cause of their wives' public humiliation; c) to assert that their joblessness and helplessness do not negatively affect their wives' respect and appreciation of them, and do not distort the prevailing image of male domination.

The reversal in mother to daughter-in-law relations is reflected in young daughters-in-law visibly enacting in public the role of primary family provider, while mothers-in-law enact their more domestic role as the supporter of daughters-in-law. The centrality of the young wives' positions in family provision has, nevertheless, been perceived as unsatisfactory and unpleasant by the majority of them. Most young wives experience their search for sources of survival as humiliating and exploitative. They assert that their previous gender position of being dependent on their husbands was a better position to be in. Their new position as family provider has undermined their feminine sense of self-respect, as a wife and mother. They also emphasise that the new tasks they handle for the sake of family survival do not add any value to their senses gendered self. They would rather prefer to return to the *normal* gender order, by which men practise their manhood as the primary provider of the family, and women practise their womanhood by being respectable housewives.

Although the changing gender relations within the family during the Second Intifada imply the degeneration of the structural basis of the patriarchal Gazan family, both men and women struggle to maintain the ideological image of patriarchy by the enhancement of cooperation between family members. Mother to daughter-in-law contestation has shifted to cooperation. Mothers-in-law have lost their material and social sources of power over their daughters-in-law due to the joblessness and helplessness of their sons, while daughters-in-law have gained the social legitimacy to provide for the family. Both mothers and their daughters-in-law realise the importance of family connectedness as a long-term strategy to maintain the stability of the family and the security of all its members. The historical experience of Gazan women shows that family connectivity is not contradictory with contestations based on gender. The former appears to be more strategic, while the latter is more practically linked with specific times and places within women's life cycles. Women's lack of interest or desire to act purely as autonomous individuals, and their concerns to remain connected with others, even those who oppress them at certain phases of their life cycle, have shaped their intra-family relationality and the process of production and reproduction of notions of personhood and agency.

Chapter 6
Conclusion: Gazan Women – between the Masculinising of their Enactment and the Feminising of their Selfhood

> I don't really need his love or his material support, but I need people to say that I have a real husband. I want my children, especially my sons, to grow up with a strong model of their father as a real man. This makes sons powerful too, and I become more respected by others. (Sawsan, 32 years old, from El-Shujae'ya)

> Believe me, I would accept my husband's violence if he was actually a real man and respected by his children and others. (Um Iyad, 48 years old, from the Beach camp)

> It would be *irhram law Ana armala* (a mercy for me if I were a widow), rather than to see my husband with all his *afiato* (physical well- being), unable to do anything. (Um-Muhammad, 29 years old from, the Beach camp)

> Who said that I want to *atlah men el beit we ahki ma' el nas ashan yekoon eli qeema* (be out of my home and making myself valuable) as those women in the associations tell us in their lectures? I had a sense of value and self-respect in the past, but not now. (Manal, 32 years old, from El-Shujae'ya)

I have chosen these women's words to start this concluding chapter. What are the ideological and subjective implications of these narrations, if we assume that they reflect a mode of gendered knowledge, or self-consciousness that women in Gaza have constituted through the historical interplay of the different forms of oppression and resistance in their day-to-day lives? Are women in Gaza seduced by subordination? I assume not. But then how can we then explain that the dislocation of socio-economic and political structural arrangements, based on male domination and patriarchy during the Second Intifada, has not significantly affected historically and ideologically constructed images of feminine selfhood as inferior, versus masculine selfhood as superior? Do Gazan women's desires to act and to be presented as if part of a 'merger with another' (Bartky 1990: 2), as opposed to desiring to be autonomous, constitute a disempowering of their agency?

Before reviewing the findings of my research, I want to say that the research also reflects the trajectory of my own life, including my struggles as a female activist, the wife of a political prisoner who became a martyr, and the dedicated mother of two children. For the first time in my professional and political life, I have to acknowledge that the meaning of my own agency has better theorised my pursuit of the interpretation of my research subject. The women and men who participated in my research inspired me to unravel my own personal and political history, in order to better understand the fears and desires that lay beneath the contradictory practice of my own agency. They also helped me to understand why I freely supported my husband, who was deeply involved in the Palestinian national struggle and subsequently spent many years in Israeli prisons, whilst also dedicating myself to raising my two children. According to my research participants, the answers to these questions were tied in with my own need for a source of long-term personal and familial security; which, for a Palestinian refugee woman, can only be provided by her immediate family. My personal desire, embodied in the social and cultural history of my people, has been to live as a dedicated mother and giver of love to my family, even if this consciously involves compromising some of my own gender needs and interests. Both the women research participants and I have strategised our gender performance, whether as empowered or subordinated, in order to operate within a variety of contradictory subject positions that we possess either forcefully or freely, within the given political context. We do so in order to meet the necessities of living – with consideration for differences in class and social status – and without losing our moral feminine selfhood.

I seek to use these research findings to contribute to the ongoing theoretical debate about the relationship between structure, individual practice and the constitution of the gendered subject and subjectivity. In Chapter 2, I argued that this debate has primarily focused on the definition of women's agency or subjectivity, and I questioned whether women's subjectivity always needs to be tied to a liberal notion of the individualised autonomous self that resists the system of male domination. In the empirical chapters (3, 4, and 5) I have attempted to show the paradox between the contextual situational change in gendered structures of power and the constitution of gendered selves. The findings and analysis of these chapters reveal that it is not domestic-public gender stereotyping that threatens women's self-determination, as argued by many liberal feminist scholars (Azmon 1981, Bartky 1990). The individualised autonomous self is exemplified in Bartky's term 'authentic choice of self' (1990: 22–23) and presented as universal, necessarily implying a changing feminine consciousness always associated with changing actions. Women in Gaza have contradicted Bartky's argument of universality, especially during the Second Intifada. They have demonstrated a great capacity to transcend socially constructed gender stereotyping, as well as gaining the social legitimacy to act differently. Nevertheless, they have continued to over-value the historically embodied subjective aspects of differentiated femininity and masculinity.

An Overview of the Research Findings

The empirical analysis and findings show that poor and vulnerable women and men in Gaza have struggled to rescue the historically embodied images of their gendered selves from the consequences of the dislocation of socio-economic gendered structural arrangements, as a direct result of Israel's military occupation of Gaza and its destruction of Gaza's political economy. As shown in chapters 4 and 5, this dislocation has affected the structural and historical basis of livelihood management based on male domination and patriarchy within households and local community based organisations (CBOs). This has been exemplified by men losing their economic capacity to provide for the family, being defeated in their desires to provide security for their family members, losing their influence in kin and community institutions, as well as losing public recognition as activists in the Palestinian national resistance.

Older Gazan men and women have been replaced by younger men and women in family provision, and in decision-making processes within the family and in wider community organisations. Marriage has become a project for livelihood survival, rather than a symbol of the persistence of patriarchy. The shift in livelihood sources, from the domestic sphere of the household economy and informal sector to the public sphere of humanitarian aid provided mostly by CBOs, has forced women to reconfigure their gender roles and activities.

Gazan women are acting as the primary family providers, and as the core decision makers in both the domestic sphere and in CBOs. Many women have also become active in supporting Islamic political discourse, led in Gaza by Hamas and other religious groups. Women have become significant participants in mosque activities and raising religious awareness during Hamas elections at both local and national levels.[1]

The disturbance of gender roles, as they have played out against the actual interests and desires of both men and women, for the sake of household /family survival, has created means of resistance reflecting individual subjective gendered images. This is illustrated by women and men's presentation of their desired gendered subject positions: women want to return to their gendered position as respected housewives, dependent on their husbands, whilst men want to be able

1 The theme of women's participation in religious mobilisation and their demonstration of the discourse of political Islam led by Hamas is significant with regard to the shaping of women's agency and subjectivity in the context of Gaza during the Second Intifada. I have not been able to do justice to this theme in this book, although comments about it are integrated throughout the empirical analysis of chapters 4 and 5. As the reader may notice, I have tried to cover this thematic gap by linking women's return to Islam with their return to gender traditions – acting as ideal housewives and mothers appears to be consistent with their actions as faithful Muslim women. For further relevant details on this theme, see Islah Jad (2005) 'Between Religion and Secularism: Islamist Women of Hamas', in *Shifting Ground: Muslim Women in the Global Era*, edited by F. Nouraie-Simone.

to fulfil their family obligations and maintain their economic and social authority within the family and in the public sphere. The empirical evidence suggests that gender relational arrangements within the family and in the local community before the Second Intifada were regarded as more satisfactory by both women and men, compared with the reconfigured gender arrangements during the Second Intifada. Women asserted that they were more respected and lived in dignity whilst living as housewives, dependent on their husbands' income.

Gazan women, especially the poor and vulnerable, asserted that the changing livelihood context has affected their perceptions of self and of the other. However, they also acknowledge that they were oppressed by their men and by the patriarchal structure of the family before the Second Intifada, although this oppression took different forms. Nevertheless, they previously had more space for subtle negotiations within stable gender relations of power: and also had powerful men and/or parents-in-law to rely on, whether materially or symbolically, in order to negotiate and accumulate power within the family and in the wider community before the Second Intifada. In the context of Gaza, the stability of gender order at the micro level has played a facilitating role for women to negotiate their actual power from within the system of dividing responsibilities according to gender. The disturbance of the gender order at the micro level, in contrast, has undermined women's space to negotiate such divisions of responsibility, while the changing political economy has affected both public and private spheres, which no longer operate 'normally' in order to reproduce each other. Rather, women are morally obliged to bear the material and psychological consequences of the crisis of male bread-winners: standing beside their helpless husbands and sons during the harsh times imposed on them by the wider oppressive colonial system of the Israeli military occupation.

The specific context of the Second Intifada created new forms of gender inequality. Women's enactment of men's traditional roles in household management have taken place in a situation where men have lost their sources of economic power, and where family and kin relations have lost their potential to provide personal and familial support. Whilst pursuing sources of livelihood that are mostly dependent on humanitarian aid, women have embraced dual responsibilities in both the domestic and public spheres, while men have become resourceless as well as helpless. The new gender relational dynamics that have accompanied these changes – for example, the new freedom of women's public mobility, the centrality of young wives and the marginality of older mothers, the tolerance and cooperation of husbands with their wives – that women might have experienced as empowering, have instead been regarded by them as disempowering. In their evaluations and interpretations of how these changes have affected their lives, Gazan women have asserted that the new gender dynamics of the Second Intifada have added further additional burdens to gender relations.

During the Second Intifada, poor and vulnerable women focused on the loss of the moral aspect of their femininity, particularly the self-respect and dignity entailed in acting as *musatatat* (respected housewives and mothers), efficiently enacting their gender roles and responsibilities, while depending on their men to provide for, and to protect, the family. They have lost the social status of being wives of recognised and authoritative husbands, while mothers have lost the power gained through their adult sons. These were substantive sources of power on which poor housewives depended before the Second Intifada.

The enactment of women's agency, in practising the socially recognised position as the primary family provider and its core decision-maker, as well as their status in CBOs, while men have lost these positionalities, is not regarded as satisfactory by Gazan women. Rather, it is presented as a mode of unfair gender positioning that has led to a devaluing of both women's and men's selfhood. Women in Gaza have re-affirmed their gendered subjectivity by the presentation of their gender preferences and desires as being contradictory to the actual gender practice imposed on them during the livelihood crisis. For example, many women asserted that they prefer to have a secure marriage at the expense of further education and employment; they would prefer to return to their respected domesticated positions rather than to be humiliated by searching for aid coupons in public; they would also prefer to return to their dependence on their husband's authority as the determinant of their social status, and to maintain family connectedness, even if this jeopardises their personal preferences and desires to live in autonomous nuclear households.

However, the findings of chapters 3 and 4, suggest that these preferences are both contextual and fluid. They have been influenced by the multiple discourses and positionalities that women have experienced and pursued, whether freely or forcefully, throughout their lives within the family and in wider society.

The specific model of agency and subjectivity relevant to women in Gaza is Teresa De Lauretis' (1986) description of the notion of the subject, as 'multiple, shifting, and often self-contradictory' (quoted in Moore 1994: 58). Also of relevance is the way in which both Henrietta Moore (1994) and Saba Mahmood (2001, 2005) define agency and subjectivity in relation to structure, individual practices and discourses. Henrietta Moore, for example, emphasises that the gendered subject is, contextually as well as biographically, a by-product of 'the co-existence of multiple discourses of gender' within the system of each culture, and in which some discourses over-determine others at certain times and in certain social sites (Moore 1994: 59). In the context of Gaza, this may be seen in terms of where Islamist discourses – there is not a singular Islamist discourse – gain ascending over secular nationalist and liberal discourses that were dominant before the Second Intifada. However, Islamist discourses do not operate in isolation from secular discourses; they have been contextually and historically influenced by them, such that the latter have in turn facilitated Islam's presentation of its distinctiveness, and as a result, resulted in its achievement of hegemony.

Sara Roy (2000) and Islah Jad (2005) point out that, in this respect, Hamas, as an Islamist political and social movement, has succeeded in turning its Islamic ideology into a hegemonic discourse, by investing in the experiences of other secular nationalist movements. By shifting its emphasis from political and military struggle to the social sector, where women have been encouraged to participate, Hamas has used a pragmatic and non-confrontational strategy of public mobilisation. Large numbers of women's organisations affiliated to Hamas have been established in Gaza, aiming to provide services for poor families, based on Islamic values and principles, especially when, owing to their corrupt practices, secular parties have failed to achieve these goals (Roy 2000: 26, Jad 2005: 1).

The Islamist discourse has attracted mostly poor women because it addresses both their material interests in family survival, and their desire to be respected housewives from the perspective of Islamic values and principles of gender. This means that women's subjectivity has been shaped by the intersection of socio-economic and political factors and the changing positionalities of women within the existing multiple discourses, or the dominant discourse, in order to achieve satisfaction, pleasure and rewards.

Conceptualizing Gender Subjects in Gaza

Key features of women's subject position and subjectivity in Gaza are characterised by consistency in self-presentation and contradictions in practice. In other words, the contradictory practices of domination and subordination operate within a consistent presentation of a gendered self. Women are often in conflict between what they desire – to be feminine as socially and originally conceived (Moore 2007: 20) – and what they are compelled to do in situations of necessity, which from their viewpoint is masculine. Women in Gaza have historically weaved between two models of agency: that of the conscious strategiser of gender performance, shaped in multiple contradictory positions (dominant and subordinate) following the degree of investment in, and the expected material and social outcomes of, their evaluation of the social setting, and the moral feminine self, embedded in a web of relations with others. Being an efficient strategiser of her individual and familial life, in both the short and long-term, requires a woman to handle both masculine and feminine tasks and responsibilities simultaneously, whilst consistently presenting herself within the moral boundaries of femininity as *set muhtarama* (a respected woman).

For women in Muslim Middle Eastern societies, including Palestine, moral femininity is structured by their gendered practice, which is rooted in the ideological overlap between tradition and Islam.[2] This moral practice, illustrated in their self-sacrifice for the sake of their children and families is, however, explained by several feminists as a sign of gender oppression (Bartky 1990, Rubenberg 2001), or as a reflection of social inferiority (Abu-Lughod 1992: 203). Virginia Held (1987, 2006), Sara Ruddick (1994) and Saba Mahmood (2001), however,

2 See the details in Israr Ahmad (2003) 'Religious Obligation of Moslem Women', and in Devi Ze'evi (2006) 'Producing Desire: Changing Sexual Discourse in the Ottoman Middle East, 1500'.

analyse the moral practice of women as wives and mothers, whether they follow the ideology of Islam or not, as a sign of their agentive power. Saba Mahmood argues, for example, that women's experience of patience during suffering, is not a sign of their passivity. Rather, it reflects their capacity 'to endure in the face of hardship without complaint' (Mahmood 2001: 220). Gazan women's endurance of the livelihood crisis contradicts the liberal notion that describes women's self-sacrifice only as a sign of their passivity and submission (Bartky 1990). The endurance, tolerance and sacrifice of women in Gaza have enabled them to care and provide for their family members, which has been the only means of ensuring the material and emotional survival of their children.

At the same time, women in Gaza have successfully wielded their power within the family and in both informal and formal public institutions, by taking up multiple roles as child bearers and carers, income earners and managers of the household economy, without transcending the ideological discourse and normative images of femininity and masculinity. This is reflected in a popular and contemporary Palestinian women's saying: 'I act like ten men, but I keep my reputation as a respected woman'. As argued by Henrietta Moore (1994), the concept of reputation is not only connected to women's self-presentation and social evaluation, but also to their potential for power and agency. Women's reputations in Gaza, especially those of young women, are primarily constructed around the concept of their modest physicality, particularly with regard to how they dress and communicate with men. Reputation is also used as an instrument for strategising gendered relations of power. For example, in a relatively stable context in Gaza, the reputation of young wives is reflected in their domestic modesty. But in a situation of livelihood scarcity it is reflected in their modesty in communicating with strangers in public, especially men. In other words, their reputations in Gaza do not have a fixed content, but are modified in order to legitimise their needs for mobility and public communication. The definitions of women's reputations also shift as their positions change, acting as a critical intermediary between practical and moral models of their subjectivity, and serving the re-stabilisation of gender imaginaries in the face of dramatic structural changes.

The multiple modality of women's agency in Gaza, composed of both masculine and feminine aspects of gender practice as they are socially constructed, implies several economic, social, ideological and moral goals. Women's 'masculine' practice of agency appears more contextual and situational, especially amongst poor women, who use it in order to survive and stabilise their households in a prolonged situation of insecurity and uncertainty. However, their feminine practice is ideological as well as moral. Women's gendered subjectivity is both contradictory and complementary, both accepting and rejecting, both accommodating and resisting. Through compromise, bargaining and manoeuvring, women both internalise and externalise the socially constructed image of male domination.

In Chapter 5, it became clear that this multiplicity in women's agency in Gaza is such that the feminine aspect of self-presentation is purposely and consciously utilised to legitimise the 'unnatural' aspect of their masculine enactment, which is itself used to challenge the socially constructed, inferior meaning of femininity. Um-Sufian, for example, said: 'To be responsible for everything is not the problem, but without a husband, even if he is useless, I would be a subject of compassion by other people. It suffices to have his name as a *rejal* (a man) at home'. Her words imply that she is regarded by her local community as a powerful respected woman, not only because she efficiently provides for her family and manages her household, which is supposedly her husband's role: more importantly, it is because the enactment of this role does not contradict her position as a wife, secured by the presence of her husband, regardless of the lack of material value he provides. Here, we can see how the gender dynamics of simultaneous empowerment and subordination operate in parallel, without one replacing or threatening the other, and through which the ideology of the gender order remains intact.

The apparent contradiction between women's actual practices of gender that are socially understood as masculine and their self-presentation of their gendered subject as conforming to an ideal of femininity has been clearly illustrated in chapters 4 and 5. Young and middle aged wives actually act as the primary provider of the family, its core decision-maker and manager of the household. At the same time, they consciously refuse to present the masculine form of power as dominant or as oppressive of their husbands. The class factor amongst poor and vulnerable Gazan women has more influence than the gender factor in shaping their practice of power and agency, that is, their capacity to act for the survival of the family and to challenge the effects of the structural causes of their men's powerlessness. Women exercise their power to empower their men, even if conditions would enable them to act differently. Does this contradictory practice mean that the feminine practice of agency is submissive? Why can't we see women's endurance and self-sacrifice for the empowerment of their powerless husbands and other family members as an illustration of deliberate action and wisdom, leading to better social outcomes, or as an indication of critical and strategic agency?

My answers to these questions are based on a historical analysis of the structure of gendered relations of power in Palestinian society under Israeli military occupation, and how the meaning of masculinity and femininity has taken multiple forms of practice and presentation. The empirical findings of my research support the conceptualisation of masculine and feminine subjects as situational, and not essentially a defined singular project (Moore 1999: 15). I have also found that masculinity and femininity are more accurately analysed historically and contextually, away from the use of a singular category. Empirical evidence shows that the boundaries between what men and women do in their day-to-day lives are constantly renegotiated and redrawn in each encounter within the specific institutional context (Cornwall and Lindisfarne 1994: 17, Kandiyoti 1994: 212, Connell 2000: 24). According to Connell – who opens up the possibility of examining subordinate masculinities – masculinity and femininity need to be analysed in relation to institutions, economics and everyday life and our part of our domestic and public history (Connell 2000: 24).

The Crisis of Presentation of Gendered Selfhood

There is considerable evidence that Palestinian women have historically enhanced the symbolically differentiated meaning of masculinity and femininity as much as men, as a means for both the family unit and wider community to resist the collective threat of Israeli military occupation against the moral aspects of the Palestinian subject (Taraki 2006, Johnson 2007). In the Palestinian context, where the political economy and its structure of power relations deprives both men and women from enacting their 'normal' gender roles, and when the gendered domestic-public division has been forcefully reconfigured to serve the immediate need for family survival and security (see Chapter 4), the ideological presentation of historically embodied images of femininity and masculinity becomes one of the only options available for both men and women to maintain significant meanings for their socio-cultural existence.

For further articulation of the conceptualisation of the specific model of Gazan women's agency, I refer to Henrietta Moore's (1994) analysis of the problematic relationship between the social and the individual. For Moore, this relationship 'resides in the intersection of the personal history of men and women with collective situations, discourses and identities' (Moore 1994: 50). This argument implies that the individual subject, man or woman, is influenced by several individual and societal factors that determine gendered and non-gendered practice. The subject's practice involves both resistance and accommodation in order to deal with the contradictory discourses created and experienced throughout the life history of individuals and social groups.

During the crisis of masculinity and femininity of the Second Intifada, poor women in Gaza have purposively drawn on the historical image of their gendered selves as subordinated and inferior, to facilitate their access to humanitarian aid on the one hand, and to psychologically support the masculinity of their jobless and helpless husbands on the other. Men who have historically internalised the ideology of domination have resisted their powerlessness by demonstrating their sense of masculine identity (Moore 1994: 69). As revealed in chapters 4 and 5, jobless and helpless husbands and brothers reconstruct the historical images of domination and superiority by presenting their women's role in family provision and in community organisations as an inferior role that cannot be undertaken by men. They also legitimise their wives' and daughters' intensive mobility and public participation by emphasising that these actions are not contradictory with Islam – because, for example, women scrupulously follow the Islamic dress code, and they go raise their own religious awareness through local Islamic CBOs. This recourse to Islamic legitimisation enhances the cultural and religious superiority of men.

The gendered enactments and strategies used by women in Gaza are not unconscious practices, which only reflect practical logic (Bourdieu 1990). In addition to the moral aspect of agency as stressed by Mahmood, we need also to consider the dynamic aspect of a woman's subjectivity, when as a conscious agent she questions her enactment on a continuous basis and modifies her techniques of gender negotiation, in order to achieve her strategic goals.

Drawing on James C. Scott's (1979,1985) work on subaltern forms of resistance, I argue that oppressed women in Gaza do not resist their subordination, but question and evaluate it, when deciding how to act in order to achieve their personal and familial goals, without losing their desired moral feminine self. Poor and vulnerable Gazan women realise from their life experience that they can achieve their goals without necessarily engaging in open conflict with the hegemonic system of power when they have no other resources or available support. The interplay of the two notions of agency – masculine and feminine – suggests that women's desire and preference to present themselves as subordinate and inferior is not masochistic or a question of female shame (Bartky 1990: 2), neither is it a reflection of their incapacity to enact the masculine form of power. Poor and vulnerable women think about power, because it is reflected in their day-to-day practices, but do not publically reveal this. This, as argued by Scott, is the 'hidden transcript' (1990: 4) against the holders of power. I argue that poor and vulnerable Gazan women do not openly want to resist the hegemonic system of male domination, because they are aware that they practise their 'hidden transcript' of power within a system of male domination. Rather, they practically and consciously prioritise non-gendered interests and preferences that meet the desirable moral constitution of their feminine self, to show themselves as givers of care and love, dedicated to the lives of others, which is signified by their connectedness with others, including those who historically and contemporaneously subordinate them.

This practice of willing subordination on the part of women in Gaza is based on relations of dependence according to gender. Their sense of righteousness and happiness depends on a similar sense of righteousness and happiness in their husbands. Thus, Gazan women are concerned with strengthening the masculinity of their men during crises in a way that also strengthens their own feminine selfhood, which is characterised as being self-sacrificing care and love givers. Their reward for this practice is their husbands' respect and appreciation and the support and protection of their mothers-in-law, whilst at the same time maintaining their social status within socially constructed and recognised constraints.

Gazan women have played a critical role in challenging potential upheavals of gender subjectivity during the Second Intifada. They have efficiently practised the dual gender roles of family provision and family reproduction activities, and ask only that their men provide them with 'respect and love', which from a Gazan woman's perspective has a double meaning: First, it is a sign of real manliness in the absence of male economic sources of power. Respect and love from their husbands is an important element that enables wives to feel secure about their marriage and their children. It can also be a symbol of women's interest in showing that the practice of male domination is not oppressive and exploitative.

If a husband respects and loves his wife, she will reciprocally respect and obey him and relish his authority. However, the term 'a woman's obedience' to her husband does not express the western liberal feminist ideas of a woman being forced to obey her husband because she is economically, socially, and/or psychologically dependent on him (Bartky 1990, Mullet 1988). In the context of Gaza, women use this term to reflect a different meaning unrelated to economic dependence, as this is self-evidently not achievable. They rather consider the social outcomes and rewards beyond the use of this term. 'Women's obedience' is more an ideological term, referring to the provision of care and appreciation in a situation where its structural meaning has been eroded. In the context of the crisis of masculinity, women's obedience is not understood as implying exploitation and oppression, but is a term used by women to reflect their desire for a respectful, authoritative and masculine husband. As such, it is part of the reciprocal exchange of gender power, regardless of the disturbance in the distribution of economic sources of power.

From the perspective of Gazan women, when a husband respects his wife, gender contestation in the family is diminished and wives gain respect from other members of the family and the local community. In the situation of a crisis of masculinity, the reciprocity of exchanges of power is understood by both genders as one in which a woman enhances the sense of masculinity of her man in public, while he provides her with the love and respect to maintain her social status in the family and the wider society.

Second, the concept of love and respect from husbands also creates a sense of parity regarding the representation of gendered selfhood, in a situation where both masculinity and femininity are in a crisis of representation. While Gazan women are capable and socially legitimised to take up their men's role as primary provider for the family in a situation in which men's sources of income have been lost, their men should in turn provide them with respect and love inside their homes and in public. This provision, however, is a moral aspect of power. In a situation where men have been collectively deprived of practising their normative masculine roles and activities, this form of moral support is considered by women as their motivation for holding dual gender responsibilities without distorting public images of femininity and masculinity.

As has been clearly observed among the research participants, women with respectful and tolerant husbands, who practise their masculinity without oppression, appear to be more confident and powerful than women with violent husbands, despite the similarity in men's diminished economic capacity. Men's violence is a manifestation of male domination. However, male domination or authority does not necessarily entail violence. I have argued that the reason women in Gaza justify their husbands' violence is related to the changing subjective position of both men and women. Husbands' violent enactment and wives' justification of this violence reflects the crisis of presentation of gendered selfhood (Moore 1994). Both women and men have, during the crisis of the Second Intifada, acted to enhance the self-presentation of each other, in order to achieve 'the successful management of modes of gender subjectivity' (Moore 1994: 67–68).

The Strategisation of Women's Enactment

Bourdieu was right when he stressed the insufficiency of material possessions as the basis of power. He asserted that the strategisation of material power requires legitimisation. For Bourdieu, the latter is only achieved by the power of structural norms, and he argued that the structures govern both practices and the concomitant presentations (Bourdieu 1990: 21). This is reflected in the practice of femininity and/or masculinity, which is always 'misrecognition' of the actors' gender interests: that is, the interest to resist the stereotypical norms of gender relations of domination and subordination (ibid. 242–243). Misrecognition, for Bourdieu, refers to the traditional Marxist idea of false consciousness that denotes denial of the economic and political interests present in a set of practices. Bourdieu analysed the symbolic practice of male violence and women's inferiority as a reflection of the misperception of both men and women's gender interests to change the structure of domination (ibid.).

However, the context of Gaza disputes Bourdieu's theory of practice. Gazan women have enhanced the presentation of their feminine selfhood as subordinate and inferior, not in order to support stereotypical gender norms, which have already changed during the Second Intifada: they have rather done so in order to ideologically and culturally reject structural changes in stereotypical gender norms and the reconfiguration of power relations between men and women. This ideological presentation aims to maintain the portrayal of their powerless men as dominant in public. Subordinate and marginalised men, on the other hand, have enhanced the presentation of their superior masculinity, either by becoming more violent, or else more cooperative and compassionate with their wives.

Hence, the experience of women in Gaza suggests a different analysis from Bourdieu's theory of practice. It shows that men and women's practices and presentations of domination and subordination are a conscious act, and as such they reflect their consciousness of the advantages beyond maintaining certain ideological positions and values. Women's enactment has been strategised in relation to what is achievable within the prevailing oppressive system, based not only on gender, but also on other socio-economic and political factors (Scott 1990), especially in this situation of chronic insecurity and uncertainty. Within this context, gender is an intermediary resource, used to carry out practices in order to achieve certain ends, which may be non-gendered but strategic, for example, those of long-term personal and familial security. This analysis overlaps with the analysis of women's practice of everyday life in the work of de Certeau (1984) and Andrea Cornwall (2007).

The empirical evidence of my research shows that Gazan women's life choices have remained influenced by contingent circumstances, where inter-subjective relations with intimates, including those which are historically patriarchal and hierarchical, are invoked and invested. Andrea Cornwall grounds her analysis on the distinction that de Certeau makes between strategic and tactical choices. Cornwall points out that women's strategic choices cannot only be analysed from an individual dimension, because these choices are always influenced by contingent circumstances in which strategic gender choices are restricted in a situation of uncertainty in favour of tactical choices. For Cornwall, these tactical choices are illustrated in women's sociability and the web of interpersonal relations with intimates (Cornwall 2007: 28 and 42). Intersubjective relations play a critical role in how women shape and reshape their life choices. Economic and political contingencies in Gaza have historically constrained women to pursue their strategic gender choices for the sake of the survival and security of their family members. For example, poor women have learnt throughout their lives to avoid any long lasting tension between their exercise of agency to achieve their autonomy – supposedly a strategic gender goal – and their dependence on family connectedness, because they need to be able to invoke the latter in situations of uncertainty.

In a situation of collective threat against the family and the whole society, gender oppression is both normalised and undermined when people are faced with the consequences of colonial oppression. Iris Jean-Klein describes the everyday resistance of ordinary women and men in Palestinian society, and argues that the continuity of their domestic activity is neither invariably a gender-specific phenomenon, or exclusively counter-hegemonic. The everyday experiences of Palestinians, 'represented both a counter-hegemonic, liberational current and, at the same time, a hegemonising exercise' (Jean-Klein 2001: 91). This means that gender is intentionally and simultaneously resisted and accommodated by both men and women, in order to achieve recognised interests, whether these are gender specific or not. A woman in Gaza feels happier and more powerful when she is dependent on a powerful man who is practising his masculine authority at home and in public. Within this relation of subordination, it becomes not only a social responsibility, but more importantly a moral obligation for a woman to act as an ideal wife and mother. This practice of femininity, which is inseparable from the practice of masculinity, brings women in Gaza a sense of parity in relation to historically constituted ideas of masculinity and femininity. Or, as described by Saba Mahmood, this relation of subordination creates the conditions for women to act to achieve 'continuity, stasis and stability' (2001: 212).

In Gaza, women have been influenced by multiple ideological discourses of modernity, tradition, nationalism and Islam. Through these different positions that women have either gained from, or had imposed upon them by dominant discourses, they have experienced and built up multiple forms of consciousness and enactments. This has been described in the empirical analysis of Chapter 4, where women have shown a high capacity to invest in the different forms of institutions and resources developed by the changing economic and political structure in Gaza; and to bargain and negotiate their power within the different conflictual political discourses (secular or Islamist), in order to fulfil their personal and familial needs.

Generations of women in Gaza have enhanced their feminine inferior status in order to maintain their husbands' calmness, tolerance, respect and love: they have also used this status to legitimise their public activism. They become emotionally connected with their extended families in order to gain their mother-in-laws' support with childcare; they enhance their husbands' authority in order to resist their mother-in-laws' domination; they borrow money or secure credit in their names to create the image that their husbands are earning income; and they are committed to Islamic dress codes and sanctioned behaviour in order to facilitate their mobility, education and political participation. These multiple strategies reflect the multiple contradictory discourses and positionalities of gender, and are simultaneously and carefully utilised by women in order to minimise risks and maximise rewards.

The form and meaning of autonomy for women in Gaza does not appear to contradict their interest and desire to depend on their husbands' authority. In order for a wife to be autonomous within her household, she needs to shift from depending on her parents-in-law to depending on her husband, by living with him in a nuclear family. However, in order to access better education and employment, she has to be careful not to display superiority over her husband. Gazan women do not approach this kind of autonomy as separate from their relations with, and dependence on, others: autonomy, in the liberal individualist sense, is not relevant to them. They do not jeopardise the societal values of their status based on connectedness with their intimates in order to visibly or publicly exercise individual autonomy that is independent of reliance on others. For women in Gaza this would carry a high risk of social isolation and exclusion. This calculation of risk explains why they use multiple discourses and practices, through which socially accepted forms of practice legitimise or minimise the risk of the newly emerged practice.

Gazan Women's Agency and the Context of Contemporary Palestine

The critical questions of this book are to ask why women in Gaza have not utilised the actual power they have attained, either in the situation of livelihood crisis during the Second Intifada, or through the circulation of gender power across generations, in order to enhance their individual autonomy from being dependent on family relations. Why have they not contested the image of male domination illustrated in the ideology of patriarchy and Islam? Why have the images of male domination and women's subordination remained dominant in Gazan women's self-presentation, at the same time as the socio-economic structure has changed and the socio-economic function of patriarchy and male domination has diminished? And why do they intentionally act as the transmitter of the discourses of patriarchy, male domination and Islam, whilst the actual practice of gender is contradictory with the positions these discourses offer women? What forms of threat do women encounter if they resist these images that consistently enhance male domination?

The answers to these questions cannot be generalised or universalised, because they are critically related to the specific history and context of Palestinian women and Palestinian society. At the time of writing this book the history of Israeli colonial oppression has been experienced by four generations of Palestinian men and women, for whom there has been no space for personal being (Pitcher 2003). The vast majority of the participants of this research were mothers with dependent children. Throughout the historical and contextual analysis in chapters 3, 4 and 5, these women have been shown to emphasise their ideal practice of mothering children by the presentation of self-sacrifice, and their endurance of livelihood hardship and insecurity for the sake of their children. Ideal mothering should not, however, be reducible to the notion of nature or emotions: but must instead be politicised (Lutz and Abu-Lughod 1990). In the case of Gaza this reflects, among other things, women's belonging to a wider vision for the national future when their children will have a better quality of life, produced from their mothers' intensive care and self-sacrifice. Julie Peteet's (1997) arguments about the significance of mothering in her article on the First Intifada (1987–1993) are still relevant to the Second Intifada. Peteet argues that women's self-sacrifice as mothers is 'a means of asserting moral and spiritual superiority. In crafting this superiority, women are not positing femininity or maternity as a superior position or essence; they are asserting the moral superiority of the community of Palestinians whose embodiment they represent' (Peteet 1997: 123).

The history of the prolonged Israeli military occupation of Palestine has had a critical effect regarding the shaping of gender subjectivity. Maria Holt (2003) argues that when Palestinians were forced into exile after 1948, the concept of family and personal honour became related to the loss of the land and the idealisation of women as the guardians of national dignity. Holt asserts that the specificity of the Palestinian circumstances (from the war in 1948 to the Second Intifada) has ingrained feelings of despair and powerlessness among Palestinians, particularly amongst men, who lost everything. Many Palestinian men found themselves with only one channel through which to express their authority, namely within the family. Women, on the other hand, were nationally, ideologically and morally responsible for empowering men by enhancing their masculinity, as a critical sign of the national and cultural identity of the larger society (Holt 2003: 227). Palestinian women, as noted by Nira Yuval-Davis (1997) have acted not only as the reproducers of family and its gender relations, but also as the reproducers of the nation itself.

Palestinians have historically been constituted to adapt to and resist the 'forces that challenge their humanity' (Brown 1999 as quoted in Jean Klein, 2001: 93). Nationalist resistance discourse, together with Islamic moral and political discourse, has been specifically internalised and reflected in the perpetuated practice of women's self-sacrifice and altruism for their families and their nation, and of acting as substitutes for men in family provision. 'Women's self-sacrifice' is a moral and political term that reflects the social valuation and legitimisation of women's central role in the reproduction of the family and the nation (Peteet 1997, Jean-Klein 2000). It cannot be denied, however, that it contributes to Gazan women being deprived of any space between the values and desires of their selves, as agentive actors in both private and public spaces, and the values and desires of significant others, such as family members and the nation (Joseph 1993, Massad 1995). The dilemma here is the specific forms according to which women's self-hood in the contemporary Palestinian context has been ideologically and morally constituted to meet the interests and the desires of others which, over time, have also become theirs.

Moreover, women's insistence, in their public presentations, of sending the message that what they do as primary provider is a humiliation of their femininity, and that their 'men will not stay jobless forever', should not be seen from the singular dimension of reflecting their internalisation of gender oppression. I do not necessarily see this gender dynamic used by women, as Naila Kabeer (1999) argues, as a justification or a reflection of actual gender oppression, or as stated by Bourdieu (1990), as a misconception of women's interests. Within the specific context of the Second Intifada it appears to be the most effective and deliberate means that poor women have to accumulate and maintain their actual power in certain aspects of family life, and in the local community, with the least, or minimal, levels of confrontation with the dominant ideological system.

The changing gender configurations in the context of the crisis of masculinity in Gaza are difficult for both men and women, as they create new form of discrimination against women in particular. In this situation women intentionally need to maintain the image of male domination, in order to create a symbolic sense of parity in the presentation of the gendered self, at the same time as the actual complementary practice of gender, as conceived by women, has been disturbed. Is this not a strong indication that the specific history of Palestinian women has shaped them as critical actors? They are able to rationalise their gender relations, as well as to maintain their emotional sensitivity, by focusing on the power and happiness of others as a signifier of self.

Another critical point that reflects the historical complexity of women's agency in Gaza is their preference to present themselves as victims of the victimisation of their men by the oppressions of Israeli military occupation, but not as victims of male domination. This form of presentation has a political dimension, by which women can use the social image of their subordination and inferiority in order to attain sympathy at the community level (Meyer 2004), and to influence politics at national and international levels, while still carrying the material and psychological burdens they bear as a result of their men's joblessness. This is not only a survival strategy aimed at obtaining material support, but also present indication of how Gazan women perceive their inferiority. They feel inferior because of the implicit inferiority of their husbands and sons, and the inferiority of their nation. Throughout the history of Palestinian women, they have borne the martyrdom and imprisonment of their husbands and sons for generations, becoming solely responsible for providing for their families, without feeling inferior. The difference in the Second Intifada is the double intensity of their feelings of inferiority: that is, the association of women's subordination with the inferior position of their men. This challenges the constitution of gender subjectivity, as both men and women become unable to balance between their actual practice of agency and the desirable constitution of their selves.

Although the specific history of Gazan women has dispossessed them from shaping an independent sense of gendered self, this history has also created a rewarding and positive sense of otherness amongst them. The literature on Palestinian women's agency, as referred to earlier, confirms the findings of my empirical research that the sense of otherness characterising Palestinian women's selfhood has significantly contributed to rescuing the Palestinian family from fragmentation, and has enabled male and female children across generations to stand against continuous physical, social, and psychological threats to their safety and security. The findings in chapters 4 and 5, for instance, clearly illustrate that women's enhancement of men's sense of masculinity, particularly during the Second Intifada, has in many cases been accompanied by more respect and intimacy in male–female relationships, and less contestation within the family itself. It has also enhanced gender and generational changes, by which young wives have gained more legitimacy from their husbands and their mothers-in-law to practise decision-making powers, and to manage their household affairs. On the other hand, the increasing domination of Islamic discourse and institutions during the Second Intifada is also found to be associated with women's enhancement of men's practice of guardianship over them. In some of the women's narrations this discourse has been implicitly associated with the revival of their religious faith, when they consider themselves to be acting as ideal wives and mothers, while their husbands act as the primary family provider, in order to satisfy the orders of Qur'an and *Sunna.*[3] I argue here that the process of construction of gendered selfhood in this specific context supports Henrietta Moore (1994) in her assertion that the construction of gendered selfhood can never be standardised. It rather results from the interconnection between the personal histories of women's practices, the collective situations lived, and the multiple contradictory discourses pursued (Moore 1994: 50).

The final concluding point I would like to suggest in relation to the specific context of the Second Intifada, is that in a context where the dominant structure is visibly destroyed, and the material sources that shape the relations of power are also decomposed, people have no means to maintain their social existence, except by enhancing the dominant ideology as a set of meanings. The gender order is a combination of structure and ideology, both operating in a process to constitute gendered selfhood. The destruction of structural sources of male domination does not automatically lead to a shrinking of the ideology of male domination. It may

3 See Israr Ahmad's (2003) interpretation of the Qur'an in relation to women's Islamist obligations as faithful women. Ahmad argued that 'the major responsibility entrusted to the mother is that of imparting purposeful education and moral values to her children. To seek other avenues at the cost of this major responsibility is certainly not admissible. If, however, her circumstances are such that she can spare some time, she should definitely practise *Da'wah* (preaching) outside her home (Ahmad 2003: 29).

work in reverse, by enhancing ideology as a means to re-stabilise the disturbed gendered structure. In Gaza, the practice of masculinity and femininity based on gendered divisions of labour and responsibility, and the separation between the domestic and public spheres as the principal elements of the ideology of patriarchy (tradition) and Islam, have by no means been distorted by the destruction of the overall socio-economic structure. The distortion of this ideology, however, remains invisible, unless, as argued by Ernesto Laclau, 'the incarnating meaning and incarnating body would be entirely commensurable with each other' (Laclau 1996: II).

Women and men in Gaza bear the responsibility of keeping the distorted ideology of male domination, as illustrated in the crisis of masculinity and the reconfiguration of gender roles, invisible. Both sexes maintain the presentation of their gendered selves, in order to reflect the ideological image of male domination as the only source of power remaining and thus re-stabilise the dislocated social structure. Both men and women have collectively enhanced the presentation of masculinity and femininity in such a fashion as to 'activate' or realise symbolically the element of material power implicit in the fantasy of masculine identity (Moore 1994: 69). In the situation of collective threat against Gazan families and their whole society, I would suggest that both men and women equally contribute, by their presentation of self, to the perpetuation of the image of male domination. Men's tolerance and cooperation with their wives, and their support of their mobility and public participation, is found not to be ideologically threatening, if women in turn enhance their men's masculine image in public. This also explains the return of some research participants to the practice of veiling and piety associated with their participation in public activities, particularly in Islamic mobilisation, in a context dominated by Islamic ideology and discourse(s). The earlier practice appears to legitimise the latter, as a means for poor women to achieve consistency between the practice of their agency and the presentation of ideological gendered meaning beyond that practice.

The research sample was purposively selected to investigate the meaning of agency and subjectivity among women who have never experienced being in recognised positions in public, or being collectively organised in a social movement, which definitely creates different interests and desires, and may be a different mode of agency. My arguments in this book are, therefore, most specific to poor and vulnerable housewives, who have not previously experienced involvement in a women's movement, or in political and national organised resistance before the Second Intifada. This may open an opportunity for further research to investigate, on a comparative basis, the effects of organised social and political activism on gender subjectivity.

Conclusion

In this book, I have attempted to contribute to feminist scholarship on the theorisation of women's agency. I have found that conceptualising women's agency can never be standardised or universalised, and confined to the liberal notion of individual autonomy and independence. Defining women's agency, or women's subjectivity, is by no means inseparable from the defining of men's subjectivity: they are both by-products of the interconnection between women's and men's personal histories and practices, the collective situations in which they live, and the multiple contradictory discourses that exist in any given context. Through my analyses, I have also demonstrated that women are always in multiple and shifting positionalities, through which their enactments and presentation of their gendered selves take contradictory and complementary characters, and simultaneously entail resistance and accommodation of the prevailing gender order.

I have also sought to contribute to an opening up of the issue of masculinity as a crucial dimension of feminist scholarship. Mainstream feminist work still presents men only with reference to domination, exploitation and oppression of women. It is time for feminist scholarship to reach beyond this hegemonic practice and discourse of femininity and masculinity, and to better contextualise and historicise the relation between the two.

The empirical analysis of the experience of Gazan women during the Second Intifada shows that women's subjectivity is a matter of tactical and strategic action aimed at maintaining a meaning for their social existence, within a continually dislocated structure. Women tactically accommodate their gendered expectations as part of their active engagement in struggles for survival, and strategically manoeuvre in order to maintain the accumulation of their actual power in the domestic sphere. They instrumentalise their gender subordination and social inferiority to socially legitimise the masculine aspect of their agency, and subjectively to moralise the feminine aspect of their agency. By this multiple masculine-feminine model of agency, women in Gaza have materially and socially sustained their families. In the context of war and a crisis of livelihood, they have consciously deconstructed one of their multiple gender identities in order to reconstruct another. They show their displeasure with the reconfiguration of gender roles and responsibilities, but underline the presentation of their gendered selfhood as ideal wives and mothers who make sacrifices for the sake of their children and their emotional connectedness with their families and community.

The defining of Gazan women's agency and subjectivity in this book is not only contextualised, but also historicised. Throughout Palestine's contemporary history, Gazan women have been influenced by multiple discourses including nationalism, liberalism, traditionalism and Islamism. They have experienced and built up multiple forms of consciousness and enactments that have enabled them to perpetually shift from one position to another, or to be in multiple positions at the same time. They have become able to rationalise their gender relations, in order to achieve personal and familiar survival and security, as well as to maintain their emotional sensitivity, by focusing on the empowerment and happiness of others as a signifier of self. Women in Gaza define their agency and their subjectivity as powerful by the empowering of others, including those who are socially and historically constructed as the oppressors of their gender. In a context of a crisis of masculinity, Gazan women's enhancement of men's masculinity has had the merit of shifting gender relations towards greater tolerance, intimacy and perhaps also to greater equity. This only happens when each gender uses its selfhood sustainably for the empowerment of the other in stable socio-economic situations.

Bibliography

Abed, G. 1988. *The Palestinian Economy: Studies in Development under Prolonged Occupation*. London: Routledge.

Abu-Bakr, O. 2001. 'Islamic Feminism: What is in a Name?' *Middle East Women's Studies Review*, Vol. 15, No. 4.

Abu-Lughod, L. 1989. 'Zones of Theory in the Anthropology of the Arab World'. *Annual Review of Anthropology*, Vol. 18, 267–306.

——— 1990. 'The Romance of Resistance: Tracing Transformations of Power through Bedouin Women'. *American Ethnologist*, Vol. 17, No. 1, 41–55.

——— 1992. 'Islam and the Gendered Discourses of Death'. *International Journal of Middle East Studies*, Vol. 25, No. 2, 187–205.

——— ed. 1998. *Remaking Women: Feminism and Modernity in the Middle East*. Princeton: Princeton University Press.

——— 2002. 'Do Muslim Women Really Need Saving?' *American Anthropologist*, Vol. 104, No. 3, 783–790.

Abu-Nahleh, L. 2003. 'Employment: Contrasts between Daughters and Daughters in law'. *Review of Women's Studies*, Vol. 1, No. 1. Ramallah, West Bank: Institute of Women's Studies, Birzeit University.

——— 2006. 'Six Families: Survival and Mobility in Times of Crisis'. In *Living Palestine: Survival, Resistance and Mobility under Occupation*, edited by L. Taraki. Syracuse: Syracuse University Press.

Adibi, H. 2006. 'Sociology of Masculnity in the Middle East'. In *Proceedings Social Change in the 21st Century Conference 2006*. Carseldine Campus: Queensland University of Technology.

Afshar, H. 1991. 'Emancipation Struggles in Iran'. In *Women, Development and Survival in the Third World*, edited by H. Afshar. London: Longman.

——— 1993. *Women in the Middle East: Perceptions, Realities and Struggle for Liberation*. New York: Macmillan Press Ltd.

——— 1995. 'Book review: Arab Women by Judith E. Tucker, Women, Islam and the State by Deniz Kandiyoti Marriage on Trial: A Study of Islamic Family Law by Ziba Mir-Hosseini'. *British Journal of Middle Eastern Studies*, Vol. 22, Nos 1&2, 197–201.

Agarwal, B. ed. 1988. *Structures of Patriarchy: The State, the Community and the Household*. London: Zed Books Ltd.

——— 1997. 'Bargaining and Gender Relations: Within and Beyond the Household'. *Feminist Economics*, Vol. 3, No. 1, 1–51.

Ahmad, I. 2003. *Religious Obligations of Muslim Women*. Translated by Khalid Mahmood. Pakistan: Lahore Markazi Anjuman Khuddam ul Qur'an.

Ahmad, L. 1984. 'Early Feminist Movement in the Middle East'. In *Muslim Women*, edited by Freda Hussain. New York: St. Martin Press.

——— 1992. *Women and Gender in Islam: Historical Roots of a Modern Debate.* New Haven, CT: Yale University Press.

Al-Ali, N. 2007. *Iraqi Women: Untold Stories from 1948 till Present*. London: Zed Books Ltd.

——— and Pratt, N. eds. 2009. *What Kind of Liberation? Women and the Occupation in Iraq.* Berkeley: University of California Press.

——— eds. 2009. *Women and War in the Middle East: Transnational Perspectives*. London and New York: Zed Books.

Al-Khayyat, S. 1990. *Honor and Shame: Women in the Modern Iraq*. London: Saqi Books.

Al-Mahadin, S. 2004. 'Jordanian Women in Education: Politics, Pedagogy and Gender Discourses'. *Feminist Review*, No. 78, 22–37.

Allen, A. 1998. 'Rethinking Power'. *Hypathia*, Vol. 13, No. 1, 21–40.

Alsop, R., Bertelsen, F.M. and Holland, J. 2006. 'Empowerment in Practice: From Analysis to Implementation'. In *Directions of Development*. Washington, DC: The World Bank Publication.

Alstott, L. 2004. *No Exit: What Parents Owe Their Children and What Society Owes Parents*. New York: Oxford University Press.

Annas, J. 1993. 'Women and the Quality of Life: Two Norms in One?' In *The Quality of Life*, edited by M. Nussbaum and M. Sen. A study prepared for the World Institute for Development Economics Research (WIDER) of the United Nations University. Oxford: Clarendon Press.

Antonius, S. 1979. 'Fighting on Two Fronts: Conversations with Palestinian Women'. *Journal of Palestine Studies*, Vol. 8, No. 3, 26–45.

Arebi, S. 1994. *Women and Words in Saudi Arabia: The Politics of Literary Discourse*. Cambridge: Cambridge University Press.

Asad, T. 1970. *The Kababish Arabs: Power, Authority and Consent in a Nomadic Tribe*. London: C: Hurst

——— 2000. 'Agency and Pain'. *Culture and Religion*, Vol. 1, 29–60.

Aswad, B. 1967. 'Key and Peripheral Roles of Noble Women in Middle Eastern Plains Village'. *Anthropological Quarterly*, No. 40, 139–152.

Azmon, Y. 1981. 'Sex, Power and Authority'. *The British Journal of Sociology*, Vol. 32, No. 4, 547–559.

Badran, M. 2007. *Feminism Beyond East and West: New Gender Talk and Practice in Global Islam*. Global Media Publication.

Barakat, H. 1985. 'The Arab Family and the Challenge of Social Transformation'. In *Women and the Family in the Middle East: New Voices of Change*, edited by E. Fernea. Austin: University of Texas Press.

Barghouti, R. 2002. 'Between Agency and Necessity: Palestinian Women Peddlers in the Bireh Market'. *Review of Women's Studies*, Vol. 1, No. 1. Ramallah/West Bank, Institute of Women's Studies, Birzeit University.

Barlas, A. 2002. *Believing Women in Islam – Unreading Patriarchal Interpretations of the Qur'an*. Austin: University of Texas Press.

Baron, B. 2005. *Egypt as a Woman Nationalism, Gender and Politics*. Berkeley: University of California Press.

Barry, K. ed. 1990. *Sexuality and War: Literary Masks of the Middle East, Feminist Crosscurrents*. New York: New York University Press.

Bartky, S. 1990. *Femininity and Domination: Studies in the Phenomenology of Oppression*. New York: Routledge.

Berger, P. and Luckman, T. 1967. *The Social Construction of Reality*. New York: Doubleday.

Boddy, J. 1989. *Wombs and Alien Spirits: Women, Men, and the Za'r cult in Northern Sudan*. Madison: University of Wisconsin Press.

Bolak, C.H. 1997. 'When Wives are Major Providers: Culture, Gender, and Family Work'. *Gender and Society*, Vol. 11, No. 4.

Bordo, S. 1993. *Unbearable Weight: Feminism, Western Culture, and the Body*. Berkeley, CA: University of California Press.

Bourdieu, P. 1990. *The Logic of Practice*. Stanford: Stanford University Press.

——— 1998. *Pascalian Mediations*. Cambridge: Cambridge University Press.

——— 2001. *Masculine Domination*. Translated by Richard Nice. Stanford: Stanford University Press.

——— and Passeron, J.C. 1977. *Reproduction in Education, Society and Culture*. Translated by Richard Nice. London: Sage Publications.

Bowie, F. 2000. *The Anthropology of Religion*. Oxford: Blackwell Publishing.

Brown, K. 1999. 'Marginal Narratives and Shifty Natives: Ironic Ethnography as Anti-National-ist Discourse'. *Anthropology Today*, Vol. 15, No. 1, 13–16.

Bucar, M.E. 2010. 'Dianomy: Understanding Religious Women's Moral Agency as Creative Conformity'. *Journal of the American Academy of Religion*, Vol. 78, No. 3, 662–686.

Butler, J. 1990. *Gender Troubles: Feminism and the Subversion of Identity*. New York: Routledge.

——— 1993. *Bodies that Matter: On the Discursive Limits of Sex*. New York: Routledge

——— 1997a. *Excitable Speech: A Politics of the Performative*. New York: Routledge

——— 1997c. Further Reflection on Conversations of our Time. *Diacritics*, Vol. 27, No. 1, 13–15.

Cavaglieri, S. 2005. Livelihood Strategies and Food Security. Master's thesis, University of Roma Tre, Department of Economics. Rome, Italy.

Chant, S. 1997. *Women Headed Households: Diversity and Dynamics in the Developing World*. New York: Macmillan Press Ltd.

Chatty, D. 2000. 'Women Working in Oman: Individual Choice and Cultural Constraints'. *Journal of Middle East Studies*, No. 32, 241–254.

Cheal, B. 1988. 'Refugees in the Gaza Strip, December 1948 – May 1950'. *Journal of Palestine Studies*, Vol. 18, No. 1, 138–157.

Cheater, A. ed. 1999. *The Anthropology of Power: Empowerment and Disempowerment Changing Structures*. London: Routledge.

Cheref, A. 2006. 'Engendering or Endangering Politics in Algeria'. *Journal of Middle East Women's Studies*, Vol. 2, No. 2, 60–85.

Chodorow, N. 1978. *The Reproduction of Mothering.* Berkeley: University of California Press.

Cohen, R. 1970. 'The Political System'. In *Handbook of Method in Cultural Anthropology*, edited by R. Narroll and R. Cohen. Garden City, NY: Natural History Press.

Cooke, M. 2000. 'Women, Religion, and the Postcolonial Arab Women'. *Cultural Critique*, No. 45, 150–184.

Collins, J. 2004. *Occupied by Memory: The Intifada Generation and the Palestinian State of Emergency*. New York and London: New York University Press.

Hill Collins, P. 2000. *Black Feminist Thought: Knowledge, Consciousness, and the Politics of Empowerment.* New York: Routledge.

Connell, R.W. 2000. *Masculinities*. Sydney: Allen and Unwin.

Cornwall, A. 2007. 'Myth to Live By? Female Solidarity and Female Autonomy Reconsidered'. *Development and Change*, Vol. 38, No. 1, 149–168.

——— 2007. 'Choice, Chance and Contingency: Career Strategies and Tactics for Survival'. *Social Anthropology*, No. 15, 127–146.

——— and Lindisfarne, N. eds. 1994. *Dislocating Masculinity: Comparative Ethnographies*. New York: Routledge.

Crehan, K. 2002. *Gramsci, Culture and Anthropology.* Berkeley: University of California Press.

Crewe, E and Harrison, E. eds. 1998. *Whose Development: An Anthropology of Aid.* London: Zed Books Ltd.

Cudd, A. 2006. *Analysing Oppression*. New York: Oxford University Press.

Davis, S. 1983. *Patience and Power: Women's Lives in Moroccan Village.* Cambridge, MA: Schenkman Publishing Company.

de Beauvoir, S. 1970. *The Second Sex (1949*). New York: Bantam.

de Certeau, M. 1984. *The Practice of Every Day Life.* Berkeley: University of California Press.

de la Rocha, G.M. 2007. 'The Construction of the Myth of Survival'. *Development and Change*, Vol. 38, No. 1, 45–66.

Deeb, L. 2006. *An Enchanted Modern: Gender and Public Piety in Shi'i Lebanon.* Princeton: Princeton University Press.

Delaney, C. 1991. *The Seed and Soil: Gender and Cosmology in Turkish Village Society.* Berkeley: California University Press.

Development Studies Program. 2004. *Palestine Human Development Report 2004.* Prepared by Development Studies Program in cooperation with the Palestinian Ministry of Planning and funded by UNDP.

Duval, S. 1998. 'New Veils and New Voices: Islamist Women's Groups in Egypt'. In *Women and Islamisation: Contemporary Dimensions of Discourse on*

Gender Relations, edited by A. Karin and M, Tjornsland. Oxford and New York: Berg, 45–72.

Early, E. 1993. *Baladi Women of Cairo: Playing with an Egg and Stone.* Boulder, Co: Lynne Reinner

El Kholy, H. 2002. *Defiance and Compliance: Negotiating Gender in Low-Income Cairo.* New York and Oxford: Berghahn Books.

Elisha, E. 2006. *The West Bank and Gaza Strip: A Geography of Occupation and Disengagement.* London: Routledge.

Emadi, H. 2002. *Repression, Resistance, and Women in Afghanistan.* London: Praeger.

England, K. 1994. Getting Personal: Reflexivity, Positionality, and Feminist Research. *The Professional Geographer*, Vol. 46, No. 1, 80–89.

Erlanger, S. 2006. 'Palestinian Landslide: The Elections; Hamas Routs Ruling Faction, Casting Pall on Peace Process'. Article published in the *New York Times*, 27 January 2006.

Esim, S. and Kuttab, E. 2002. *Women Informal Employment in Palestine: Securing a Livelihood Against all Odds.* ERF working papers series, paper 0213.

Farrag, A. 1971. 'Social Control amongst the Mzabite Women of Beni-Isguen'. *Middle Eastern Studies*, No. 3, 317–327.

Farsakh, L. 2002. 'Palestinian Labor Flows to the Israeli Economy: A Finished Story?' *Journal of Palestine Studies*, Vol. 32, No. 1, 13–27.

Fernea, W.E. ed. 1985. *Women and the Family in the Middle East: New Voices of Change.* Austin: University of Texas Press.

Fowler, B. ed. 2000. *Reading Bourdieu on Society and Culture.* Oxford: Blackwell.

Foucault, M. 1980. 'Truth and Power'. In *Power and Knowledge: Selected Interviews and Other Writings 1972–1977*, edited by C. Gordon. New York: Pantheon Books.

——— 1983. 'Subject and Power'. In *Michel Foucault Beyond Structuralism and Hermeneutics*, edited by H. Dreyfus and P. Rabinow. Chicago: University of Chicago Press.

——— 1985. *The Use of Pleasure: The History of Sexuality, Volume Two.* Translated by Robert Hurley. New York: Random House.

——— 1997. *Ethics, Subjectivity and Truth, Vol. 1. Essential work of Foucault, 1954–1984*, edited by P. Rabinow. New York: The New Press.

——— 2000. *Power: Essential Writings of Foucault 1954–1984.* Volume 3, edited by J.D. Faubion. New York: The New Press.

Friedman, M.A. 1993. *What are Friends For?: Feminist Perspectives on Personal Relationships and Moral Theory.* Ithaca: Cornell University Press.

Gabbay, R.E. 1959. *A Political Study of the Arab–Jewish Conflict: The Arab Refugee Problem (A Case Study).* Geneva: Droz.

Garry, A. and Pearsall, M, eds. 1996. *Women, Knowledge and Reality.* New York: Routledge.

Gerson, J.M. and Peiss, K. 1985. 'Boundaries, Negotiation, Consciousness: Reconceptualizing Gender Relations'. *Social Problems*, No. 32, 317–331.

Ghouas, N. 2004. *Understanding Anthropology through Interpretation of Symbolic Forms of Expression*. Post-Doctoral Research 2003–2004, European Research Institute, German Research Institute.

Giacaman, R., Jad, I. and Johnson, P. 1996. 'For the Public Good? Gender and Social Citizenship in Palestine'. *Middle East Reports*, Vol. 26, No. 1, 11–17.

——— and Johnson, P. 2002a. 'Characteristics of Head of Households, Household Composition, and Household Labor Patterns'. In *Inside Palestinian Households: Initial Analysis of a Community-Based Household Survey*, edited by R. Giacaman and P. Johnson. Birzeit, West Bank: Birzeit University, institute of Women's Studies and Institute for Community and Public Health.

——— and Johnson, P. eds. 2002b. *Inside Palestinian Household: Initial Analysis of a Community-Based Household Survey.* Vol. 1. Birzeit, West Bank: Birzeit University.

Giddens, A. 1979. *Central Problems in Social Theory: Action, Structure and Contradiction in social Analysis*. London: Macmillan.

——— 1991. *Modernity and Self-Identity: Self and Society in the Late Modern Age*. Stanford: California University Press.

Gilmore, D.D. 1990. *Manhood in the Making: Cultural Concepts of Masculinity*. New Haven: Yale University Press.

Glenn, N.E. 1992. 'From Servitude to Service Work: Historical Continuities in the Racial Division of Paid Reproductive Labor'. *Signs*, Vol. 18, No. 1, 1–43.

Gluck, B.S. 1995. 'Palestinian Women: Gender Politics and Nationalism'. *Journal of Palestine Studies*, Vol. 24, No. 3, 5–15.

Goffman, E. 1963. *Behavior in Public Places: Notes on the Social Organisation of Gatherings*. New York: Collier-Macmillan Ltd.

——— 1983. 'The Interaction Order'. *American Sociological Review*, No. 48, 1–17.

González de la Rocha, M. 2007. 'The Construction of the Myth of Survival'. *Development and Change*, Vol. 38, No. 1, 45–66.

Gran, J. 1977. 'The Impact of the World Market on Egyptian Women'. *MERIP Report*, No. 58, 3–7.

Gutmann, C.M. 1997. 'Trafficking in Men: The Anthropology of Masculinity'. *Annual Review of Anthropology*, No. 26, 385–409.

Haddad, Y.Y. 1980. 'Palestinian Women: Patterns of Legitimation and Domination'. In *The Sociology of the Palestinians*, edited by Kh. Nakhla and E. Zuriek. London: Croom Helm.

——— and Esposito, L.J. eds. 1998. *Islam, Gender and Social Change*. Oxford and New York: Oxford University Press.

——— eds. 2000. *The Pitfalls of the Nationalist Discourses on Citizenship in Egypt*. Oxford: Oxford University Press.

Haj, S. 1992. 'Palestinian Women and Patriarchal Relations'. *Signs: Journal of Women in Culture and Society*, Vol. 17, No. 4, 761–778.

Hale, S. 1986. 'Sudanese Women and Revolutionary Parties: The Wing of Patriarch'. *Middle East Report*, No. 138, 25–30.

Hammami, R. 1990. 'Women, the Hijab, and the Intifada'. *Middle East Report*, No. 164/165, 24–30/71–78.

——— 1994. *Between Heaven and Earth: Transformation in Religiosity and Labor among Southern Palestinian Peasant and Refugee Women, 1920–1993*. PhD Dissertation Submitted to the Temple University Graduate Board.

——— 1998. 'The Cultural Construction of Gender Work and Culture: Palestinian Rural Women's Work Experience in the Pre-Nakba'. In *Women's Time and Alternative Memory*, edited by H. Sadda et al. Cairo: Women and Memory Forum.

——— 2001. 'Gender Segmentation in the West Bank and Gaza Strip: Explaining the Absence of Women from the Formal Labor Force'. In *the Economics of Women and Work in the Middle East and North Africa*, edited by M. Cinar. Amesterdam: JAI Press.

——— 2004. 'On the Importance of Thugs: The Moral Economy of a Checkpoint'. *Middle East Report*, No. 231, 26–34.

——— Taraki, L. and Kandyoti, D. 1995. *Gender and Society: Working Papers*. Birzeit, Ramallah/West Bank: Birzeit University, Institute of Women's Studies (IWS).

Hamman, M. 1981. 'Labor Migration and the Sexual Division of Labor'. *MERIP Report*, No. 95, 3–5.

Hampton, J. 1993. 'Feminist Contractarianism'. In *A Mind of One's Own*, edited by Antony and Witt. Oxford: Westview, 227–256.

Hannerz, U. 1992. *Cultural Complexity: Studies in the Social Organisation of Meaning*. Colombia: Colombia University Press.

Hapke, M.H. 2001. 'Development, Gender and Household Survival in a Kerala Fishery'. *Economic and Political Weekly*, Vol. 36, No. 13, 1103–1107.

Hartsock, N. 1983. 'The Feminist Standpoint: Developing the Ground for a Specifically Feminist Historical Materialism'. In *Discovering Reality: Feminist Perspectives on Epistemology, Metaphysics, Methodology, and the Philosophy of Science*, edited by S. Harding and M. Hintikka. Dordrecht: D. Reidel, 283–310.

——— 1983. *Money, Sex and Power: Toward a Feminist Historical Materialism*. Boston: North Eastern University Press.

——— 1990. 'Foucault on Power'. In *Feminism and Postmodernism*, edited by N. Hartsock. New York: Routledge.

——— 1996. 'Community/Sexuality/Gender: Rethinking Power'. In *Revisioning the Political: Feminist Reconstructions of Traditional Concepts in Western Political Theory*, edited by N.J. Hirschmann and C. Di StefaNo. Boulder, CO: Westview Press.

Hasselknippe, G. and Tviet, M. 2007. *Against the Odds: How Palestinians Cope through Fiscal Crisis, Closures, and Boycott*. FAFO Report No. 41. Oslo: FAFO Institute for Applied International Studies.

——— Atallah, A., El Dada, H., et al. 2008. *Surveying Palestinian Opinions March 2008*. FAFO Tabulation Report. Oslo: FAFO.

Hasso, S.F. 1998. 'The 'Women's Front': Nationalism, Feminism, and Modernity in Palestine'. *Gender and Society*, Vol. 12, No. 4, 441–465.

Hatem, M. 1988. 'Egypt's Middle Class in Crisis: The Sexual Division of Labor'. *Middle East Journal*, No. 42, 407–22.

—— 1993. 'Toward the Development of Post-Islamist and Post-Nationalist Feminist Discourses in the Middle East'. In *Arab Women: Old Boundaries*, edited by J.E. Tucker, 29–48. Bloomington: Indiana University Press.

—— 2002. 'Gender and Islamism in the 1990s'. *Middle East Report*, No. 222, 44–47.

Haugaard, M. ed. 2002. *Power: A Reader*. Manchester: Manchester University Press.

Hayward, C. 2000. *De-Facing Power*. Cambridge: Cambridge University Press.

Hegland, E.N. 1991. 'Political Roles of Aliabad Women: The Public-Private Dichotomy Transcended'. In *Women in Middle Eastern History: Shifting Boundaries in Sex and Gender*, edited by N.R. Keddie and B. Baron. New Haven and London: Yale University Press.

Hegland, M. 1998. 'Flagellation and Fundamentalism: (Trans)forming Meaning, Identity, and Gender through Pakistani Women's Rituals of Mourning'. *American Ethnologist*, Vol. 25, No. 2, 240–266.

Heiberg, M. and Ovensen, G. 1993. 'Palestinian Society in Gaza, West Bank and Arab Jerusalem: A Survey of Living Conditions'. *FAFO Report* 151. Oslo: Fafo.

Held, V. 1987. 'Non-contractual Society: A Feminist View'. In *Science, Morality and Feminist Theory*, edited by M. Hanen and K. Nielsen. *Canadian Journal of Philosophy*, Supplementary No. 13, 111–137.

—— 1993. *Feminist Morality: Transforming Culture, Society, and Politics*. Chicago: University of Chicago Press.

—— 2006. *The Ethics of Care: Personal, Political, Global*. Oxford: Oxford University Press.

Herb, M. 1999. *All in the Family: Absolutism, Revolution and Democracy in the Middle Eastern Monarchies*. Albany: State University of New York Press.

Hilal, J. 1992. 'West Bank and Gaza Strip Social Formation under Jordanian and Egyptian Rule (1948–1967)'. *Review of Middle East Studies*, No. 5, 33–73.

Hilterman, J. 1991. *Behind the Intifada*. Princeton, NJ: Princeton University Press.

Hoagland, S.L. 1988. *Lesbian Ethics: Toward a New Value*. Palo Alto, CA: Institute of Lesbian Studies.

Hochschild, A. 1989. *The Second Shift: Working Parents and the Revolution at Home*. New York: Viking.

Hollywood, A. 2004. 'Gender, Agency, and the Divine in Religious Historiography'. *The Journal of Religion*, Vol. 84, No. 4, 514–528.

Holt, M. 2003. 'Palestinian Women, Violence, and the Peace Process'. *Development in Practice*, Vol. 13, No. 2/3, 223–238.

Homans, G. 1958. 'Social behaviour as exchange'. *American Journal of Sociology*, No. 63, 597–606.

Hopkins, S.N. ed. 2003. *The New Arab Family. Cairo Papers in Social Science*, Vol. 24, Nos 1&2. Cairo and New York: The American University of Cairo.

Institute of Women's Studies (IWS). 2001. *Women's Income Generating Projects Survey.* Ramallah, West Bank: Birzeit University.

——— 2008. *The Impact of Israeli Mobility Restrictions and Violence on Gender Relations in Palestinian Society: 2000–2007.* Ramallah, West Bank: IWS, Birzeit University (unpublished research).

International Crisis Group. 2007. *Inside Gaza: The Challenge of Clans and Families*. The International Crisis Group Report, Jerusalem.

Jacabsen, B.L. 2004. 'Educated Housewives Living Conditions among Palestinian Refugee Women'. *FAFO Report* 425. Oslo: FAFO.

Jackson, C. and Palmer, J.R. 2000. *Work Intensity, Gender and Well Being.* Geneva: UNRISD.

——— 2007. 'Restoring Risk: Marriage and Creative Conjugality'. *Development and Change*, Vol. 38, No. 1, 107–129.

Jad, I. 2005. 'Between Religion and Secularism: Islamist Women of Hamas'. In *Shifting Ground: Muslim Women in the Global Era*, edited by F. Nouraie-Simone. New York: Feminist Press.

——— 2009. 'The Politics of Group Wedding in Palestine: Political and Gender Tension'. *Journal of Middle Eastern Women's Studies*, Vol. 5, No. 3, 36–53.

Jean-Klein, I. 1997. 'Palestinian Militancy, Martyrdom and Nationalist Communities in the West Bank during the Intifada'. In *Martyrdom and Political Resistance*, edited by J. Pettigrew, 85–110. Amsterdam: VU University Press, Comparative Asian Studies Series 18.

——— 2000. 'Mothercraft, Statecraft, and Subjectivity in the Palestinian Intifada'. *American Ethnologist*, Vol. 27, No. 1, 100–127.

——— 2001. 'Nationalism and Resistance: The Two Faces of Everyday Activism in Palestine during the Intifada'. *Cultural Anthropology*, Vol. 16, No. 1, 83–126.

Johnson, P. and Hilal, J. 2001. *Gender and Poverty in Palestine: Critical Issues.* Paper for a workshop organized by Gender directorate, the Palestinian Ministry of Planning and International Cooperation, Ramallah (June 2001).

——— and Kuttab, E. 2001. 'Where Have All the Women (and Men) Gone? Reflection on Gender and the Second Intifada'. *Feminist Review*, No. 69, 21–43.

——— 2002. Palestinian Participatory Poverty Assessment Project Policy Briefing Paper, Women, Gender and Poverty in Palestine: Learning about Family Crisis, Survival and Development from Poor Women, Men and Children. Ramallah, West Bank: Palestinian Ministry of Planning and international cooperation, UNDP and DFID.

——— and Hilal, J. and Musa, R. 2002. *In the Public Interest: Public Revenues, Social Allocations and Social Needs*. Paper for the Forum for Economic and Social Policy Research in Palestine. Ramallah: PRIP.

——— and Hilal, J. eds. 2003. An Annual Review of Gender Studies. Ramallah, West Bank: Institute of Women's Studies, Birzeit University.

——— 2006. 'Living Together in a Nation of Fragments'. In *Living Palestine: Family Survival, Resistance, and Mobility under Occupation*, edited by L. Taraki. New York: Syracuse University Press.

——— 2007. 'Tales of Strength and Danger: Sahar and the Tactics of Everyday Life in Am'ari Refugee Camp, Palestine'. *Signs: Journal of Women in Culture and Society*, Vol. 32, No. 3, 597–619.

——— 2008. 'What Rosemary Saw: Reflections on Palestinian Women as Tellers of the Palestinian Present'. *Journal of Palestine Studies*, Vol. 38, No. 4, 29–46.

——— 2009. 'Unmarried in Palestine: Embodiment and (dis)Empowerment in the Lives of Single Palestinian Women'. Pathways of Women's Empowerment: Changing Narratives of Sexuality'. A paper presented in a conference entitled: *Pathways of Women's Empowerment Project: What Are We Learning?* Cairo: American University of Cairo in cooperation with IDS/Sussex University (20–24 January 2009).

Joseph, S. 1986. 'Women and Politics in the Middle East'. *MERIP Middle East Report*, No. 138, 3–7.

——— 1993. 'Connectivity and Patriarchy among Urban Working-Class Arab Families in Lebanon'. *Ethos*, Vol. 21, No. 4, 452–484.

——— 1993. 'Gender and Relationality among Arab Families in Lebanon'. *Feminist Studies*, Vol. 19, No. 3, 465–486.

——— 1993. 'Fieldwork and Psychosocial Dynamics of Personhood'. *Frontiers: A Journal of Women Studies*, Vol. 13, No. 3, 9–32.

——— 1994. 'Brothers/Sisters Relationships: Connectivity, Love and Power in the Reproduction of Patriarchy in Lebanon'. *American Ethnologist*, Vol. 21, No. 1, 50–73.

——— 1996. 'Patriarchy and Development in the Arab World'. *Gender and Development*, Vol. 4, No. 2, 14–19.

——— 1997. 'The Public/Private: The Imagined Boundaries in the Nation/State/Community: The Lebanese Case'. *Feminist Review*, No. 57, 73–92.

——— 1999. *Intimate Selving in Arab families: Gender Self and Identity.* Syracuse: Syracuse University Press.

——— ed. 2000. *Gender and Citizenship in the Middle East.* Syracuse: Syracuse University Press.

——— 2004. 'Conceiving Family Relationship in Post-War Lebanon'. *Journal of Comparative Family Studies*, No. 2, 272–293.

——— and Slyomovics, S. eds. 2001. *Women and Power in the Middle East.* Philadelphia: University of Pennsylvania Press.

Kabeer, N. 1999. 'Resources, Agency, Achievements: Reflections on the Measurement of Women's Empowerment'. *Development and Change*, Vol. 30, No. 3, 435–464.

——— 2000. *The Power to Choose: Bangladeshi Women and Labour Market Decisions in London and Dhaka*. London/New York: Verso.

Kandiyoti, D. 1988. 'Bargaining Patriarchy'. *Gender and Society*, Vol. 2, No. 3, 274–290.

——— 1990. 'Women and Household Production in Turkey'. In *The Rural Middle East*, edited by K. and P. Glavanis. London: Zed Books.

——— 1991. *Women, Islam and the State.* London: Macmillan.

——— 1991a. 'Introduction'. In *Women, Islam and the state*, edited by K. and P. Glavanis. London: Macmillan.

——— 1991c. 'Islam and Patriarchy: A Comparative Perspective'. In *Women in Middle Eastern History: Shifting Boundaries in Sex and Gender*, edited by N. Keddie and B. Baron. New Haven, London: Yale University Press.

——— 1994. 'The Paradoxes of Masculinity: Some Thoughts on Segregated Societies'. In *Dislocating Masculinity: Comparative Ethnographies*, edited by A. Cornwall and N. Lindisfarne. New York: Routledge.

——— 1995. Book Review of 'The Eloquence of Silence: Algerian Women in Question', by Marnia Lazreg. *Contemporary Sociology*, Vol. 24, No. 5, 617–619.

——— 1995. 'Contemporary Feminist Scholarship and the Middle East Studies'. *Working Papers: Gender and Society*. Ramallah, West Bank: Birzeit University, Women's Studies Program.

——— 1996. *Gendering the Middle East: Emerging Perspectives.* London and New York: I.B. Tauris & Co. Ltd.

——— 1998. 'Gender Power and Contestation: Rethinking "Bargaining with Patriarchy"'. In *Feminist Visions of Development: Gender Analysis and Policy*, edited by C. Jackson and R. Pearson. London: Routledge, 135–152.

Kaplan, A.M. 1973. *On Freedom and Human Dignity: The Importance of the Sacred in Politics.* Morristown, NJ: General Learning Press.

Karam, M.A. 1998. *Women, Islamisms, and the State: Contemporary Feminisms in Egypt.* New York: St. Martin's Press.

Keddi, N. and Baron, B. eds. 1991. *Women in Middle Eastern History: Shifting Boundaries in Sex and Gender.* New Haven, CT: Yale University Press.

Khoury, P.S. and Joseph, K. eds. 1990. *Tribes and State Formation in the Middle East.* Berkeley: University of California Press.

Kinoshita, F. 1995. 'Household Size, Household Structure, and Developmental Cycle of a Japanese Village: Eighteenth to Nineteenth Centuries'. *Journal of Family History*, Vol. 20, No. 3, 239–260.

Kuttab, E. 2006. 'The Paradox of Women's Work'. In *Living Palestine: Family Survival, Resistance and Mobility under Occupation*, edited by L. Taraki. Syracuse: Syracuse University Press.

Laclau, E. 1996. 'The Death and Resurrection of the Theory of Ideology'. *Journal of Political Ideologies*, Vol. 1, No. 3, 201–220.

Lang, E. and Muhanna, A. 1992. *Women and Work in the Beach Camp.* Jerusalem: Arab Thought Forum.

Lazreg, M. 1994. *The Eloquence of Silence: Algerian Women in Question.* New York/London: Routledge.

Lesch, A.M. and Tessler, E. 1987. *Israel, Egypt and the Palestinians: From Camp David to Intifada.* Bloomington: Indiana University Press.

Lewin, E., Collier, J., Rosaldo, M. and Fjellman, J. 1971. Power Strategies and Sex Roles. Paper presented at the 70th Annual Meeting of the American Anthropological Association, New York.
Lloyd, G. 1992. 'Maleness, Metaphor, and the Crisis of Reason'. In *A Mind of One's Own*, edited by L. Antony and Ch. Witt. Boulder: Westview Press.
Litvak, M. 1998. 'The Islamisation of the Palestinian-Israeli Conflict: The Case of Hamas'. *Middle Eastern Studies*, Vol. 34, No. 1, 148–163.
Lovell, T. 2000. 'Thinking Feminism with and Against Bourdieu'. In *Reading Bourdieu on Society and Culture*, edited by B. Fowler. London: Blackwell Publication.
——— 2002. 'Power and Agency. A book review'. *British Journal of Sociology*, Vol. 53, No. 3, 491–496.
Lutz, C. and Abu-Lughod, L. 1990. *Language and the Politics of Emotion.* Cambridge: Cambridge University Press.
Macleod, E.A. 1991. *Accommodating Protest: Working Women, the New Veiling and Change in Cairo.* New York: Colombia University Press.
Mahmood, S. 2001. 'Feminist Theory, Embodiment, and the Docile Agent: Some Reflections on the Egyptian Islamic Revival'. *Cultural Anthropology*, Vol. 16, No. 2, 202–236.
——— 2005. *Politics of Piety: The Islamic Revival and the Feminist Subject.* Princeton and Oxford: Princeton University Press.
——— 2006. 'Secularism, Hermeneutics, and Empire: The Politics of Islamic Reformation'. *Public Culture*, Vol. 18, No. 2, 323–347.
Malti-Douglas, F. 1991. *Women's Body, Women's Word: Gender and Discourse in Arabo-Islamic Writing.* Princeton, NJ: Princeton University Press.
Massad, J. 1995. 'Conceiving the Masculine: Gender and Palestinian Nationalism'. *Middle East Journal*, Vol. 49, No. 3, 467–483.
Mataria, A. 2008. *Analyzing Health Equity in the West Bank and Gaza.* World Bank, Health Policy Report, Jerusalem.
Mayer, T, ed. 1994. *Women and the Israeli Occupation: the Politics of Change.* London: Routledge.
McCall, L. 2001. *Complex Inequality: Gender, Class, and Race in the New Economy.* New York: Routlede.
McLaren, A.M. 2002. *Feminism, Foucault, and Embodied Subjectivity*. Albany: State University of New York Press.
Meriwether, M. 1999. *The Kin who count': Family and Society in Ottoman Aleppo, 1770–1840.* Austin: University of Texas Press
Mernissi, F. 1987. *Beyond the Veil: Male-female Dynamics in a Modern Muslim Society.* Indiana: Indiana University Press
——— 1991. *Women and Islam: An Historical and Theological Enquiry.* Oxford: Basil Blackwell
Meyers, D. 2002. *Gender in the Mirror: Cultural Imagery and Women's Agency.* Oxford: Oxford University Press.

——— 2004. *Being Yourself: Essays on Identity, Action, and Social Life*. Lanham, MD: Rowman and Littlefield.

Miller, P. 1987. *Domination of Power*. London and New York: Routledge & Kegan Paul.

Mir-Hosseini, Z. 1993. *Marriage on Trial: A Study of Islamic Family Law, Society and Culture in the Modern Middle East*. London & New York: I.B. Tauris.

——— 1996. Stretching the Limits: A feminist Reading of the Shari'a Post-Khomeini Iran. In *Feminism and Islam: Legal and Literary Perspectives*, edited by M. Yamani, 285–319. London: Ithaca Press.

Mitchell, E.L. 2009. 'Making Ends Meet: Gender and Household Coping Strategies in the West Bank'. *FAFO Report* 2009:48. Oslo: FAFO.

Moghadam, M.V. 1992. 'Patriarchy and the Politics of Gender in Modernizing Societies: Iran, Pakistan and Afghanistan'. *International Sociology*, Vol. 7, No. 1, 35–53.

——— 1993. *Modernizing Women: Gender and Social Change in the Middle East*. Boulder: Lynne Rienner Publishers, Inc.

——— 1996. *Patriarchy and Economic Development: Women's Positions at the End of the Twentieth Century*. Oxford: Clarendon Press.

——— and Sadiqi, F. 2006. 'Women Activism and the Public Sphere: An Introduction and Overview'. *Journal of Middle East Women's Studies*, Vol. 2, No. 2, 1–7.

Moore, H. 1994. *Passion for difference: Essays in Anthropology and Gender*. Cambridge: Polity Press.

——— 1999. *Anthropological Theory Today*. Cambridge: Polity Press.

——— 2007. *The Subject of Anthropology: Gender, Symbolism and Psychoanalysis*. Cambridge: Polity Press.

Moors, A. 1990. 'Countrywomen in the West Bank: A Study of the Gender and Economic Division of Labor'. *Afaq Filastiniyya* (Summer 1990): 130–145.

——— 1995. *Women, Property and Islam: Palestinian Experiences 1920–1990*. Cambridge: Cambridge University Press.

Morriss, P. 1987. *Power: A Philosophical Analysis*. Manchester: Manchester University Press.

Moustakas, C. 1994. *Phenomenological Research*. Thousand Oaks: Sage.

Mullet, S. 1988. Shifting Perspectives: A New Approach to Ethics'. In *Feminist Perspectives: Philosophical Essays on Method and Morals*, edited by L. Code, S. Mullet, and C. Overall. Toronto: University of Toronto Press.

Nahas, M.K. 1954. 'The Family in the Arab World'. *Marriage and Family Living*, Vol. 16, No. 4, 293–300.

Najmabadi, A. 1998. 'Crafting an Educated Housewife in Iran'. In *Remaking Women: Feminism and Modernity in the Middle East*, edited by L. Abu-Lughod. Princeton: Princeton University Press.

Narayan, U. 1997. *Dislocating Cultures: Identities, Traditions and Third World Feminism*. New York: Routledge.

Nassar, N.J. and Heacock, R, eds. 1990. *Intifada: Palestine at the Crossroads*. New York: Praeger.

Nelson, C. 1973. 'Women and Power in Nomadic Societies of the Middle East'. In *The Desert and the Town: Nomads in the Greater Society*, edited by C. Nelson. Berkeley: Institute of International Studies, University of California, 43–59.

—— 1974. 'Public and Private Politics: Women in the Middle Eastern World'. *American Ethnologist*, Vol. 1, No.3, 551–563.

Obermeyer, M.C. 1995. *Family, Gender and Population in the Middle East: Policies in Context*. Cairo: the American university of Cairo Press.

O'Brien, L. and Pickup, F. 2002. 'Forgotten Villages: Struggling to Survive under Closure in the West Bank'. *Oxfam Briefing Paper* No. 28. New York: Oxfam Publication.

OCHA Special Focus. 2007. 'The Closure of the Gaza Strip: the Economic and Humanitarian Consequences'. December 2007.

Ortner, S. 1974. 'Female to Male as Nature is to Culture?' In *Women, Culture and Society*, edited by MZ. Rosaldo and L. Lamphere. Stanford: Stanford University Press.

—— 2006. *Anthropology and Social Theory: Culture, Power and the Acting Subject.* Duke University Press: Durham and London.

Ouzgane, L. 2006. *Islamic Masculinities.* London & New York: Zed Books.

Oxfam GB. 2006. Assessment Report of the Humanitarian Situation in Gaza Strip. Oxfam office in the Occupied Territories, Jerusalem.

—— 2007. *Breaking the Impasse: Ending the Humanitarian Stranglehold on Palestine.* Oxfam Briefing Note (November 2007). Jerusalem: Oxfam-GB office.

—— 2009. *Rebuilding Gaza: Putting People before Politics.* Briefing Paper (June 2009). Jerusalem: Oxfam office, Jerusalem.

Ovensen, G. 1994. 'Responding to Change: Trends in Palestinian Household Economy'. Oslo: FAFO.

Palestinian Center for Human Rights (PCHR). 2008. Human Rights Situation in Occupied Palestinian Territories in the year 2008. Gaza Strip: PCHR Publications.

Palestinian Central Bureau of Statistics (PCBS). 1999e. *Labour Force Survey, Annual report*. Ramallah, West Bank: Palestinian Central Bureau of Statistics.

—— 2000d. *Labour Force Survey, annual reports 1997–2000*. Ramallah, West Bank: Palestinian Central Bureau of Statistics

—— 2002. *Housework, Child Care and Community Service.* Ramallah, West Bank: Palestinian Central Bureau of Statistics.

—— 2004b. *Health Survey 2004: Summary of Main Indicators.* Ramallah, West Bank: Palestinian Central Bureau of Statistics.

—— 2005. *Palestinian Children: Issues and Statistics. Annual Report, series No. 8*. Ramallah, West Bank: Palestinian Central Bureau of Statistics.

—— 2006. *Palestinian Family Survey.* Ramallah, West Bank: Palestinian Central Bureau of Statistics.

——— 2007. *Indicators of the Labor Force in the Palestinian Territory.* Ramallah, West Bank: Palestinian Central Bureau of Statistics.

——— 2007. *Poverty and Living Conditions in the Palestinian Territory.* Ramallah, West Bank: Palestinian Central Bureau of Statistics.

——— 2009. *Press Release on Labor Force Survey Results (January-March 2009).* Ramallah, West Bank: Palestinian Central Bureau of Statistics.

Palestinian Ministry of Planning. 1998. *Palestinian National Poverty Report.* Ramallah, West Bank: Palestinian Ministry of Planning and International Cooperation.

——— UNDP and DFID. 2002. National Report on Participatory Poverty Assessment (*Voice of the Palestinian Poor*). Ramallah, West Bank: Palestinian Ministry of Planning and International cooperation, UNDP and DFID.

Palestinian Working Women Society (PWWS) and Palestinian Center for Public Opinion (PCPO). 2001. *Public Opinion Survey on the Issue of Violence against Women*. Ramallah and Beit Sahour, 19–22 April.

Palestinian Trade Centre (PalTrade). 2007. *Investing in Palestinian Economic Reform and Development.* Ramallah, West Bank: Ramallah, West Bank: PalTrade.

——— 2008. *Gaza Terminals Movement Monitoring, 2007 Annual report.* Ramallah, West Bank: PalTrade.

Paidar, P. 1995. *Women and the Political Process in Twentieth-Century Iran.* Cambridge: Cambridge University Press.

Parson, T. 1951. *The Social System*. London: Routledge.

Pateman, C. 1988. *The Sexual Contract.* Stanford: Stanford University Press.

Peteet, J. 1986. 'Women and the Palestinian Movement: No Going Back?' *MERIP Middle East Report*, No. 138, 20–44.

——— 1991. *Gender in Crisis: Women and the Palestinian Resistance Movement.* New York: Colombia university press

——— 1994. 'Male Gender and Rituals of Resistance in the Palestinian 'Intifada': A cultural Politics of Violence'. *American Ethnologist*, Vol. 21, No. 1, 31–49.

——— 1997. 'I cons and Militants: Mothering in the Danger Zones'. *Signs*, Vol. 23, No. 1, 103–129.

——— 2000. 'Male Gender and Rituals of Resistance in the Palestinian Intifada: A Cultural Politics of Violence'. In *Imagined Masculinities: Male Identity and Culture in the Modern Middle East*, edited by M. Ghoussoub and E. Sinclair-Webb. London: Saqi Books.

Pitcher, L. 2003. ''The Divine Impatience': Ritual, Narrative, and Symbolisation in the Practice of Martyrdom Palestine'. *Medical Anthropology Quarterly, New Series*, Vol. 12, No. 1, 8–30.

Radcliffe, A. S. 1986. 'Gender Relations, Peasant Livelihood Strategies and Migration: A Case Study from Cuzco, Peru'. *Bulletin of Latin American Research*, Vol. 5, No. 2, 29–47.

Rassam, A. 1984. 'Introduction: Arab Women: The Status of Research in the Social Sciences and the Status of Women'. In *Social Science Research and*

Women in the Arab World. Paris: the United Nation Educational, Scientific and Cultural Organisation (UNESCO), 122–136.

Razavi, S. 1999. 'Gendered Poverty and Well-Being: Introduction'. *Development and Change*, Vol. 30, No. 3, 409–433.

Rew, A. 1997. *Discourses in Developmental Anthropological Perspective.* Oxford and New York: Berg.

Rhode, D. 1997. *Speaking of Sex: The Denial of Gender Inequality*. Cambridge: Harvard University Press.

Rogers, C.S. 1975. 'Female Forms of Power and the Myth of Male Dominance: A Model of Female/Male Interaction in Peasant Society'. *American Ethnologist*, Vol. 2, No. 4, 727–756.

Rohdhe, A. 2006. Opportunities for Masculinity and love: Cultural Production in Ba'thist Iraq during the 1980s. In *Islamic Masculinities*, edited by L. Ouzgane. London and New York: Zed Books.

Rosenfeld, H. 1960. 'On the Determination of the Status of Arab Village Women'. *Man*, No. 60, 66–70.

——— 1968. 'Change, Barriers to Change, and Contradictions in the Arab Village Family'. *American Anthropologist, New Series*, Vol. 70, No. 4, 732–752.

Rosenfeld, M. 2002. 'Power Structures, Agency, and Family in a Palestinian Refugee Camp'. *International Journal of Middle East Studies*, Vol. 34, No. 3, 519–551.

Roy, S. 1987. 'The Gaza Strip: A Case of Economic De-Development'. *Journal of Palestine Studies*, Vol. 17, No. 1, 56–88.

——— 1989. 'Changing Political Attitudes among Gaza Refugees'. *Journal of Palestine Studies*, Vol. 19, No. 1, 72–82.

——— 1991. 'The Political Economy of Despair: Changing Political and Economic Realities in the Gaza Strip'. *Journal of Palestine Studies*, Vol. 20, No. 3, 58–69.

——— 1999. 'De-development Revisited: Palestinian Economy and Society since Oslo'. *Journal of Palestine Studies*, Vol. 28, No. 3, 64–82.

——— 2000. The Transformation of Islamic NGOs in Palestine. *Middle East Report*, No. 214, 24–26.

——— 2006. *The Economy Of Gaza.* Reported to The Palestine Center, USA (9 October 2006).

——— 2007. *Failing Peace: Gaza and the Israeli-Palestinian Conflict.* London: Pluto Press.

——— 2009. *The Peril of Forgetting Gaza.* Available at: www.thecrimson.com/article.aspx?ref=528434 [accessed 20 October 2009].

Rozmarin, M. 2005. 'Power, Freedom, and Individuality: Foucault and Sexual Difference'. *Human Studies*, Vol. 28, No. 1, 1–14.

Rubenberg, A.C. 2001. *Palestinian Women: Patriarchy and Resistance in the West Bank.* Boulder/London: Lynne Rienner.

Ruddick, S. 1994. Thinking of Mothers/Conceiving Birth'. In *Representations of Motherhood*, edited by B. Donna, et al. New Haven: Yale University Press.

Rugh, A.B. 1985. 'Women and Work Strategies and Choices in a Lower Class Quarter of Cairo'. In *Women and the Family in the Middle East: New Voices of Change*, edited by W.E. Fernea. Austin: University of Texas Press.

Sa'adallah, S. 2001. *Gender and Power in Muslim Societies: Issues for Development Practice.* SIDA Studies No. 3.

Sa'adawi, N. 1993. 'Women's Resistance in the Arab World and in Egypt'. In *Women in the Middle East: Perceptions, Realities and Struggle for liberation*, edited by H. Afshar. New York: Macmillan press Ltd.

Sa'ar, A. 2004. 'Many Ways of Becoming a Woman: The Case of Unmarried Israeli-Palestinian "Girls"'. *Ethnology*, Vol. 43, No. 1, 1–18.

Saler, B. 1997. 'E.B. Tylor and the Anthropology of Religion'. Paper Presented for the 95th Annual Meeting of the American Anthropological Association, San Francisco, 21 November 1996. *Marburg Journal of Religion*, Vol. 2, No. 1, 1682–1700.

Samed, A. 1976. 'The Proletarianisation of Palestinian Women in Israel'. *MERIP* Reports, No. 50, 10–26.

Sawicki, J. 1991. *Disciplining Foucault: Feminism, Power and the Body.* New York: Routledge, Chapman and Hall, Inc.

Sayigh, R. 1979. *Palestinians from Peasants to Revolutionaries.* London: Zed Books

——— 1983. 'Women in Struggle: Palestine'. *Third World Quarterly*, Vol. 5, No. 4:880–886.

——— 1985. 'Encounters with Palestinian Women under Occupation'. In *Women and the Family in the Middle East: New Voices of Change*, edited by W.E. Fernea. Austin: University of Texas Press.

——— 1998. 'Gender, Sexuality, and Class in National Narrations: Palestinian Camp Women Tell Their Lives'. *A Journal of Women's Studies*, Vol. 19, No. 2.

Scott, J.C. 1979. *The Moral Economy of the Peasant: Rebellion and Subsistence in Southeast Asia.* Yale: Yale University Press.

——— 1985. *Weapons of the Weak: Everyday Forms of Peasant Resistance.* Yale: Yale University.

——— 1990. *Domination and the Art of Resistance: Hidden Transcripts.* New Heaven and London: Yale University Press.

Sharoni, S. 1995. *Gender and the Israeli-Palestinian Conflict: The Politics of Women's Resistance.* Syracuse: Syracuse University Press.

Shaw, J. 1991. A Survey of Palestine: Prepared in December, 1945 and January, 1946 for the Information of the Anglo-American Committee of Inquiry. Institute for Palestine Studies (volume 1 of 3).

Shehada, N. 2009. 'House of Obedience: Social Norms, Individual Agency, and Historical Contingency'. *Journal of Middle East Women's Studies*, Vol. 5, No. 1, 24-49.

Shilling, C. 1999. 'Towards An Embodied Understanding of the Structure/Agency Relationship'. *British Journal of Sociology*, Vol. 50, No. 4, 543–562.

Sholkamy, H. 2003. 'Rationales for Kin Marriage in Rural Upper Egypt'. In *The New Arab Family*, edited by N. Hopkins. Cairo: American University of Cairo Press, 62–79.

SIDA Studies. 2001. 'Discussing Women's Empowerment'. Report No. 3/24 www.sida.se/shared/jsp.

Singerman, D. 1995. *Avenues of Participation: Family, Politics and Network in Urban Quarters of Cairo*. Princeton: Princeton University Press.

——— 2006. 'Restoring the Family to Civil Society: Lessons from Egypt'. *Journal of Middle East Women's Studies*, Vol. 2, No. 1, 1–32.

Sletten, P. and Pedersen, J. 2003. 'Coping with Conflict: Palestinian Communities, Two years into the Intifada'. *FAFO report*, 408. Oslo: FAFO.

Smith, E. D 1999. *Writing the Social: Critique, Theory, and Investigations*. Toronto: University of Toronto Press.

Sprague, J. and Hays, J. 2000. 'Self Determination and Empowerment: A feminist Standpoint Analysis of Talk of Disability'. *American Journal of Community Psychology*, Vol. 28, No. 5, 671–695.

Starrett, G. 1998. *Putting Islam to Work: Education, Politics and Religious Transformation in Egypt*. Berkeley: University of California Press.

Stokke, L. 2001. 'Marriage patterns'. In *Growing Fast: The Palestinian Population in the West Bank and Gaza Strip*, edited by J. Pederson, S. Randal and M. Khawaja, FAFO report 353. Oslo: Fafo Institute for Applied Social Sciences.

Stowasser, B.F. 1996. *Women in the Quran: Traditions and Interpretations*. Oxford University Press.

Swartz, D. 1997. *Culture and Power: The Sociology of Pierre Bourdieu*. Chicago: The University of Chicago Press.

Swedenburg, T. 1990. 'The Palestinian Peasant as National Signifier'. *Anthropological Quarterly*, Vol. 63, No. 1, 18–30.

Talhami, G. 1984. 'Palestinian Women: the Case for Political Libration'. *Arab Perspectives*, Vol. 4.

Taraki, L. ed. 2006. *Living Palestine: Family Survival, Resistance, and Mobility under Occupation*. Syracuse: Syracuse University Press.

Tayler, C. 1985. *Philosophy and the Human Sciences: Philosophical Paper 2*. Cambridge: Cambridge University Press.

Thompson, L. 1991. 'Family Work: Women's Sense of Fairness'. *Journal of Family Issues*, No. 12, 181–196.

Thornhill, T. 1993. 'The Interrogation of Palestinian Women Detainees by the Israeli General Security Services'. In *Women in the Middle East: Perceptions, Realities and Struggle for Liberation*, edited by H. Afshar. New York: The Macmillan Press Ltd.

Torab, A. 1996. 'Piety as Gendered Agency: A Study of Jalaseh Ritual Discourse in an Urban Neighborhood in Iran'. *The Journal of the Royal Anthropological Institute*, Vol. 2, No. 2, 235–252.

——— 2006. *Performing Islam: Gender and Ritual in Iran*. Boston: Brill Academic Publishers.

Treacher, A. and Shukrallah, H. 2001. 'The Realm of the Possible: Middle Eastern Women in Political and Social Spaces'. *Feminist Review*, No. 69, 4–14.

Tucker, J. 1978. *Women in Nineteenth Century Egypt*. Cambridge: Cambridge University Press.

——— ed. 1993. *Arab Women: Old Boundaries, New Frontiers*. Bloomington and Indianapolis: Indian University Press.

United Nation Development Program (UNDP). 2007. Development Time: Poverty in the Occupied Territories, July 2007: No. 1. Jerusalem: UNDP.

——— 2008. Development Time: Unemployment in the Occupied Palestinian Territories, March 2008: No. 2. Jerusalem: UNDP, www.undp.ps.

UNRWA. 2007. UNRWA Emergency Appeal 33rd Progress Report, July – December 2007. Gaza: UNRWA Headquarter office, Department of External Relations. www.unrwa.org.

——— 2007. Job Creation Programme: Humanitarian Context. Gaza: UNRWA Headquarter office.

——— 2007. UNRWA: Emergency Appeal 2007. Thirty Third Report, July – December 2007, 33. Gaza: UNRWA Headquarter Office.

——— 2008. Impact and Market Research Report for UNRWA's Microfinance and Micro Enterprise Program in the Palestinian Territories. Planet Finance: the Micro Finance Platform.

Verdon, M. 1998. *Rethinking Households: An Atomistic Perspective on European Living Arrangements*. London and New York: Routledge.

Wadud, A. 1999. *Qur'an and Woman: Rereading the Sacred Text from a Woman's Perspective*. Oxford and New York: Oxford University Press.

Walby, S. 1996. 'The Declining Significance' or the Changing Forms of Patriarchy'. In *Patriarchy and Economic Development: Women's Positions at the End of the Twentieth Century*, edited by V.M. Moghadam. Oxford: Clarendon Press.

Warnock, K. 1990. *Land Before Honor: Palestinian Women in the Occupied Territories*. London: Macmillan.

Warren, C.A.B. 1988. *Gender Issues in Field Research*. Newbury Park, CA: Sage.

Wassef, N. 2001. 'On Selective Consumerism: Egyptian Women and Ethnographic Representations'. *Feminist Review*, No. 69, 111–123.

Weber, M. 1978. *Economy and society: An Outline of Interpretive Sociology*. USA: University of California Press.

Whitehead, A. 1981. 'I am hungry, Mum: the Politics of Domestic Budgeting'. In *Of Marriage and the Market: Women's Subordination in International Perspective*, edited by K. Young, C. Wokowitz and R. McCullagh. London: CSE Books, 88–111.

WFP, FAO and UNRWA. 2008. Rapid Food Security Survey conducted March/ April 2008 as reported in World Food Program, 'Food Security and Market Monitoring Report', July 2008: Report 19.

World Bank. 2002. *Fifteen Months – Intifada, Closures and Palestinian Economic Crisis – An Assessment*. Washington: World Bank Publication.

——— 2004. *The Shrinking Role of NGOs in Gaza and West Bank.* Jerusalem: World Bank publication.
——— 2007. West Bank and Gaza Strip Investment Climate Assessment. Unlocking the Potential of the Private Sector. Document of the World Bank, Report No. 39109 (March, 2007). Finance and Private Sector Development Group & Social and Economic Development Department, Middle East and North Africa Region. Washington, DC: World Bank publication.
——— 2007b. Two Years after London: Restarting Palestinian Economic Recovery. Washington, DC: World Bank Publication.
——— 2008. Recent Developments and Prospects in the Occupied Palestinian Territories. Jerusalem: World Bank Publications.
——— 2008 and 2009. Palestinian Economic Prospects: Aid, Access and Reform. Jerusalem: World Bank publication.
Youssef, N. 1974. *Women and Work in Developing Societies: Population Monograph Series.* Berkeley: University of California at Berkeley.
Yuracko, K. 2003. *Perfectionism and Contemporary Feminist Values*. Bloomington: University of Indiana Press.
Yuval-Davis, N. 1980. 'The Bearers of the Collective: Women and Religious Legislation in Israel'. *Feminist Review*, No. 4, 15–27.
——— 1997. *Gender and Nation*. London: Sage Publications.
Za'ateri, Z. 2006. 'The Culture of Motherhood: An Avenue for Women's Civil Participation in South Lebanon'. *Journal of Middle East Women's Studies*, Vol. 2, No. 1, 33-64.
Zarkov, D. 2007. *The Body of the War: Media, Ethnicity, and Gender in the Break-up of Yugoslavia.* Durham: Duke University Press.
Zebiri, K. 1993. *Mahmud Shaltut and Islamic Modernism*. Oxford: Clarendon Press.

Web-Based References

All FAFO Reports. Available at: http://www.fafo.no/ais/middeast/opt/.
'Development Times' Reports. Available at:www.undp.ps/en/focusareas/crisis/crisisprev.html [accessed 18 August 2009].
Human Rights Watch, *Razing Rafah: Mass Home Demolitions in the Gaza Strip*, October 2004. Available at: http://www.hrw.org/reports/2004/rafah1004/ [accessed 2 July 2009].
Information on the Peace Process Negotiations. Available at: http://www.mideastweb.org/campdavid2.htm.
Mir-Husseini, Z. and Shalkomy, H. 2010. Available at: http://www.contestations.net [accessed May 2010].
Population Census 2007. Available at: http://www.pcbs.gov.ps/Portals/_pcbs/census2007/ind_loca_09.pdf.

Rosenthal, G. 2009. The Narrated Life Story: On the Interrelation between Experience, Memory and Narration. Available at: http://eprints.hud.ac.uk/4894 [accessed 23 May 2010].

Sara Roy Article on Gaza. Available at: www.thecrimson.com/article.aspx?ref=528434 [accessed 20 October 2009].

The Annual Reports of the Palestinian Centre of Human rights 2007 and 2008. Available at: http://www.pchrgaza.org/.

The PCBS Official Statistical Reports. Available at: http://www.pcbs.gov.ps/.

UNRWA Reports and Publications. Available at: www.un.org/unrwa/overview.

Arabic References

Abu-Namel, H. 1979. 'Qita' Ghazza, 1948–1967'. [*The Gaza Strip, 1948–1967*]. Beirut: Palestine Liberation Organisation Research Centre.

Al-Sourani, Gh. 1991. 'Qita' Ghazza, 1948–1956: al-'Awda' al-Ijtimai'yya al-Siyasiyya'. [*The Gaza Strip, 1948–1956: The Economic and Social Context*]. *SAMED Economist* (April – June), Vol. 13, No. 84, 12–29.

Hammami, R. and Kuttab, E. 1998. 'Towards a New Strategies for the Women's Movement, Democratic Transformation and Independence'. In *After the Crisis: Structural Changes in Palestinian Political Life*. Ramallah: MUWATIN, the Palestinian Institute for the Study of Democracy.

Hilal, J. and Malki, M. 1997. The Informal Social Security System in Gaza and West Bank. Ramallah, West Bank: The Palestinian Centre for Economic Policy Research (MAS).

Malki, M., Shalabi, Y. and Ladadwa, H. 2004. *The Palestinian Society in Resisting the Occupation: The Sociology of Resistance during the Second Intifada.* Ramallah, West Bank: MUWATIN, the Palestinian institute for the study of Democracy.

Palestinian Ministry of Health (MOH). 2004. *The Impact of the Second Intifada on Health Sector in Gaza Strip*. Gaza: Palestinian Ministry of Health Annual report.

Palestinian Ministry of Social Affairs (MOSA). 2003. *The Organisational Policy Paper Proposed for Social Welfare System*. Ramallah, West Bank: MOSA.

PCBS. 2009. Population Indicators by Type of Locality and Selected Indicators – 2007. Ramallah, West Bank: PCBS.

Women's Affairs Centre (WAC). 2007. 'Violence against Women'. Al-Ghayda'a' Quarterly magazine (Winter 2007), no: 20. Gaza: WAC.

Women's Affairs Centre (WAC). 2007. *Women in Gaza Strip: Closure, Impoverishment, and Security Chaos*. Gaza: WAC.

Women's Affairs Centre (WAC). 2008. *The Impact of Closure and Political Chaos on Family Relations in Gaza Strip*. Gaza: WAC.

Women's Center for Research and Documentation (WCRD) and PCBS. 2008. *The Challenges of Women's Participation in Labor Force, and Recommendations for Interventions*. West Bank, Ramallah: PCBS.

Index